Astene
Publications 2

Fig. 1. Bedouin encampment on the front cover of John Kitto's *Palestine: the physical geography and natural history of the Holy Land* (London, 1841).

We travel not for trafficking alone:
    By hotter winds our fiery hearts are fanned:
for lust of knowing what should not be known
    We make the Golden Journey to Samarkand

[James Elroy Flecker, 'Golden Road to Samarkand']

Acknowledgements

Thanks are due to Peter McConochie for creating the cover of the book and to Paul Starkey for providing the photographs. The front cover is of Alanya castle on the south coast of Turkey, taken in 1984, and the back cover is of a street in Old Jerusalem, taken in August 2000. Thanks to Penguin Books, Harmondsworth, for permission to publish the portrait of Gell, originally published by Penguin; to Mr Tom North, for permission to publish the illustrations to 'The Norths in Syria, Egypt and Palestine'; to the Cartographic Unit, University of Southampton for producing Maps 2 and 3. The maps of Cook's tours to Egypt (Map 971(12)) and that of Cook's Tours in Palestine (Map 48840(40)) are reproduced by permission of The British Library. Thanks to the School of Modern European Languages and the Centre for Middle Eastern and Islamic Studies at the University of Durham for providing support; to Janet and Paul Starkey for their assistance in preparing the volume for publication and to ASTENE for supporting this venture.

Travellers in the Levant:
Voyagers and Visionaries

edited by
Sarah Searight and Malcolm Wagstaff

ASTENE 2001

©ASTENE

Published by ASTENE
CMEIS, University of Durham
South End House
South Road
Durham DH1 3TG

Charity number: 1067157
Registered address:
Association for the Study of Travel in Egypt and the Near East
26 Millington Road, Cambridge CB3 9HP

ISBN 0 9539700 1 9

Contents

List of Maps	vi
List of Illustrations	vii
Preface, *Paul Starkey Series Editor*	ix
Introduction *Sarah Searight and Malcolm Wagstaff*	xi

I. Colonel Leake and Associates

Introduction	1
Colonel Leake: traveller and scholar, *Malcolm Wagstaff*	3
William Martin Leake and the Greek Revival, *Hugh Ferguson*	17
Leake in Kythera, *Davina Huxley*	35
Straddling the Aegean: William Gell 1811–1813, *Charles Plouviez*	42
The Anger of Lady Hester Stanhope: some letters of Lady Hester, John Lewis Burckhardt and William John Bankes, *Norman N. Lewis*	57
Jacob Jonas Björnståhl and his Travels in Thessaly, *Berit Wells*	71

II. From Pilgrimage to Tourism

Introduction	85
Levels of Contact between East and West: pilgrims and visitors to Jerusalem and Constantinople from the ninth to the twelfth centuries, *Peter Frankopan*	87
Muslim Travellers to *Bilad al-Sham* (Syria and Palestine) from the thirteenth to the sixteenth centuries: Maghribi travel accounts, *Yehoshu'a Frenkel*	109
Italian Travellers to the Levant: retracing the Bible in a world of Muslim and Jews, 1815–1914, *Barbara Codacci*	121

The Norths in Syria, Egypt and Palestine, 1865–1866,   140
    Brenda Moon
The Pilgrimage to Budding Tourism: the role of Thomas   155
    Cook in the rediscovery of the Holy Land, *Ruth Kark*

III. Fact and Fantasy

Introduction   175
J.F. Lewis 1805–1876: mythology as biography,   177
    Emily Weeks
Edward Lear's Travels to the Holy Land: visits to   197
    Mount Sinai, Petra and Jerusalem, *Hisham Khatib*
'Oriental novellas' in the works of Gérard de Nerval, 1840s,   213
    Marianna Taymanova

List of Contributors   225
Index   227

List of Maps

1. 'The Nearer East— Land Surface Features', from D.G. Hogarth, *The Nearer East* (London: Henry Frowde, 1905), opposite page 128; prepared by The Edinburgh Geographical Institute by J.G. Bartholomew.   x
2. Map of the region visited by the Ionian Mission, 1811–1813   47
3. Björnståhl's route through Thessaly, from Callmer, 161.   78
4. Cook's Tours to Egypt. The Nile, Turkey, Greece &c, Map 971(12), 1873, reproduced by permission of The British Library.   156
5. Cook's Tours in Palestine, Map 48840(40), 1873, reproduced by permission of The British Library.   168

List of Illustrations

1 Bedouin encampment on the front cover of John Kitto's *Palestine: the physical geography and natural history of the Holy Land* (London, 1841). — i

2 Portrait of Colonel Leake, a contemporary miniature in the author's possession, based on the portrait by C.A. Jensen, 1838, now in the National Portrait Gallery — 4

3 Sir Robert Smirke, R.A. (1781–1867), with permission from the R.I.B.A. — 19

4 William Wilkins, R.A. (1778–1839), with permission from the R.I.B.A. — 20

5 C.R. Cockerell, R.A. (1788–1863), with permission from the R.I.B.A. — 22

6 Thomas L. Donaldson FRIBA (1795–1885), with permission from the R.I.B.A. — 27

7 Avlemon from the chapel of Ayios Georgios. The *Mentor* was wrecked just outside the promontory on the left of the harbour mouth, from a photograph by Davina Huxley. — 37

8 Avlemon harbour today, from a photograph by Davina Huxley — 40

9 Portrait of Sir William Gell, *c.* 1814. Artist unknown. Originally published in Edith Clay, *Sir William Gell in Italy* (London: Hamish Hamilton, 1976). Reproduced by permission of Penguin UK. — 42

10 Plaster cast of medallion of Jacob Jonas Björnståhl made by Johan Tobias Sergel in Rome in 1772. The cast was presumably one of the eight original medallions made in the early 1950s and now hangs ion the entrance hall of the Swedish Institute in Athens. Photo by Marie Mauzy. — 72

11 Marianne North, photograph reproduced by permission of Mr Tom North. — 140

12 Frederick North, photograph reproduced by permission of Mr Tom North. — 140

13 Frederick North in the Hotel, Beirut, photograph reproduced by permission of Mr Tom North. — 142

14 Jerusalem, photograph reproduced by permission of Mr Tom North. 149

15 Near Hebron, photograph reproduced by permission of Mr Tom North. 150

16 Barber Saphed, photograph reproduced by permission of Mr Tom North. 152

17 Tripoli, photograph reproduced by permission of Mr Tom North. 153

18 Jewish festival at Meiron, 2 May 1865, photograph reproduced by permission of Mr Tom North. 154

19 Photograph of J.F. Lewis, undated, — photographed by Elliott and Fry (National Portrait Gallery, London). 182

20 Photograph (albumin print) of J.F. Lewis in Eastern dress, undated (Private Collection). 183

21 John Frederick Lewis — 'The Hosh [Courtyard] of the House of the Coptic Patriarch, Cairo', 1864, oil on canvas (Private Collection). 184

22 John Frederick Lewis — 'The Mid-Day Meal', 1875, oil on canvas (Private Collection). 185

23 John Frederick Lewis — 'A Frank Encampment in the Desert of Mount Sinai, 1842 ... ', 1856, watercolour and bodycolour (Yale Center for British Art, New Havant, CT). 187

24 Sir Thomas Phillips — 'Lord Byron in Albanian dress', after 1835, oil on canvas (National Portrait Gallery, London). 192

25 Count d'Orsay — pencil drawing of Lord Byron, 1823 — location unknown,, reproduced in Doris Langley Moore, 'Byronic Dress', *Costume: the Journal of the Costume Society*, 5 (London: Victoria & Albert Museum, 1971), 1-13. 193

26 Edward Lear — 'Jerusalem from Mount of Olives, Sunrise', 1859, oil on canvas. 198

27 Edward Lear — 'Mount Sinai', watercolour. 201

28 Edward Lear — 'Petra — the amphitheatre', oil on canvas. 205

29 Edward Lear — 'Petra — The Treasury', 13 April 1858, pencil and watercolour. 206

30 Edward Lear — 'Jerusalem from the Mount of Olives', watercolour heightened with white. 208

Preface

Paul Starkey, Series Editor

It is a pleasure to introduce the second of a series of publications to appear under the imprint of the Association for the Study of Travel in Egypt and the Near East (ASTENE). The Association was founded in 1997, following successful conferences on this theme in Durham (1995) and Oxford (1997) and aims to bring together researchers from a wide variety of disciplines relevant to the study of travel in the area. Papers from the Durham and Oxford conferences have already been published, as *Travellers in Egypt* (London, I.B. Tauris, 1998) and *Unfolding the Orient* and Interpreting *the Orient* (Reading, Ithaca Press, 2001) respectively.

The present volume is the second in a series of three containing papers developed from the Association's 1999 Cambridge conference. The first of these volumes, *Desert Travellers*, edited by Janet Starkey and Okasha El Daly (ASTENE, 2000), discussed a variety of desert travellers covering both a wide geographical area and an enormous timespan, from the classical writer Herodotus to the twentieth-century adventurer T.E. Lawrence. The two other volumes in the series have a somewhat narrower geographical focus: the present volume discusses a number of travellers to the Levant, from the ninth to the twentieth centuries, while *Egypt through the Eyes of Travellers*, edited by Paul Starkey and Nadia El Kholy (scheduled to appear later in 2001) will focus on a variety of Western views of Egypt, mainly in the nineteenth century. Together, these volumes provide a fascinating array of perspectives on a complex set of political, literary and cultural issues.

Grateful thanks are due to Sarah Searight and Malcolm Wagstaff for editing the papers in the present volume, and for helping to make them available to a wider audience. It is hoped that they will prove as stimulating to the reader as to those who enjoyed the original papers at the Cambridge conference.

Map 1. The Middle East and its Deserts: 'The Nearer East— Land Surface Features', from D.G. Hogarth, *The Nearer East* (London: Henry Frowde, 1905), opp. page 128; prepared by The Edinburgh Geographical Institute by J.G. Bartholomew.

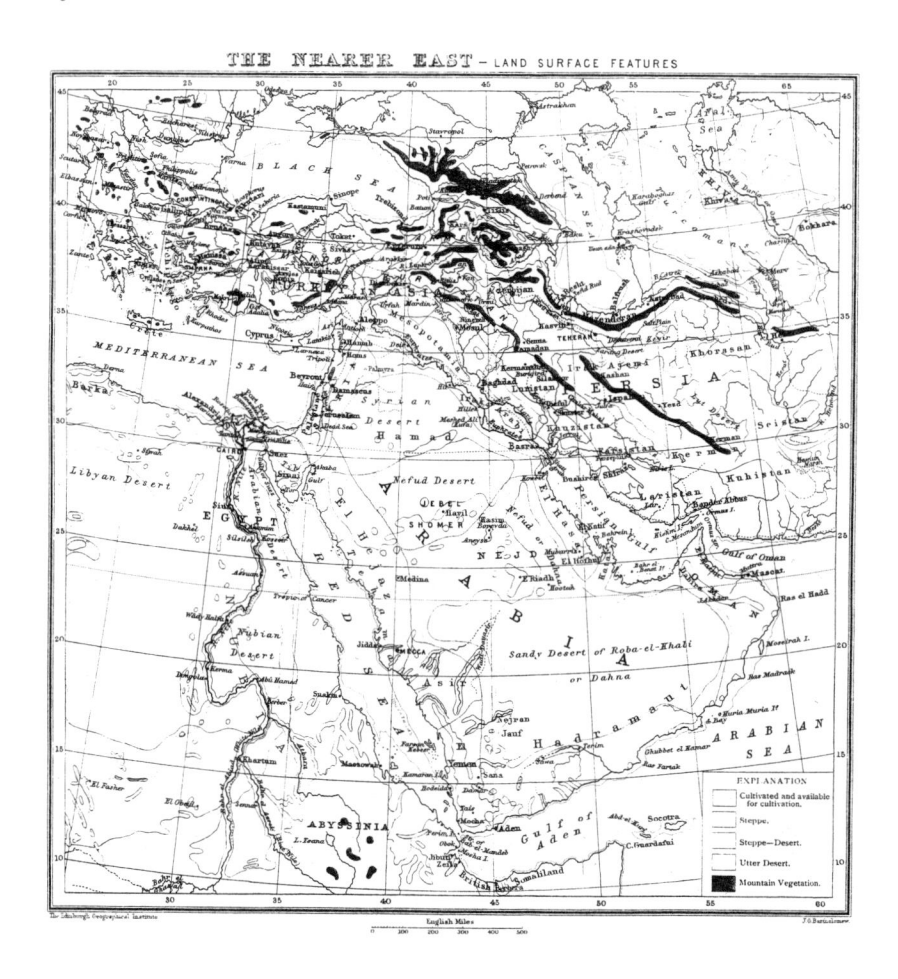

General Introduction

Malcolm Wagstaff and Sarah Searight

Levant, from the French *lever* 'to rise', is a slightly archaic English term for the eastern basin of the Mediterranean Sea. We use it here because of its currency in western Europe at the time when most of our travellers were active. As a geographical region, the Levant covers the coastal areas of the Mediterranean from Greece to Asia Minor (Anatolia), Syria, Palestine and Egypt and embraces the great islands of Crete and Cyprus, as well as the smaller ones of the Aegean and the islets off the Syrian coast. By extension, the Levant can also include inland areas as well.

The papers included in this volume illustrate the diverse character of travellers to the Levant since Europe's Middle Ages, the variety of their experiences and the range of writing which they produced. Most of the travellers discussed here travelled on their own, although usually with the personal servants and guides to whom they owed so much but who were rarely mentioned in their master's or mistress's accounts. Travel arrangements and itineraries were often privately arranged on an individual basis, but they made use of an established infrastructure which provided transport animals, accommodation and security. Perhaps originally evolving to meet the needs of commerce, the system facilitated the movements of the post and the military, but was exploited by pilgrims of all three Abrahamic faiths. The demands of pilgrims led to improved facilities for travellers, which underwent considerable extension and improvement from the middle of the nineteenth century as railways and steam ships increased the numbers of people visiting the region, specifically demanding westerners. Something of the transition can be seen in the travels of Frederick North and his daughter, Marianne, and the evolution of the travel company, Thomas Cook. By the late nineteenth century a certain sameness had emerged in the travellers' itineraries, as well as in the things seen, experienced and eagerly anticipated which they recorded in their journals. Scientific expeditions, such as those funded by the Egyptian Exploration Society and the Palestine Exploration Fund and anticipated by the Society of Dilettanti, diminished the scope for personal research of the type conducted by Leake. Individuals, of course, could still have significant encounters like those between Thackeray and Lewis or between Lady Hester Stanhope and Bankes and Burckhardt.

The travellers represented in this volume range from little-known Muslim and Christian pilgrims to celebrated north European scholars. Whilst the former travelled for religious motives, the latter had professional reasons for their journeys. The pilgrims used well-travelled routes to the Holy Land, comparatively well provided with facilities, but the scholars often followed each other along relatively unfrequented routes, to a number of favoured Classical sites. The scholars included the Swedish linguist, Björnståhl, and the English archaeologist, Gell, as well as a number of architects. Burckhardt can be added to the group since he was in Syria to improve his knowledge of Arabic and Islam. Leake is representative of another category of professional, the soldiers and diplomats who visited the region for diplomatic and military purposes, including espionage, but frequented left no published record of their work. J.F. Lewis is typical of the artists who drew much of their inspiration from travel and residence in the Levant. Thackeray and de Nerval were amongst the many writers who visited the region and tended to present a romantic view of it. The search for adventure and the exotic doubtless drew Lady Hester Stanhope, and she is representative of a class of romantic exile, as well as the 'grand' tourist.

The output from the travellers varied widely. The Ionian Expedition led by Gell produced hundreds of drawings, and the text was added later to those selected for publication. Other travellers produced sober, factual accounts of their experiences and observations based on their journals. Although Leake's works, *Travels in the Morea* and *Travels in Northern Greece*, are exceptional in range and detail amongst the travellers included here, the European travel narrative assumed a standard format during the late eighteenth century, while in the nineteenth century the type of information to be recorded was codified by the Royal Geographical Society's *Hints for Travellers*, first published in 1854. As Frenkel shows, however, standardisation was already apparent amongst the narratives *(riḥla)* of Muslim pilgrims of the thirteenth to sixteenth centuries. These formed a distinct art form in which travelling was always described as a hardship and undertaken in response to the strictures of the Qur'an and the wish to expand personal religious knowledge. The output of other travellers was more factitious. Later travellers developed the genre of the exotic oriental tale. Gérard de Nerval, for instance, wrote two romantic oriental tales, as well as his documentary account of his actual travels, and used them to present his philosophical and aesthetic ideas. Thackerary's account of his encounter with Lewis is less obviously fiction, but Weeks argues that it was not a strictly factual account of the artist and his work either. Nonetheless, it was influential in establishing Lewis' reputation for producing accurate depictions of oriental people and their daily life. Edward Lear, by contrast, concentrated on topography.

Real and imaginative worlds were often confused for past travellers to the Levant. Unlike Mark Twain who spotted the humbug early on, most were reluctant to accept the different world which they actually found. They described what they were expected to do and see, though servants helped to shelter them from too much reality. Disappointment and frustration, however, show through from time to time in their accounts, particularly those left by Europeans, such as Marianne North.

On the whole, the papers presented here do not explore this dimension of Near Eastern travel writing. Nor do they engage in the debate about orientalism and the way in which it may have influenced both the perceptions of contemporary writers and also the expectations and outlook of their public. On the one hand, they tend to emphasise the incidents of travel and their outcomes (e.g. the anger of Lady Hester Stanhope, Greek Revival architecture, the economic development of the Holy Land, the reputation of John Frederick Lewis) and the biographies of the travellers themselves (eg. Björnståhl, Gell and Leake). On the other hand, several papers deal with generalised experience and genre output (e.g. pilgrims, tourists, oriental scenes in stories and pictures). Together they illustrate the delight and interest to be found in studying travellers to the old Levant.

Colonel Leake and his Associates

Lieutenant-Colonel William Martin Leake has a considerable reputation as a careful observer of the topography and socio-economic scene in the Levant, especially Greece, at the beginning of the nineteenth century. But he was also a formidable scholar in the historical geography of Classical antiquity. Despite his reticence, he became a respected member of the 'unseen college' of scholars, writers and men of affairs which flourished in early nineteenth century London, and had wide contacts in the worlds of art (he knew Lear, for example), architecture, literature, and politics, as well as classics, geography and numismatics. Wagstaff outlines Leake's career and reviews his activity as a scholar. It is often forgotten that he was an artillery officer, not a gentleman traveller, and visited the region for professional reasons, initially as a member of the British Military Mission to Turkey and then as a military advisor and diplomat. His lengthy scholarly career really began only after his retirement from the army.

Ferguson's paper shows how Leake interacted with a group of influential British architects. They travelled in Greece and came to lead the Greek Revival in architecture. Huxley reveals the adventurous side of Leake's travels in Greece by focussing on one incident, his shipwreck in 1802 on the island of Kythera when in transit with a shipment of Lord Elgin's marbles. Leake returned to the island in 1806 while on passage from Corfu to Mount Athos. He remained in contact with some of the islanders and, in due course, published on the ancient topography of their homeland. Leake travelled with Gell on several occasions when they were in Greece during 1805 and, like him, became a member of the Society of Dilettanti which sponsored Gell's Ionian expedition of 1811—1813 described by Plouviez.[1] Leake served on the publications' committee of the Society that eventually saw the third volume of *Ionian Antiquities* appear in 1840. Bankes and Burckhardt, both of whom raised the anger of Lady Hestor Stanhope, the subject of Lewis' contribution, were also known to Leake. Bankes was also a member of the Dilettanti (from 1821) and the African Association (from 1826), serving on the committee with Leake (1826–1829).[2] Bankes and Leake corresponded, for example on the price edict of Diocletian. Leake gave evidence for Bankes in the libel action which his former travelling companion, James Silk Buckingham, brought against him in 1826. A decade earlier, however, Bankes had irritated Lady Hestor by his conversation (which at least some of his contemporaries thought could eclipse even that of Sidney Smith) and angered her by ignoring her well-intentioned advice about travelling to Palmyra and trying to poach her physician, Dr Meryon. Leake knew Burckhardt, whose gossip about her also angered Lady Hester, only indirectly. As the secretary of the African Association (1822–1831), Leake began the formidable task of editing Burckhardt's papers and journals for publication. By contrast, Leake did not know Björnståhl at all and does not appear to have been aware of his work. What they have in common, though a quarter of a century apart, is travel through Thessaly and a traverse of the romantic Vale of Tempe.

[1] Gell was elected to the Society of Dilettanti in 1807 and Leake in 1814, L. Cust, *History of the Society of Dilettanti*, (London: 1919).

[2] Ibid.; *Minutes of the Association for Promoting the Discovery of the Interior Parts of Africa*, Cambridge University Library, Add. 7087.

Colonel Leake: traveller and scholar

Malcolm Wagstaff

Lieutenant-Colonel William Martin Leake (1777–1860), generally known simply as Colonel Leake, is remembered today chiefly for two or possibly three books: *Travels in the Morea*, 3 volumes (1830), *Travels in Northern Greece*, 4 volumes (1835), and possibly *Journal of a Tour in Asia Minor*, one volume (1824).

Despite their titles, these volumes are major works of historical geography and attempt to unravel, usually with considerable success, the topography of Greece and Asia Minor as described by the ancient Greek and Latin authors. Nonetheless, they form only a part of Leake's scholarly output. This ranges from the study of the languages spoken in Greece at the beginning of the nineteenth century,[3] the *Topography of Athens*[4] and the outbreak of the Greek War of Independence,[5] to early work towards the decipherment of Egyptian hieroglyphics,[6] the study of inscriptions[7] and numismatics.[8] As travel writing, the three books identified report only a selection of Leake's journeys. He also visited the West Indies,

---

[3] W. Martin Leake, *Researches in Greece* (London: John Booth, 1814).

[4] W.M. Leake, *The Topography of Athens with Some Remarks on its Antiquities* (London: John Murray, 1821; 2nd ed. J. Rodwell, 1841).

[5] W.M. Leake, *An Historical Outline of the Greek Revolution* (London: John Murray, 1826). This was first published anonymously in 1825.

[6] C. Yorke and W. Martin Leake, 'On some Egyptian monuments in the British Museum and other collections', *Transactions of the Royal Society of Literature*, 1:1 (1829), 205–227.

[7] For example, W.M. Leake and J. Squire, 'An account of the Greek inscription on Pompey's Pillar', *Archaeologia* 15 (1806), 59–64. This was probably Leake's first article.

[8] Especially W.M. Leake, *Numismata Hellenica* (London: John Murray, 1856, 1859).

Fig. 1. A portrait of Colonel Leake, a contemporary miniature in the author's possession, based on the portrait by C.A. Jensen, 1838, now in the National Portrait Gallery.

travelled up the Nile and journeyed in Palestine and Syria. Greek islands, including Corfu and Kythera, were included in his itineraries. Malta and Sicily engaged his attention. He crossed Italy and France on his return from his first tour of duty in the Near East and subsequently travelled up the Rhine and visited parts of Switzerland as British military advisor to the army of the Swiss Cantons during Napoleon's 'Hundred Days'. Finally, in his early sixties he made a continental wedding tour which took him to some of the places he had first seen as a young man.

Unlike many of his contemporaries, Leake frequently travelled on official business. The aim of this contribution is to outline the reasons for his Near Eastern travels and to link them to his output as a scholar.

The primary reason for Leake's travels was military. He was a professional soldier from 1792, when he joined the Royal Military Academy at Woolwich, aged fifteen, until his retirement from the Royal Artillery by the sale of his commission as a Lieutenant-Colonel in 1823, when he was forty-six. Leake entered the army somewhat unwillingly, as his father noted in an autobiographical memoir;[9] he left as a result of the 'downsizing' of the officer corps in the Artillery ordered by the Duke of Wellington, as Master General of the Ordnance,[10] though ill health was also a factor. He later regretted his decision.[11]

After service in the West Indies, Leake was selected for service in the Ottoman Empire as a member of a British Military Mission.[12] The Military Mission (principally gunners and engineers, but also including surveyors) formed a part of the British response to the French invasion of Egypt (1798), and was designed to provide training and stiffening to the Ottoman forces.[13] When the British soldiers reached Constantinople, the Porte did not know what to do with them and their presence in the

[9] John Martin Leake, *Memoir of his Father and his Family*, Hertfordshire County Record Office, Microfilm M3.
[10] H.W.L. Hime, *History of the Royal Regiment of Artillery, 1815–1853* (London: Longmans, Green and Co., 1908), 14–36.
[11] Hertfordshire County Record Office, Acc.599/85782 (Draft Petition, 1855) and 85783 (Draft letter to Sir Charles Yorke).
[12] Public Record Office, *Koehler's Papers*, FO 78/25.
[13] Public Record Office, *Koehler's Papers*, FO78/25-27; W. Wittman, *Travels in Turkey, Asia Minor, Syria* ...(London: Richard Phillips, 1803).

vicinity of the city was a political embarrassment. After several false starts, the Mission was eventually allowed to provide support to the Ottoman army gathering at Jaffa prior to an attack upon the French in Egypt. When the news came through, the Mission's commander, General Koehler, decided to link up with the Ottoman army as soon as possible. As a result a small advanced party, including Leake, dashed off across Asia Minor in disguise (January 1800), leaving the rest of the Mission to proceed by sea.[14] The group reached Cyprus only to find that a convention had been arranged at al-Arish on 24 January, 1800 for the withdrawal of French troops from Egypt. Koehler decided to return to Constantinople. When his party reached Alanya on the south coast of Asia Minor, Leake was ill with jaundice. He was left behind to recover. Once restored to health, he made a leisurely return to Constantinople, calling at several islands and mainland ports on his way.[15]

Whilst Leake was away, the Convention of al-Arish had been repudiated by the British government and the French commander, General Kléber.[16] Military operations had resumed. The entire Military Mission had transferred to Jaffa. Leake eventually rejoined it sometime between 4 August and 15 October 1800.[17] Whilst waiting for the Ottoman troops to regroup and be reinforced after their defeat at Heliopolis (20 March 1800), Leake accompanied General Koehler on a visit to Jerusalem and Bethlehem in October 1800. The re-advance of the Ottoman army into Egypt along the coastal route through Sinai and the frontal assault on

---

[14] W. Martin Leake, *Journal of a Tour in Asia Minor* (London: John Murray, 1824), 1–50, 93–129. W.M. Leake, 'Journey through some provinces of Asia Minor in the year 1800', in R. Walpole (ed.), *Travels in Various Countries of the East; being a continuation of Memoirs Relating to European and Asiatic Turkey* (London: Longman, Hurst, Rees, Orme and Brown, 1820), 185–263.

[15] Leake, *op. cit.* (1824), 127–29.

[16] A.B. Rodger, *The War of the Second Coalition, 1798 to 1801* (Oxford: Clarendon Press, 1964), 133–40.

[17] Leake was not on the muster roll of 4 August 1800 annexed to a letter from Koehler to Grenville, dated 2 August 1800 (Public Record Office, W01/344) but Wittman (*op. cit.* (1803), 150) includes him on the excursion to Jerusalem.

the Delta by British forces under Lieutenant General Sir Ralph Abercromby resulted in the defeat for the French and their evacuation of Egypt.[18] Leake accompanied the Ottoman army and saw action at the battle of El Hanka near Cairo on 16 May 1801. Once in Egypt, Leake and his friend William Richard Hamilton (1777-1859), Lord Elgin's private secretary, had an opportunity to follow the Nile up to Aswan (October 1801-February, 1802).[19] Given an escort of British soldiers, Leake and Hamilton were not on a pleasure trip. Charting the course of the Nile was one objective,[20] but more important was Hamilton's diplomatic mission to one of the Mamluk beys, Muhammad Alfi Bey. He had survived the French occupation and, following the murder of many beys after the departure of the French, had retreated into Nubia where he was manoeuvring to fill the power vacuum which would be left in Egypt with the evacuation of the British forces. There was diplomatic purpose also behind the visit to Syria which the friends made in April-June, 1802.[21] It was on their way home from Syria that Leake first visited southern Greece and Athens, where Hamilton helped to organise the shipping of some of Lord Elgin's marbles, as well as Kythera and Corfu. The visit to the Ionian Islands was unintended. Leake and Hamilton were on the *Mentor* brig with a consignment of marbles bound for Malta when it foundered in a storm off Kythera (16 September 1802).[22] Whilst Hamilton stayed to organise the recovery of the marbles, Leake made his way to Corfu on his way home.[23]

[18] P. Mackesy, *British Victory in Egypt, 1801* (London: Routledge, 1995).
[19] W. Hamilton, *Remarks on Several Parts of Turkey. Part I: Aegyptica, or Some Account of the Antient [sic] and Modern State of Egypt as Obtained in the Years 1801, 1802* (London: Payne, Cadwell and Davies, 1809).
[20] Hamilton, *ibid.*, iv-v.
[21] Hertfordshire County Record Office, Acc. 599/85490; Public Record Office, FO 78/32; J. Squire, 'Travels through part of antient [sic] Coele Syria', In R. Walpole (ed.), *Memoirs Relating to European and Asiatic Turkey* (London: Longman, Hurst, Rees, Orme and Brown, 1818), 293-352.
[22] A.H. Smith, 'Lord Elgin and his collection', *Journal of Hellenic Studies*, 36 (1916), 163-372.
[23] W.M. Leake, Miscellaneous a. 'Cerigo to England, 1802,3', Leake Collection, Classical Faculty Library, University of Cambridge.

Leake went out to Greece in his own right in 1804. This time he was operating directly under the British Foreign Office. With breakdown of the Peace of Amiens (April 1802–May 1803), the French stepped up their diplomatic offensive to pressure the Sultan and the powerful semi-independent governors in the Balkan provinces to side with them in the renewed conflict.[24] Both the Ottoman and the British authorities anticipated that the threat of a French attack on the Ottoman Empire could become reality and that the blow would fall on either Albania or the Morea. This threat provides the context for Leake's mission. He was part of the British counter-measures to French machinations and, until the Ottoman Empire changed sides in 1807, operated with the approval of the Porte. He had specific instructions to advise the Ottoman authorities in Greece and Albania in military matters, to assess the degree of support that the local people might give to the French if a landing took place, and to investigate the routes north-eastwards towards Constantinople from possible landing places on the west coast.[25] Information on landing places and routes would be necessary to organise local resistance to a French advance and, if necessary, to deploy British troops. Leake's job, then, required him to assess local and regional topography from a military point of view. Whilst written descriptions were useful, mapping was also important. Accordingly, there are frequent references in Leake's *Travels in the Morea* and *Travels in Northern Greece* to survey work from vantage points and the use of telescope, theodolite and compass. His itineraries make careful note of the time, whilst his manuscript journals record experiments in timing the distance covered by different types of horses. This was essential information, for dead-reckoning provided an estimate of the distance travelled and was thus basic to his map-making activities.

---

[24] S.J. Shaw, *Between Old and New. The Ottoman Empire under Sultan Selim III, 1789–1807* (Cambridge, Mass.: Harvard University Press, 1971), 328–64.

[25] Hertfordshire County Record Office, Acc. 599/85492 (Leake's Instructions); Public Record Office, FO 78/57 ('Captain W.M. Leake. Turkey and Egypt').

Leake published several maps compiled on the basis of bearings and travel times, but a number of manuscript maps seem to have disappeared.[26]

Leake's journeys, then, between December 1804, when he left Corfu for the Albanian mainland, and February, 1807 when he was put under house-arrest in Salonica for nine months, were given strategic shape by his military and diplomatic work. The detail, however, was often shaped by his interest in ancient topography. He deliberately set out to identify places mentioned by the ancient Greek and Latin authors, to assign ancient names to ruins pointed out to him or spotted as he rode along, to visit them when he could and to plan them when opportunity offered and there was not too much opposition from his escort or local people. In part he was acting in accordance with his instructions; in part he was following his personal inclinations.[27]

When Leake returned to Greece in 1809, for what turned out to be the last time, it was as British resident at the court of 'Ali Pasha of Yannina. The objectives were to secure 'Ali's support for British operations in the Adriatic Sea and against the French-held Ionian Islands, as well as to counter French influence in the region.[28] Leake was probably chosen because he was already known to the formidable Pasha, with whom he seemed to be on reasonable terms. Despite his diplomatic work, he had time to travel.[29] His journeys were controlled partly by his relations with

---

[26] For example, 'The Morea, anciently Peloponnesus' published in volume one of Leake's *Travels in the Morea* (London: John Murray, 1830) and 'Suli, with the Adjoining Mountains and the Course of the Acaeron through the Defile' included at the end of volume one of his *Travels in Northern Greece* (London: J. Rodwell, 1835).

[27] Public Record Office, FO 78/57 (Draft Instructions). A more candid revelation than most is this: 'The route which I have just followed from Salona to 'Epacto was chiefly undertaken with a view to illustrate a part of the history of Thucydides, which contains, with the exception of a passage in Livy, and a few words by the geographical writers, almost all that the ancients have left us descriptive of Locris and Aetolia' (Leake, *op. cit.* (1835), II, 611).

[28] Hertfordshire Country Record Office, Acc. 599/85506 (Instructions from George Canning).

[29] Martin Leake, *op. cit.* (1835), III, 488–578 and the whole of volume 4.

Ali Pasha, either seeking an interview or trying to avoid one,[30] and partly by Leake's wish to complete his topographical survey of central Greece. In the end, Leake left Epirus in a hurry, apparently thinking that ʿAli was about to make good his threats to kill the Englishman.

Throughout his travels, Leake kept a journal in small notebooks bought for the purpose in London. These are now in the Library of the Classics Faculty in the University of Cambridge. They record for each day's travel the time taken and the nature of the terrain crossed, sometimes with a note of the weather, especially when it changed. Information about any archaeological sites seen or visited is normally recorded too, along with socio-economic and political material when this could be obtained from his hosts and travelling companions. The journals were usually written up in ink at the end of each day, though sometimes a run of several days was written up together. They must have been compiled from rough notes actually made whilst riding along for it is difficult to imagine Leake remembering everything, including times, in minute detail. Continuous prose is used in the notebooks, though common words are often abbreviated. Sketch maps and measured plans sometimes appear, but landscape and architectural drawings are extremely rare. The notebooks were edited in due course by Leake to produce the chronological and topographical basis for his books, but the two texts are remarkably close, with two main exceptions.

The first exception is the omission from the published version of the travels of the names of most of the people encountered. Initial letters are generally used instead. The other and more conspicuous difference between the two versions, manuscript and published, is the extended analysis of the ancient topography of the various areas visited. This is a major element in the published travels. It is, however, only a minor component of the manuscript texts. Although Leake clearly carried some of the basic classical texts with him, including one of Pausanias, he had neither the access to a full range of reference works nor probably the time to deal with all the problems of ancient topography which emerged from his journeys. Nonetheless, Leake's discussion of ancient topography, based

---

[30] Public Record Office, Kew, 78/65.

on field work and exhaustive study not only of the ancient texts but also of epigraphic and numismatic evidence, is the basis for his reputation as a scholar. His identification of ancient sites, whether of names occurring in the ancient authorities or of sites without known ancient names, is particularly important for scholars today but attention must also be paid to his observations on the location and topography of ancient battlefields such as Marathon and Pharsala.[31]

Leake's scholarly methods were not particularly unique. They involved the careful comparison of the topographical information in the ancient texts, often very sparse, with the actual situation as he had seen it, travelling through the landscape. The evidence of coins and inscriptions was brought in to fix locations, where relevant. Where his own field work proved inadequate, he resorted to already published travel accounts and sought the help of contemporaries who had also been in Greece. These certainly included John Hawkins (1761-1841)[32] but probably also John Morritt of Roxeby (1772-1843) and Lord 'Athenian' Aberdeen (1784-1860). Leake knew these men through the Society of Dilettanti which he joined in 1814, on Hamilton's recommendation.[33]

In time Leake was recognised as a formidable authority on the topography of ancient Greece, but he took his time in bringing his work to publication. In part this must be due to the detailed and patient nature of his scholarship. I presume that he read and collated the ancient

[31] On Marathon: W.M. Leake 'On the demi of Athens', *Transactions of the Royal Society of Literature*, 1:2 (1829), 114-283; W. Martin Leake, *On Some Disputed Questions of Ancient Geography* (London: John Murray, 1857), 53-55. Compare with N.G.L. Hammond, 'The campaign and battle of Marathon', *Journal of Hellenic Studies*, 88 (1968), 13-57. On Pharsala: Leake, *op. cit.* (1835), IV, 476-84; W. Martin Leake, 'On the military operations of Caesar in Greece, ending with the battle of Pharsalia', *Transactions of the Royal Society of Literature*, 2nd series, 4 (1851), 68-87. Compare with C.B.R. Pelling, 'Pharsalus', *Historia*, 22 (1973), 249-59.

[32] Some of the correspondence survives in the West Sussex County Record Office, Hawkins Ms., Vol. 2, Pt. 2.

[33] Society of Antiquaries, Minute Book of the Dilettanti Society, 6 June 1813; 6 February 1814. The author is grateful to the Late Sir Brinsley Ford for permission to use the Dilettanti Papers.

authorities for himself, though he admits to using an amanuensis to produce a manuscript for the publisher, John Murray.³⁴ It seems likely that he had some form of index system. In part, his delay in reaching publication may have been the result of being discouraged by the savage review of his first work, *Researches on Greece* (1814), in the *Quarterly Review*, possibly written by Hobhouse at the instigation of Byron.³⁵ The reviewer attacked Leake's scholarship and it may be that he felt that each statement which he made about ancient topography in his subsequent works had to be carefully supported and meticulously checked. Leake may also have needed time to improve his ancient Greek. His Latin was probably adequate, for he must have been taught enough to take the entrance examination for the Royal Military Academy, even though the subject was no longer part of the curriculum when he was a gentleman cadet.³⁶ According to the contemporary Greek scholar, Athanasios Psalidas, Leake's modern Greek was better than that of 'any of the English tourists' to visit Ioannina at the beginning of the nineteenth century,³⁷ but was it based on the foundation of a schoolboy study of the ancient language? We know nothing of his education before Woolwich.

The slowness of the scholarly process was not the only reason for the delayed publication of Leake's travel works. He had other work to do. Leake became secretary of the Africa Association in 1822 and then a vice-president of the Royal Geographical Society during the formative years, 1830–1835, when he frequently chaired meetings of its council. In

---

34 Letters from Leake to John Murray, 15 August 1829 and 26 April 1833, John Murray Archives.
35 *Quarterly Review*, 11 (1814), 458–80. Leake's response, 'Answer to the observations on The Researches in Greece, in No. XXII of the Quarterly Review' was published in the *Classical Journal*, 10 (1814), 402–12. For the possible authorship of the review, see Hobhouse to Byron 2 February and 8 March 1815, P.W. Graham (ed.), *Byron's Bulldog: the letters of John Cam Hobhouse to Lord Byron* (Columbus: Ohio State University Press, 1984), 153–7 and 178–80.
36 W.D. Jones, *Records of the Royal Military Academy, Woolwich* (Woolwich: F.J. Catermole, 1851).
37 Quoted by S.S. Wilson, *A Narrative of the Greek Mission* (London: John Snow, 1839), 505.

addition, Leake was a member of the Dilettanti's publication committee from 1823, the same year in which he became a foundation vice-president of the Royal Society of Literature. This was the year in which he resigned from the army, but up until that date he does not appear to have been on the half-pay list and must be assumed to have had active duties to perform.[38] The nature of these is not yet clear, though he liaised with the army of the Swiss Cantons during Napoleon's 'Hundred Days' and did not return to Britain until 1816.[39] In addition, as noted earlier, he wrote more widely than his modern reputation as a travel writer might suggest. Finally, illness probably slowed him down. His jaundice attack occurred when he was twenty-three, and he collapsed with fever on his way to Avlona in Albania when he was twenty-eight.[40] He may never have recovered completely from these illnesses, despite the belief which he and his wife had in the 'blue pill'.[41]

Bibliography

Anon., 'The Researches in Greece', *Quarterly Review*, 11 (1814), 458–80.

Graham, P.W. (ed.), *Byron's Bulldog: the letters of John Cam Hobhouse to Lord Byron* (Columbus: Ohio State University Press, 1984).

Hammond, N.G.L., 'The campaign and battle of Marathon', *Journal of Hellenic Studies*, 88 (1968), 13–57.

Hime, H.W.L., *History of the Royal Regiment of Artillery, 1815–1853* (London: Longmans, Green and Co., 1908).

Jones, W.D., *Records of the Royal Military Academy, Woolwich* (Woolwich: F.J. Catermole, 1851).

---

[38] *A List of the Officers of the Army and the Royal Marines*, 1813–1823 (The Army Lists).

[39] Hertfordshire Country Record Office, Acc. 599/85542–85552 (Correspondence Relating to Switzerland, 1815); Public Record Office, Kew, FO 78/43, Colonel Leake. Military.

[40] Leake, *op. cit.* (1835), I, 379–80.

[41] Leake to Finlay, 27 December 1858, J.M. Hussey (ed.), *The Journals and Letters of George Finlay* (Camberley: Porphyrogenitus, 1995), II, 753–5 (753).

Leake, W. Martin, *Researches in Greece* (London: John Booth).

———, 'Answer to observations on The Researches in Greece, in N° XXII of the Quarterly Review', *Classical Journal*, 10 (1814), 402–12.

———, 'Journey through some provinces of Asia Minor in the year 1800', in R. Walpole (ed.), *Travels in Various Countries of the East; being a continuation of Memoirs Relating to European and Asiatic Turkey* (London: Longman, Hurst, Rees, Orme and Brown, 1820), 185–263.

———, *The Topography of Athens with Some Remarks on its Antiquities* (London: John Murray, 1821; 2nd ed., London: J. Rodwell, 1841).

———, *Journal of a Tour in Asia Minor* (London: John Murray, 1824).

———, *Historical Outline of the Greek Revolution* (London: John Murray, 1826).

———, 'On the Demi of Athens', *Transactions of the Royal Society of Literature*, 1:2 (1829), 114–283.

———, *Travels in the Morea*, 3 vols (London: John Murray, 1830).

———, *Travels in Northern Greece*, 4 vols (London: J. Rodwell, 1835).

———, 'On the military operations of Caesar in Greece, ending with the battle of Pharsalia', *Transactions of the Royal Society of Literature*, 2nd series, 4 (1851), 68–87.

———, *On Some Disputed Questions of Ancient Geography* (London: John Murray, 1857).

———, *Numismata Hellenica. A Catalogue of Greek Coins* (London: John Murray, 1856, 1859).

Leake, W. M. and J. Squire, 'An account of the Greek inscription on Pompey's Pillar', *Archaeologia*, 15 (1806), 59–64.

Mackesy, P., *British Victory in Egypt, 1801* (London: Routledge, 1995).

Pelling, C.B.R., 'Pharsalus', *Historia*, 22 (1973), 249–59.

Rodger, A.B., *The War of the Second Coalition, 1798 to 1801: a strategic commentary* (Oxford: Clarendon Press, 1964).

Shaw, S.J., *Between Old and New: the Ottoman Empire under Sultan Selim III, 1789–1807* (Cambridge, Mass: Harvard University Press, 1971).

Smith, A.H., 'Lord Elgin and his Collection', *Journal of Hellenic Studies*, 36 (1916), 163–372.

Squire, J., 'Travels through part of antient [sic] Coele Syria', in *Memoirs Relating to European and Asiatic Turkey*, edited by I.R. Walpole (London: Longman, Hurst, Rees, Orme and Brown, 1818), 293–352.

Wilson, S.S., *A Narrative of the Greek Mission* (London: John Snow, 1839).

Wittman, W., *Travels in Turkey, Asia-Minor, Syria ...* (London: Richard Phillips, 1803).

Yorke, C. and W. Martin Leake, 'On some Egyptian monuments in the British Museum and other collections', *Transactions of the Royal Society of Literature*, 1:1 (1829), 205–27.

William Martin Leake and the Greek Revival

Hugh C.S. Ferguson

Very few Europeans, and only a handful of British subjects among them, had travelled in the eastern Mediterranean by the first half of the eighteenth century. The only travel book on Greece in English available in that period was one of 1682. Strictly speaking, the Grand Tour in the eighteenth century did not extend to Greece. It was virtually inaccessible since passage had to be obtained on Levant Company or naval vessels, while permits to travel in the Ottoman provinces had to be secured from Constantinople. Local governors were uncooperative. Malaria and outbreaks of bubonic plague made much of Greece unhealthy. Bandits by land and pirates by sea made it dangerous to explore. Athens was little visited and the interior of Greece hardly at all. Many apparently considered a tour of the islands enough to say that they had seen Greece.

It was when wars with France closed that country and Italy that British travellers turned to Greece, and illustrated travel books about it emerged as a new *genre*. After 1800 the numbers of dilettanti travellers increased greatly as the Napoleonic Wars meant that Europe was closed to Grand Tourists, who normally travelled in the Low Countries, France and Italy. Following Nelson's victory at the Nile (1798) and the success of British land forces in the Battle of Alexandria (1801), which resulted in British and Ottoman armies driving the French out of Egypt (then an Ottoman province), the grateful Porte removed all restrictions on British travellers to Greece. In a period of greatly improved relations with the Ottoman authorities, the dilettanti travellers were soon followed by the professionals — artists, architects and archaeologists. In the period 1800–1821 British architect-archaeologists enjoyed a near monopoly of access to the Greek monuments as the Continental architects were not free to travel to Greece while Europe was at war. After 1821, the Greek War of Independence closed the country to students of the monuments. At this time British, French and German architects diverted to Sicily where there were Greek temples of the archaic period to study. This series of historical events meant that British architects were the first to study and publish the Athenian monuments. From the 1750s Greek art and architecture had begun to overtake Roman as the focus of antiquarian study, and in the latter part of the eighteenth century interest in the antique turned away from classical literature and textual study to exploration and archaeology. By 1800 taste and antiquarian interest had shifted from Rome to Greece, and to Athens in particular, as part of a larger European movement.

Colonel Leake was part of this development. As a young man he had been engaged in military map-making in Egypt during 1801–1802 and in the following year had travelled with his friends, Lt John Squire and Richard William Hamilton, to Syria and Greece. They spent some time in and around Athens. From late 1804 until early 1810 Leake explored Greece more fully while engaged on missions of a military and political character for the British government and again visited Athens (January 1806). Leake used his travels on official business to visit ancient sites and, where opportunity offered, to make measurements of ancient structures, particularly of stadia and theatres. He carefully measured the drums of fallen columns and calculated the height at which they must have stood. In the preface to his *Travels in the Morea* he expressed the hope that his representation of the descriptions of the decoration, monuments and art of ancient Greece by the second century traveller, Pausanias, would be useful

> to the cultivators of the fine arts in general; that they might have a tendency to assist the public discrimination on these subjects; and that they are particularly worthy of the attention of those upon whom depends the erection of monuments and public works of every kind, in regard to which few persons

will be so hardy as to assert, that the good taste of this nation has kept pace with its wealth and expenditure.[1]

This opening decade of the nineteenth century, when Leake was exploring Greece, coincides with greatly increased archaeological activity by British architects in Athens, including C.R. Cockerell, who was to become Leake's life-long friend. Among the other young architects of note to visit Athens in the same decade were Robert Smirke and William Wilkins.

Fig. 3. Sir Robert Smirke, R.A. (1781-1867), with permission from the R.I.B.A

Robert Smirke (1781-1867) was a pupil of Sir John Soane (1753-1837) and between 1801 and 1805 he made two visits to the Continent,

---

[1] W.M. Leake, *Travels in the Morea* (London: John Murray, 1830), I, viii-ix.

travelling in Italy, Sicily and Greece. He was knighted in 1832 and was both a Royal Academician and a Fellow of the Royal Society. His major design was the British Museum (1823–1846; Greek Ionic style). Smirke was in Athens during 1802, when Lord Elgin's agents had begun to remove sculptures from the Parthenon. Elgin and Leake were there in the same year but it is not known whether their paths crossed that of Smirke.

Fig. 4. William Wilkins, R.A. (1778–1839), with permission from the R.I.B.A.

William Wilkins (1778–1839) was a Fellow of Caius College, Cambridge, and travelled in Italy, Greece and Asia Minor between 1801 and 1805. He subsequently became a member of the Society of Dilletanti (to which Leake later belonged) and Professor of Architecture at the Royal Academy, 1837–1839. Wilkins' published works include *Antiquities of*

Magna Graecia and *The Civil Architecture of Vitruvius*.[2] While the latter established his reputation as an interpreter of conundrums in the ancient text, his main hypotheses were disproved by archaeological discoveries made in the Parthenon during 1837. Perhaps the most scholarly of the architects of the Greek Revival,[3] his scholarship did not prevent a certain weakness in the composition of such large designs as the National Gallery (1833-1838) and, in Greek Doric style, University College, London (1826-1830).

Cockerell arrived in Greece somewhat later, but of this triumvirate of leading British architects and promoters of the Greek Revival style he was the most important, both for his buildings and his archaeological work. Charles Robert Cockerell (1788-1863) trained in his father's office and was for a time an assistant to Smirke before making a Continental tour devoted to architecture and archaeological study in Asia Minor, Greece, Malta, Sicily and Italy[4]. He subsequently became Professor of Architecture in the Royal Academy (1839-1857) and President of the Royal Institute of British Architects. A member of the Society of Dilettanti, his principal publications were *The Antiquities of Athens*[5] and *The Temple of Jupiter Olympius at Agrigentum*.[6] His work on the temples at Bassae and on Aegina, which he excavated, did not appear until 1860, by which time interest in classical antiquities had waned.[7] Cockerell was architect to the

[2] W. Wilkins, *Antiquities of Magna Graecia* (Cambridge: Cambridge University Press, 1807); W. Wilkins, *The Civil Architecture of Vitruvius* (London: Longman, Hurst, Rees, Orme and Brown, 1813 and 1817 [title page 1812]).

[3] R. W. Liscombe, *William Wilkins, 1778-1839*, (Cambridge: Cambridge University Press, 1980).

[4] C.R. Cockerell, *Travels in Southern Europe and the Levant, 1810-1817* (London: Longmans, 1903).

[5] C.R. Cockerell and T.L. Donaldson, *The Antiquities of Athens*, 4 vols. (London 1825-1830).

[6] C.R. Cockerell, *The Temple of Jupiter Olympius at Agrigentum* (London: Priestley and Weale, 1830).

[7] C.R. Cockerell, *The Temples of Jupiter Panhellenius at Aegina, and of Apollo Epicurius at Bassae* (London: J. Weale, 1860).

Fig. 5. C.R. Cockerell, R.A. (1788–1863), with permission from the R.I.B.A.

Bank of England (from 1833), Surveyor to St Paul's Cathedral, London (1819–1852), and designed the Ashmolean Museum and Taylorian Institute, Oxford (1841–1845). Also noteworthy was his consultancy (1826–1830) for the design of a full-size replica of the Parthenon for Edinburgh, as the Scottish National Memorial to the dead of the Napoleonic Wars (in association with the Edinburgh architect, W.H. Playfair). The project was only partially completed for lack of funds, but it now forms a landmark on Calton Hill at the east end of Princes Street. Cockerell has been described as the one English architect of true genius in the nineteenth century. He was not a revivalist in the strict sense of merely copying ancient forms, but he created a fresh style through the clever synthesis of historical elements drawn from Greece and Rome with the tradition of Wren. The result was an original English Classical style with a slight hint of Baroque.

Cockerell arrived in Greece during 1810, via Constantinople. He had travelled on a Royal Navy ship as a King's Messenger (his father had connections in the Foreign Office). It was shortly afterwards, on a journey to Ioannina, the stronghold of Ali Pasha, that Cockerell met Leake, then British resident at the despot's court and soon to leave Greece for good. Cockerell himself did not return to London until 1817, but came through Paris where his portrait was drawn by Ingres. By this time Leake was at work on his *Topography of Athens* which first appeared in 1821, and Cockerell drew the views of Athens which were engraved as illustrations for the book[8]. In addition to his expertise in architecture and Classical archaeology, Cocherell was an excellent draughtsman and watercolourist, in the strict topographical manner of the time.

For the relatively short period of the Greek Revival, research into ancient Greek buildings and the production of new buildings in Britain in the *Neo Grec* style marched hand-in-hand.[9] Measured drawings of the ancient monuments going back to Stuart and Revett provided the design details for buildings erected in Regency London and elsewhere in the country.[10]

The Greek Revival appears in some form in most European countries affected by the Neo-Classical movement. The German version of Greek Revival architecture tended to be heavy and strictly archaeological in its detail, while the French version was less pure and had symbolic political content alluding to notions of ancient democracy. The British *Neo Grec* was much lighter in spirit — one might even say light-weight, when looking at the stucco frontages of resorts like Brighton, with their serried ranks of Doric porticos. A monumental example is Eaton Square, London SW1, laid out like an ancient forum with the individual Doric porticos of the houses uniting visually to create the effect of a continuous peristyle. The general tone of architecture in Regency England was frivolous, with a succession of fads and fancies in stylistic matters. Architects experimented with the Chinese, Hindu, and Gothic styles for both interiors and exteriors, and, following the Egyptian campaigns, they flirted briefly with Egyptian. Greek and Gothic were the two styles which took root and

---

[8] W.M. Leake, *The Topography of Athens* (London: John Murray, 1821).

[9] J. Mordaunt Crook, *The Greek Revival: Neo-classical attitudes in British architecture, 1760–1870* (London: John Murray, 1972).

[10] J. Stuart and N. Revett, *The Antiquities of Athens*, Vol. 1 (London: J. Haberkorn, 1762); Vol. 2 (London: John Nicols, 1787); Vol. 3 (London: John Nicols, 1794).

became preferred for public buildings, the Gothic style superseding the Greek. In England both the Greek and the Gothic revival styles began with small garden monuments in the mid-eighteenth century, introduced into landscaped estates. The first Greek Revival building is a miniature Doric temple of 1758, designed by James Stuart, at Hagley Hall in Worcestershire, seat of Lord Cobham. After the publication of the second volume of Stuart and Revett's *The Antiquities of Athens* in 1787 recorded the buildings of the Athenian Acropolis in great detail, this source material for design became generally available to architects. More than half a century later, Leake argued in the introduction to his *Topography of Athens* for the superiority of ancient Greek art and particularly of ancient Greek architecture, and went on to suggest that the study of the 'genuine architecture of the Greeks' and the application of their rules would lead to a considerable improvement in British architecture.[11] Over this fifty year period the *Neo Grec* style gained momentum; by 1830 or so it was at its height. By the 1840s, however, the Greek style was falling out of favour. The British Museum, completed 1840, was the last major Greek Revival building, while the Euston Propylaeum (the grand portico to Euston Station) built in 1840, is the last example of monumental Doric. The commencement in 1840 of the construction of the new Houses of Parliament, marks the onset of the Gothic Revival in the design of public buildings.

Stuart and Revett's *Antiquities of Athens* (1762–1794) greatly assisted the spread of Greek Revival buildings in Britain but, more importantly, the authors' expedition to Athens in 1751 marks the beginning of scientific archaeology in Greece. The two men spent nearly four years in Athens (1751–1755) engaged on survey work. All previous publications had been of the antiquarian travelogue variety with very few remarks on ancient buildings, and no worthwhile illustrations. There had been no book in English to give a description of Athens since the late seventeenth

---

[11] W.M. Leake, *The Topography of Athens with Some Remarks upon its Antiquities* (London: John Murray, 1821), particularly cxii–cxiv.

century. This was Sir George Wheler's *A Journey into Greece*[12] and Stuart and Revett had used it to plan their survey work. They did not undertake much excavation, apart from uncovering substructures, and they were more interested in recording the surviving monuments, particularly the buildings on the Acropolis of Athens. They worked in difficult conditions. The Ottoman authorities, like their predecessors, used the Acropolis as a fortress and restricted entry. The interior was covered with buildings which lay between, and to some extent, incorporated the structures surviving from antiquity. Drawing and measuring were awkward to accomplish. Inaccuracies inevitably crept in, especially where heights were concerned — there were no long ladders to be found in the locality.

Although the publication of *The Antiquities of Athens* provided the main impetus to the Greek Revival on Britain, it was reinforced by the arrival in London in 1811–1812 of the final shipments of the Elgin Marbles, their subsequent exhibition, and eventual purchase by the British Museum (1816). The Marbles provided further momentum to the Greek Revival because they showed how low-relief motifs could be directly applied in an architectural setting. The Athenaeum Club (1827–1830), of which Leake was a founding member, and the Hyde Park Ionic Screen (1824–1825), both by Decimus Burton, incorporated the Panathenaic Frieze from the Parthenon; in the case of the Athenaeum Club the frieze runs round the top of the building under the cornice. The Reform Club (1838–1841) and the Royal College of Surgeons of England, re-modelled between 1835 and 1837, both by Sir Charles Barry, have similar but smaller-scale internal friezes.

Problems in the identification of the Parthenon sculptures had been partially solved by Leake in the first edition of *The Topography of Athens* (1821), and further elucidation of the identity of the figures in the pedimental groups was published in the second edition of 1841. C.R.

---

[12] G. Wheler [Wheeler], *A Journey into Greece* (London: W. Cademan, R. Kettlewell and A. Churchill, 1682).

Cockerell and T.L. Donaldson brought out a revised and augmented edition of Stuart and Revett's *Antiquities of Athens*, four volumes in two in a reduced format, but with several chapters of new material.[13]. In additions to sections on the Temple of Aphaia on Aegina (where Cockerell excavated the Aeginetan Marbles, now in Munich) and the Temple of Apollo at Bassae in the Peloponnesse (where he had uncovered the Bassae Marbles, now in the British Museum) there was a chapter on *entasis* in Greek buildings. *Entasis* is the convex swelling of the shaft of a Doric column which gives the profile an almost imperceptible curvature. This 1830 publication provided, for the first time, measured drawings of Doric column profiles, with dimensions, for examples from the Parthenon, the Theseum, and other Greek buildings. The data necessary to replicate 'Athenian' *entasis* thus became available to practising architects, and the feature makes its appearance in London buildings about the same date. The Pantechnicon (Motcomb Street, London SW1) and some porticos in Eaton Square seem to be the earliest examples of authentic Greek *entasis*.

Entasis had first been discovered in Greek architecture by Cockerell back in 1810 when he worked on the Temple of Aphaia on Aegina. As a result of the discovery he returned to Athens in 1814 and verified the existence in the Parthenon columns of the same subtle curvature, hitherto undetected. Leake did not discuss this phenomenon in Greek architecture, though he did remark that the purpose of *entasis* in Roman columns was quite different.

---

[13] Cockerell and Donaldson, *op. cit.*

Fig. 6. Thomas L. Donaldson FRIBA (1795–1885), with permission from the R.I.B.A.

Cockerell's collaborator, Thomas L. Donaldson (1795–1885), was Professor of Architecture at University College, London, and President of the Royal Institute of British Architects (1863–1865), but shared with Leake an interest in numismatics, to the extent of publishing a study of classical architecture as represented on ancient coins.[14] He visited Greece in 1819–1820 and independently discovered the inward vertical inclination of the columns in the Parthenon colonnade. He established by measurement that the axes of the columns on the fronts, if projected, would meet at a distant point vertically above them, and that the columns along the flanks would likewise converge inwards to the centre.

Architectural investigations on the spot were terminated by the outbreak of the Greek War of Independence in March 1821. It ended the architectural phase of Greek archaeology, and it was only with the end of the War and the establishment of the modern Greek state with Athens as its capital (1834) that archaeological activity resumed under an embryonic archaeological service. Under the direction of Ludwig Ross and his successor, Kyriakos Pittakis, the first Greek Superintendent of Antiquities, the work of clearing the Acropolis of non-Hellenic buildings and rubbish commenced. The first symbolic restoration work was on two columns in the Parthenon, and many blocks and column drums were retrieved at this time. The first major discovery was of the dismantled blocks of the small temple of Niké-Apteros ('Wingless Victory') by Eduard Schaubert. He correctly identified them and made the first reconstruction of the building.

However, the most important archaeological discovery of the period came in 1837 when the substructure and platform of the Parthenon was cleared of architectural fragments and rubbish. When the steps were cleared, an upward curvature was observed in the horizontal lines of the steps on all four sides of the temple. It was concluded that these were constructive curvatures, that is created by design and not in response to settlement or earthquake. This discovery is independently credited to John Pennethorne, an English architect, and to Joseph Hoffer, who was the first to publish a note on the curvatures in *Wiener Bauzeitung* (1838). However, the first description and discussion of the Parthenon curvatures

---

[14] T.L. Donaldson, *Architectura Numismatica: Or architectural medals of classic antiquity* (London: Day and Son, 1859).

in English actually appears in the second edition of Leake's *Topography of Athens* (1841).

The discovery of upward curvatures in the lines of the Parthenon steps almost immediately started a debate as to their original purpose, and also gave a new significance to the earlier discoveries of *entasis* and the inward vertical inclination of the columns. Instead of treating these features as unrelated curiosities of construction, the question was raised as to whether they were part of some unified design scheme involving the systematic use of visual refinements. Various motives were suggested, including perspective enhancement and the correction of optical illusions. Eventually a vast literature developed on these topics, as professional and learned journals multiplied during the nineteenth century.

London-based architects were well informed about the discoveries on the Acropolis. Kyriakos Pittakis was in regular touch with Donaldson, by that time RIBA Secretary for Foreign Correspondence. The two corresponded on a variety of archaeological topics, writing in French. Cockerell must have become aware of the discovery of the Parthenon curvatures almost immediately for later in 1837 he incorporated these features into the stonework of the lower portion of the newly-commenced Library for the University of Cambridge. The subtle upward curvatures are found in the lines of the base course at the rear of the building in Senate House Passage, off Trinity Street, and are readily observable just below eye-level.[15]

The work of clearing the Acropolis of debris and old buildings had begun during the 1836–1837 season. In an area south-west of the Parthenon the remains of an ancient workshop were uncovered. Among the finds were portions of architrave with brightly coloured ornament. The colouring had retained its original brightness, though this quickly faded in the strong sunlight. An account of the discovery was sent to

---

[15] D. Watkin, *The Life and Work of C.R. Cockerell* (London 1974), 193. The (old) Library subsequently became the Spring Law Library, and is now a college building.

London in two letters by an eye-witness, Charles Holte Bracebridge, an Englishman resident in Athens. Published as an appendix by Christopher Wordsworth to the second edition of his book on Athens and Attica,[16] the letters caused a revival of the polychromy controversy. Traces of colour on Greek buildings or architectural fragments had been noted in Athens by Stuart and Revett around 1752 and again by Wilkins in 1802. Edward Dodwell found traces of colour on the Propylaea to the Acropolis in 1805, while Joseph Woods noted traces of external painting and gilding in the Parthenon in 1818. However, these were all vestigial remains which had been exposed to the elements and were faded. The findings of 1836, with their use of polychrome decoration in strong primary colours, came as a complete revelation.

The editor of the one-volume version of Stuart and Revett's *Antiquities of Athens* (1841) wrote 'unluckily the evidence for these incredibilities is most exasperatingly clear'.[17] The French had been the first to recognise the implications around 1805, that polychromy was an integral part of ancient temple design. Jacques-Ignace Hittorff met Donaldson in Italy in 1822, and apparently it was Donaldson who first stirred his interest in the ancient Greek use of polychromy. After investigations in Sicily, Hittorff presented his developed theories on polychromy to the Académie des Beaux Arts in 1830, and a widespread controversy developed in the academies of Europe.[18] Hittorff visited London in 1836, the first of several visits to participate in the work of a special Committee set up on the initiative of the Royal Institute of British Architects (RIBA) to enquire

---

[16] C. Wordsworth, *Athens and Attica: Journal of a Residence There* (2nd ed., London: John Murray, 1837), 280–1.

[17] J. Stuart and N. Revett, *The Antiquities of Athens* (London: Leicester, 1841).

[18] Hittorff devoted the years 1827–1851 to the Greek system of polychromy and produced his *Architecture polychrome chez les Grecs* in 1851. This in turn provided many of the examples for Owen Jones's *The Grammar of Ornament* (London: Day and Son, 1856). Interest in the subject then faded but revived somewhat in 1984 with a controversial proposal to redecorate the entrance hall of the British Museum according to Smirke's original polychomatic scheme of 1846.

into the likelihood of the Parthenon sculptures being coloured in Antiquity. The Committee's remit was the 'scientific investigation into the use of colour in the decoration of the Elgin Marbles', and it met regularly between December 1836 and July 1837. The chairman was Leake's close friend, W.R. Hamilton, and its members included the scientist, Michael Faraday, the sculptor, Richard Westmacott, as well as the architects, Cockerell and Donaldson. Leake acted as a consultant and corresponded with Donaldson on particular questions. Faraday took samples and made microscopic examinations but, in the end, no trace of colour was found. The results of the Committee's work were published in the RIBA *Transactions* for 1840.

Leake had been involved in the Committee's work because he was regarded as an authority on the Parthenon sculptures. He had discussed them in the first edition of *The Topography of Athens* some twenty-five years earlier and in 1835 he is mentioned as an adviser on the installation of a copy of the Panathenaic Frieze in the saloon of a country house, Terling Place, near Maldon, Essex, for the Strutt family. Leake owned a set of casts of the Parthenon frieze, and the Terling Place copies may have been made from his originals. Leake's set of Parthenon sculpture casts was sold to the Royal Danish Museum, Copenhagen.

In 1841 a reducing machine was patented which enabled the making of two-thirds or half-size copies of sculptures and the British Museum was able to produce reduced casts of the Elgin Marbles for the provincial Schools of Design that were established between 1841 and 1852. In the Art Schools which followed after 1852, a set of Parthenon casts became a standard part of the educational equipment. Thus, belatedly, part of Lord Elgin's original plan — the promotion of art education — was given effect.

In 1842 the members of RIBA Elgin Marbles Committee of 1836–1837 were reconvened to examine and report on the fragments of marble brought from Xanthus in Lycia to the British Museum by the British government. The Committee, including Cockerell, Donaldson and Leake, was required to investigate the condition of the sculptured figures and fragments of marble with regard to the possible use of colour in their decoration. The Xanthian Marbles Committee reported in January 1843, once again inconclusively.

The second edition of Leake's *Topography of Athens* (1841) remained the standard work on the ancient city until the publication of Walter Judeich's *Topographie von Athen*,[19] which took account of the findings of excavations carried out since Leake's day. In the last quarter of the nineteenth century the foreign Schools of Archaeology became established at Athens. The French were active from 1846, when the French School was founded. Archaeological expeditions were now funded by universities and museums, and research was based on teamwork under official supervision. Thus Leake and his architect associates belong to a period when the individual investigator, with private funds and operating in a freelance way, could make a valuable contribution to knowledge. Leake's scholarly researches, backed by his practical knowledge of the region, enabled most of the important classical sites in Greece and Asia Minor to be identified. Professor W.M. Ramsay, who followed in his footsteps as the historical geographer of Asia Minor, in 1890 expressed indebtedness to Leake's pioneer work, and paid tribute to his 'wonderful topographical eye and instinct', with the words, 'Few that study Greek history ... realise what we owe to the greatest of modern Topographers. Leake ... has done more to make a real understanding of Greek life possible than any other Englishman.'[20]

Not all of the architects active in Greece after 1800 made discoveries of significance; mostly they have left a legacy of measured drawings, sketches and charming watercolours which record the life of late Ottoman Athens in the period before the Greek War of Independence. However, Cockerell, Donaldson and Wilkins did make original and significant

---

[19] W. Judeich, *Topographie von Athen*, 2 vols (Munich: Beck, 1905).
[20] R.W. Ramsay, *The Historical Geography of Asia Minor*, Royal Geographical Society Supplementary Papers (London: John Murray, 1890), IV, 98.

contributions to knowledge. Although the early publications which resulted from the architectural phase of Athenian topography were eventually superseded, H.W. Inwood's *The Erechtheion at Athens*,[21] published in 1827 and the result of survey work on the Acropolis in 1819, together with his measured drawings, remained the authoritative source for accurate details of that building until re-measurement a hundred years later by J.M. Paton and G.P. Stevens.[22] H.W. Inwood (1794–1843) corrected errors in Stuart and Revett's work and published the north doorway in large-scale detail for the first time. Together with his father, William Inwood, H.W. Inwood designed St. Pancras New Church in London (Southampton Row at Euston Road), which is a landmark of the Greek Revival in England. Inspired by the Erechtheion, the design incorporates the doorway from the north portico and the caryatid porch, while the church tower is an adaptation of the Tower of the Winds in Athens. Thus here, as in other notable buildings of the Greek Revival, the archaeological researches of the British traveller-architects were put into practical use in the design of contemporary buildings. They live on as important elements in the townscapes and landscapes of twenty-first century Britain.

Bibliography

Cockerell, C.R., *The Temple of Jupiter Olympius at Agrigentum* (London: Priestley and Weale, 1830).

———, *The Temples of Jupiter Panhellenius at Aegina, and of Apollo Epicurius at Bassae* (London: J. Weale, 1860).

———, *Travels in Southern Europe and the Levant, 1810–1817*, edited by his son, S.P. Cockerell (London: Longmans, 1903).

---

[21] H.W. Inwood, *The Erechtheion at Athens* (London: J. Carpenter, 1827).

[22] J.M. Paton and G.P. Stevens, *The Erechtheum: text and atlas* (Cambridge, Mass.: Harvard University Press, 1927).

Cockerell, C.R. and T.L. Donaldson, eds, *The Antiquities of Athens*, 4 vols (London, 1825-1830).

Crook, J. Mordaunt, *The Greek Revival: neo-classical attitudes in British architecture, 1760-1870* (London: John Murray, 1972).

Donaldson, T.L., *Architectura Numismatica; or, architectural medals of classic antiquity* (London: Day, 1859).

Hittorff, J.I., *Architecture polychrome chez les Grecs* (Paris, 1851).

Hoffer, J. 'Der Parthenon in Athen', *Wiener Allgemeine Bauzeitung*, III (1838).

Jones, O., *The Grammar of Ornament* (London: Day, 1856).

Judeich, W., *Topographie von Athen*, 2 vols (Munich: Beck, 1905).

Leake, W.M., *The Topography of Athens* (London: John Murray, 1821; J. Rodwell, 1841).

——— , *Travels in the Morea*, 3 vols (London: John Murray, 1830).

Liscombe, R.W., *William Wilkins, 1778-1839* (Cambridge: Cambridge University Press, 1980).

Paton, J.M. and G.P. Stevens, *The Erechtheum: text and atlas* (Cambridge, Mass.: Harvard University Press, 1927).

Stuart, J. and N. Revett, *The Antiquities of Athens*, Vol. 1 (London J. Haberkorn, 1762); Vol. 2 (London: John Nicols, 1787); Vol. 3 (London: John Nicols, 1794).

——— , *The Antiquities of Athens* (London: Leicester, 1841).

Watkin, D., *The Life and Work of C.R. Cockerell* (London, 1974).

Wheler [Wheeler], G., *A Journey into Greece* (London: W. Cademan, R. Kettlewell and A. Churchill, 1682).

Wilkins, W. *Antiquities of Magna Graecia* (Cambridge: Cambridge University Press, 1807).

——— , *The Civil Architecture of Vitruvius* (London: Longman, Hurst, Rees, Orme, and Brown, 1813 and 1817 [title page 1812].

Wordsworth, C., *Athens and Attica: journal of a residence there* (2nd ed., London: John Murray, 1837).

Leake in Kythera

Davina Huxley

Kythera, or Cerigo, to give it its Venetian name, is a small island in an important position. A southerly outlier of the Ionian Islands, it straddles the strait between Crete and the fingers of the Peloponnese. Colonel Leake had occasion to go there twice, and as was his custom, put each visit to good use. Years later he combined his observations on the ground with his research into the historical texts to form a small section of one of his books. So the island can provide us with characteristic glimpses of his life: first, as the young soldier on an adventurous journey; secondly, a few years later in a more responsible role in military intelligence combined with diplomatic status; and, finally, more than twenty years later as a respected scholar and author.

In September 1802 Leake reached Kythera in an unexpected and shocking fashion. He was shipwrecked on the east coast of the island, close to the village of Avlemon on the sharp rocky shore just outside the bay of San Nicolo, as it was known to the Venetians, who had built a small fort there. He and his companions were lucky to be able to scramble ashore as their ship *Mentor* went down. All their belongings and the cargo were lost, and that was especially serious because it included all Leake's notes on his recent journeys and, furthermore, the ship was carrying a consignment of the Elgin Marbles, of future fame or infamy, according to one's view. Lord Elgin, as ambassador to the Porte, had tried to help Leake in his career as a young officer.[1] He also had with him as a private secretary in Constantinople another young man, a cousin of his wife, named William Hamilton, who was the same age as Leake and with

---

[1] I am grateful to the Earl of Elgin for permission to read some of the documents referring to Leake in the Elgin Papers.

similar interests in antiquity. The two had travelled together up the Nile, in Syria and most recently in Greece itself with another soldier, an engineer officer (later Lieutenant Colonel) Squire, who was to die in the Peninsular War. They made their journeys with purpose: using surveying instruments in Greece with a view to map-making, recording inscriptions and viewing ancient battle fields.

Meanwhile, Elgin's artist Giovanni Lusieri, a topographical and archaeological draftsman of great ability most of whose work would be lost in yet another shipwreck, was supervising the loading of the ambassador's yacht *Mentor* at Piraeus. This was a delicate business. Another of Elgin's collectors had complained of 'plaguey frights' for the safety of the antiquities in his shipment. Another problem was that there was only one decent four-wheeled cart available in Athens for transporting large blocks of stone and it was often spirited away by Lusieri's rival collector, M. Fauvel, the French consul. But Lusieri at last was able to report to his employer that the ship had left for Malta on 15 September with her Scottish captain, the three passengers, crew, and seventeen cases of antiquities. A violent storm struck them off Cape Taenarum (Matapan), driving them towards Egypt with the ship making water and two men on the pumps. On 17 September they ran for shelter at Avlemon, the anchors failed to hold, they cut the cables and hoisted sail; but the ship drifted on to the rocks and sank immediately (Fig. 7).

The first items on the heavy list of expenses which Elgin had eventually to pay were for 'cloathing of Captain Leake and Mr Squire 300 Turkish piastres'. The unfortunate Hamilton was obliged to stay on the island to attempt salvage operations. Sponge divers from Kalymnos recovered one of Leake's boxes, the contents ruined, and part of the frieze from the temple of Wingless Victory. It was not until two years and many attempts later in October 1804 that the salvage was completed. Even then, we are startled to learn, the sculptures spent another four months buried on the beach at Avlemon under seaweed, brushwood and big stones for better protection from pirates and the weather. Someone building a garden wall nearby extracted a few pieces from what must have seemed to be a convenient quarry, until restrained by the British consul. Finally in 1805

Fig. 7. Avlemon from the chapel of Ayios Georgios. The *Mentor* was wrecked just outside the promontory on the left of the harbour mouth, from a photograph by Davina Huxley.

a ship was sent by Admiral Lord Nelson, commanding the Mediterranean fleet, to collect the Marbles.[2]

Leake, however, had left the island by the end of the month, but not before he had taken note of the remains of the ancient city visible on the Palaeokastro mountain a little way inland. This and other observations he would one day work into the final publication of his travels. But now in the brief interval of the Peace of Amiens (1802–1803) he was able to travel home across Europe for well-deserved leave.

Four years later, in September 1806, he found himself once more in Kythera at exactly the same season of the year, which served to remind him of his earlier disastrous visit. This one was very different. The war with France had broken out once more; the British government, anxious as ever about threats to its influence in the eastern Mediterranean and the route to India, was trying to bolster the Turks against any possible French invasion of Greece. Leake had been sent to gather military and political intelligence. After travelling in Epirus, central Greece and the Peloponnese in 1805 and much of 1806 he had hired a boat and toured round the Ionian Islands before landing at Kapsali, the port at the south end of the island, with its double harbour tucked in far below the Chora, then, as now, the chief town of the island, with the great Venetian castro dominating both.[3]

The Ionian Islands had undergone remarkable political upheavals since the Venetians had yielded them up to the French in 1797, but after a brief encounter with revolutionary ideas, the islands changed hands again and were formed into the Septinsular Republic, its autonomy guaranteed by the unusual combination of Turkey and Russia. Leake had his tent pitched in Kapsali and there met the British consul, Emanuel Calucci, who had done so much to help the shipwrecked party. In the evening they walked together up the twisting road to the town to attend a baptism in the house of the Russian vice-consul when the Prytano (the Governor), a man from Zante, stood as godfather. Leake was careful to note the Prytano as a man

[2] A.H. Smith, 'Lord Elgin and his collection', *The Journal of Hellenic Studies*, 36 (1916), 163–372.

[3] W.M. Leake, *Travels in Northern Greece*, 4 vols (London: S. Rodwell, 1835), III, 69–76.

'disinterested, liberal and impartial'. The salaries of the officials are recorded; the garrison scrutinised and found to consist of only two Russian officers with one company and a few Albanians. A few days were spent gathering information about the island's economy and many other details of the lives of the islanders: how many of the men were obliged to work seasonally in Asia Minor cultivating Turkish lands and collecting madder in the mountains which enabled them to save a little money to buy land at home. Very little meat was eaten, assisted by the 150 fast days of the Greek calendar, but there were quails and hares, and the island's famous thyme-flavoured honey. Leaving Kapsali he sailed round the west coast to look at the great cavern (the Ayia Sophia cave) below Milopotamo, where the river turned twelve mills, and then left for Melos.

This combination of a quite short visit, the political contacts, the military eye at work, the geographer's grasp of the nature of the terrain, its produce and its people is characteristic of Leake. The task is always well executed, but what makes him so remarkable is that, despite the pressures of travel in dangerous times and his official duties, he always contrives to look for signs of the historic past, and usually finds them.

Long after he had left Greece and the wars with France were over, he retired from the army and began to write his books. Now he looks at Kythera again in his mind's eye (for he never went back to Greece) and all the old experiences are recaptured from his notebooks and combined with more scholarly work on the ancient sources. Even on his journeys he had taken some texts with him and was, it seems, already formidably well read in ancient history and geography. Quietly in London he disentangles the accounts of Thucydides and Herodotus, where there are discrepancies with those of Pausanias and Xenophon, and can identify the classical city of the Kythereans with the walling he saw when travelling across the island after the shipwreck. Here was the temple of Aphrodite, the Syrian Venus of the Phoenicians, and according to Pausanias the most ancient and holy of those dedicated to the goddess in Greece.

Fig. 8. Avlemon Harbour today, from a photograph by Davina Huxley.

In old age he still had contact with Kythera for in 1850 at a meeting of the Royal Society of Literature he presented a paper which included a memoir by John Calucci, the son of the consul, about the present state of the island and new archaeological finds made there, including a remarkable cuneiform inscription, since lost. The contradictory ancient texts are discussed again by the Colonel. He notes too the presence of columns and cut blocks on the probable temple site on the Palaeokastro mountain, and adds that 'these remains would deserve an accurate examination accompanied by drawings and measurements'.[4] Just over a century later this was indeed done, although without excavation, by the British School at Athens and the University of Pennsylvania Museum, in the course of a campaign to excavate the Minoan settlement by the sea, which even the Colonel's eagle eye was not, at that date, yet trained to recognise.[5]

References

Coldstream, J.N. and G. L. Huxley (eds), *Kythera: excavations and studies* (London: Faber, 1972).

Leake, W.M., *Travels in Northern Greece*, 4 vols (London: S. Rodwell, 1835).

——, 'Some remarks on the island Cerigo, anciently Cythera', *Transactions of the Royal Society of Literature*, Second Series, 4 (1853), 255–60.

Smith, A.H., 'Lord Elgin and his collection', *The Journal of Hellenic Studies*, 36 (1916), 163–372.

---

[4] W.M. Leake, 'Some remarks on the island Cerigo, anciently Cythera', *Transactions of the Royal Society of Literature*, Second Series, 4 (1853), 255–60.

[5] J.N. Coldstream and G. L. Huxley (eds), *Kythera: excavations and studies* (London: Faber, 1972).

Fig. 9. Portrait of Sir William Gell, *c.* 1814. Artist unknown. Originally published in Edith Clay, *Sir William Gell in Italy* (London: Hamish Hamilton, 1976). Reproduced by permission of Penguin UK.

Straddling the Aegean: William Gell 1811–1813

Charles Plouviez

There is a lot about the life of William Gell that is forgotten, wrongly reported or deliberately concealed. We can be sure he was at Cambridge, but there is some confusion in the reference books about whether he graduated from Jesus or Emmanuel College, and where or when he held his fellowship. Edward Daniel Clarke, himself a Jesus man, describes Gell as 'of Jesus College', so let us give Jesus the honours. In any event, he achieved his MA in 1804 and in the same year, having already explored the site, published his first book, *The Topography of Troy*, boldly dedicated to the glamorous Georgiana, Duchess of Devonshire.[1] Described by A.C. Lascarides in his 1977 exhibition catalogue as 'the most beautiful book on Troy ever published',[2] this book is still prized by book collectors, but of small scholarly interest since, as Schliemann was to prove, he had chosen the wrong site.

Gell was the younger son of a wealthy Derbyshire landowner, and like so many younger sons was perpetually hard up. He was also a remarkably versatile scholar and *bon viveur*, whose name now crops up in unexpected contexts. As an undergraduate in 1797, he made the conventional tour of the Lake District, sketching and keeping a journal which remained unpublished until 1968, and was sufficiently enraptured to build himself a cottage overlooking Grasmere before 1800. Wordsworth, untypically,

---

[1] For Gell's life see: *DNB*, 21 (1890), 115–17; J.A. Venn, *Alumni Cantabrigienses* (Cambridge: Cambridge University Press, 1947), Part II, III, 32; W.H. Rollinson (ed.), *A Tour in the Lakes made in 1747 by William Gell* (Newcastle: Frank Graham, 1968); W. Knight (ed.), *Journals of Dorothy Wordsworth* (London: Macmillan, 1919), I, 31–60; R.R. Madden, *The Literary Life and Correspondence of the Countess of Blessington* (London: T.C. Newby, 1885).

[2] A.C. Lascarides, *The Search for Troy* (Bloomington: Indiana University Press, 1997).

approved of the cottage and he and Dorothy used to borrow Gell's boat. And in much later life Gell was host to the ailing and slightly senile Sir Walter Scott in Italy, and guided him around Pompeii. But he is probably best remembered in literary circles as a footnote to Byron, who wrote in the manuscript of 'English Bards and Scotch Reviewers':

> Of Dardan tours let Dilettanti tell,
> I leave topography to coxcomb Gell.

Byron was so impressed when he met Gell that he promoted him to 'classic Gell' before publication; then in the fifth edition, having seen the Troad for himself, downgraded him to 'rapid Gell' because he had 'topographised King Priam's dominions in three days.'

To his contemporaries, Gell became best known for his pocket itineraries of central and southern Greece, which were the first really practical travel guides since Pausanias and which can still be followed with profit; and for the first English guidebook to Pompeii. Among his wide-ranging social circle, which included the Prince of Wales' unfortunate wife Princess Caroline, he had a reputation as a witty talker and correspondent such that the poet Tom Moore, who must have known Byron's manuscript, could describe him in 1820 as 'still a coxcomb but rather amusing'.[3] No doubt this is one of the reasons why, in spite of the wide range of his studies in topography and what then passed as archaeology, the general consensus of posterity has been that, as the old *Dictionary of National Biography* puts it, 'he was not a profound scholar.' In his later years, his importance in encouraging Gardner Wilkinson's Egyptian studies has only recently been recognised,[4] but his full contribution to the foundations of Aegean studies has been seriously diminished by the effects of an unfortunate press report.

When Gell died in 1836, an obituary in the *Gentleman's Magazine* recorded that he 'received the honour of a knighthood on his return from a mission to the Ionian islands, May 14, 1803.'[5] Nearly every word in that

---

[3] Madden, *op. cit.*, 10, quoting Moore's diary of August 1820.
[4] Jason Thompson, *Sir Gardner Wilkinson and His Circle* (Austin: University of Texas Press, 1992).
[5] *Gentleman's Magazine*, new series, 5 (1836), 665–6.

statement is untrue; nonetheless, it was copied *verbatim* by the *Annual Register*, and has been repeated in every reference book and account of Gell, with one honourable exception, down to the present day. The exception was Edith Clay in the introduction to her edition of Gell's letters from Italy, and even she managed still to retain a fictitious diplomatic mission to the Ionian islands.[6]

In fact, Gell's mission was to *Ionia*, that is south-west Anatolia, not to the Ionian islands, on the western side of Greece. It was not diplomatic but archaeological, a mission properly so called because it was commissioned by the Society of Dilettanti. And Gell was knighted in 1814, not 1803, though the date of 14 May is correct. This grotesque accumulation of error was further compounded by the eccentricities of the Society's publications.

According to Horace Walpole, the Society of Dilettanti began as 'a club for which the nominal qualification is having been in Italy, and the real one, being drunk.'[7] But to show its serious nature, it had already sponsored one successful mission to the ancient Greek sites around the Aegean back in 1764–1765. Until well into the nineteenth century, most academic classical scholars had no interest in archaeology; indeed, some were positively hostile to it.[8] The Society's members, though mostly excellent classicists themselves, were chiefly artists and architects together with their moneyed patrons, the quintessential Grand Tourists. Consequently, the main objective of their archaeological studies was, as Gell later defined it, 'the improvement of architecture.'[9]

The first mission journeyed to a brief prepared by Robert Wood, of Palmyra fame, and was led by Richard Chandler, accompanied by Nicholas Revett and William Pars. Their report and drawings had been

[6] Edith Clay (ed.), *Sir William Gell in Italy* (London: Hamish Hamilton, 1976), 2.
[7] Quoted by Adolf Michaelis, *Ancient Marbles in Great Britain* (Cambridge: Cambridge University Press, 1882), 63.
[8] R. Stoneman, *Land of Lost Gods* (London: Hutchinson, 1987), 135; A. Schapp, *The Discovery of the Past* (London: British Museum, 1996), 308.
[9] *Report of the Committee of the Society of Dilettanti, appointed by the Society to superintend the expedition lately sent by them to Greece and Ionia* (London: W. Bulmer, 1814).

published in two folio volumes in 1769 and 1797, modelled on the outstandingly influential volumes of *The Antiquities of Athens* by Stuart and Revett, in which publication the Society had also played a modest role. In addition, with due acknowledgement to the Society, Chandler had published his own journals in two volumes.

Almost fifty years on, a second expedition was intended to bring Chandler's findings up to date in the light of improved knowledge. William Gell, now thirty-three years old with a string of books to his name and already a member of the Society, was chosen to lead the team.

Gell was the obvious man for the job, having already made tours in Greece and Asia Minor, and published three topographical and archaeological books. He had hands-on experience of the Ottoman Empire, a sound classical education, and some ability (if not much inspiration) as an artist. He was to be paid £50 a month plus expenses, and to be accompanied by two young architects, each paid £200 a year to act as draughtsmen: Francis Bedford, a former clerk of Soane's, and John Peter Gandy, a pupil of Wyatt and younger brother of the better-known J.M. Gandy. Gell's intimate friend, the wealthy and Honourable Richard Keppel Craven, tagged along at his own expense. Provision for the tour was lavish: bills paid in advance covered items as mundane as pencils, £1.90, or as esoteric as a gold repeater watch for Gell at £55. In addition, from his earlier experience, Gell suggested 'the propriety of carrying out with him an assortment of such Articles as would be acceptable to the men in authority in the countries they were about to visit,' and accordingly they went equipped with 'Telescopes, Pistol barrels and Locks, some articles of cut Glass, and some Shawls of British Manufacture.'[10]

---

[10] Lionel Cust and Sidney Colvin, *History of the Society of Dilettanti* (London: Macmillan, 1898), 150–1.

Map 2. Map of the region visited by the Ionian Mission, 1811–1813.

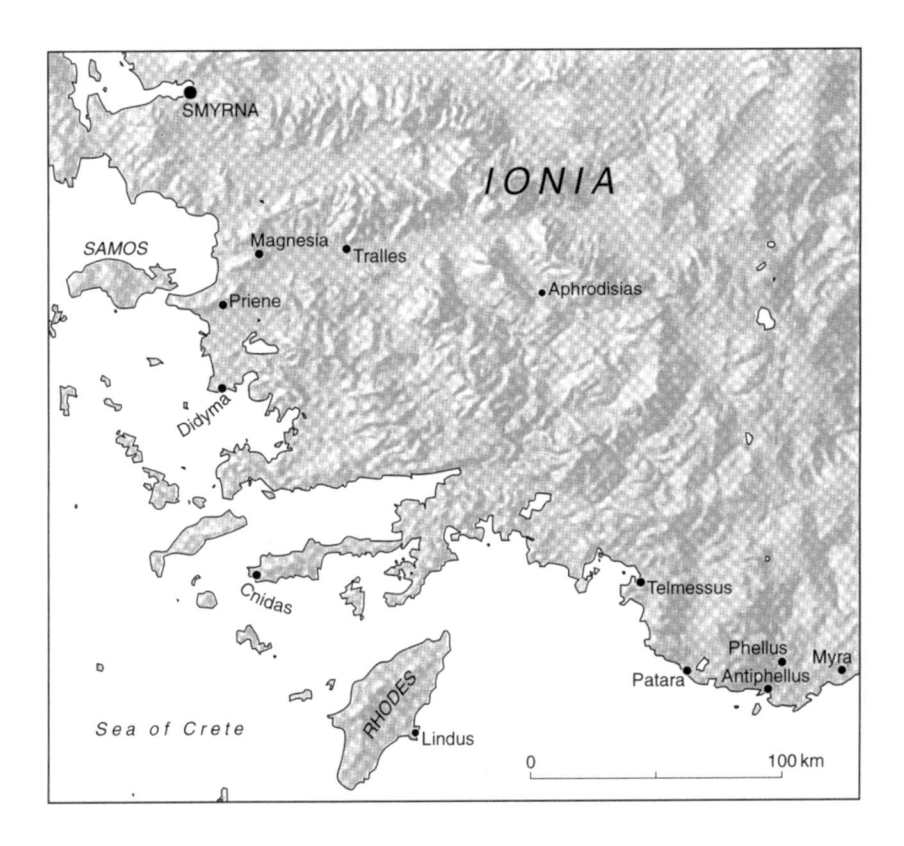

The Prince Regent, as the Society's Patron, gave the expedition his blessing, and they left London in October 1811. But the weather delayed them at Portsmouth until late November, and travelling by way of Gibraltar, they did not reach Zante until early in 1812. Being further delayed in Athens waiting for a safe passage to Smyrna, they used the time to survey and excavate the sanctuary of Demeter at Eleusis, so that it was already early summer before they reached Samos. During June, unable to get to Sardis, they examined the temple of Hera and other remains on Samos, and crossed to the mainland only around midsummer. Gell's experience was already bearing fruit, since he had recruited two men who had previously acted as his dragomans and interpreters to accompany them — one, Pietro Abuto whom he describes as a Georgian, and the other a Turk, Mustapha. Gell preferred dragomans he knew, since his grasp of languages meant that he did not need them to translate for him, but he wanted them for their ability to distract the inquisitive locals while he dug, sketched, measured and occasionally 'liberated' antiquities.

The Society had drawn up a list of nine sites in Asia Minor for Gell's party to investigate, but realistically added a sweeping get-out clause in case they should be unable to visit them all. Three of the nine sites proved inaccessible because of plague, but they managed to add another seven. Their itinerary was Samos, Didyma, Cnidus, Telmessus, Patara, Myra, Antiphellus, Phellus, Aphrodisias, Magnesia, Priene, Tralles and Lindos. They also studied four sites in Attica (one on the way out and three on the return), bringing the total score up to seventeen. Some of the sites were visited twice, and though not all the party visited every site, they must have travelled at least 300 miles overland in Asia Minor.

In May 1812, Gell wrote to the Society from Smyrna, asking for government protection from the risk of pirates in the seas around Asia Minor, but by the end of the year they were safely back in Athens, where they were again delayed, and explored Rhamnous, Thorikos and Sunion. In all they produced 274 architectural drawings and 209 views and maps in about twelve months: 'rapid Gell' indeed.

Although Gell kept a full journal as well as sending regular letters back to London, the only published account of their journey was an article, possibly by Gell, in the *Zante Gazette* which was subsequently reprinted by the Society of Dilettanti, and it tells little more than I have summarised above. The published archaeological material can be found in four large and heavy folios which, beginning in 1817, took altogether ninety-eight years to appear. Almost all of the raw material from the expedition on which they were based is now lost: three volumes of Gell's journal and five of his sketches and drawings, together with four volumes of drawings by the architects, were last recorded in the Society when they were borrowed by the distinguished traveller, William Martin Leake, in 1822. He used them for his own book on Asia Minor, and it was alleged by the authors of the final Dilettanti volume that he still had them many years later.[11]

The Society of Dilettanti were in many ways archaeological pioneers, but unfortunately they were also pioneers of some of the more persistent shortcomings of the profession, such as going over budget and delaying publication. Gell's Ionian mission exemplifies this. The team arrived back in England in the summer of 1813, and were enthusiastically thanked by the Dilettanti at their meeting of 6 February 1814. Gell was to have his portrait painted by Lawrence and in May to receive his knighthood, and the two architects were each presented with an engraved piece of silver. But they had gone at least £1500 over budget.

Although most of the Dilettanti were fairly wealthy and a substantial minority were among the greatest aristocrats in the land, their annual subscription covered little more than the cost of their no doubt ample dinners. So in 1814, the Society had acquired this massive quantity of publishable material, but had no funds. They launched an appeal in a *Report* in pamphlet form, which contained the *Zante Gazette* article, a list of all the drawings, and a proposal from the secretary, Sir Harry Englefield, for a special ten-guinea subscription for five years to finance publication. Solemn resolutions were passed, a high-powered editorial committee headed by the architect William Wilkins was set up, and ambitious plans were made; but the publication programme proved to be a century-long series of missed opportunities.

---

[11] *Antiquities of Ionia*, Part the Fifth (London: Macmillan, 1915), 6.

The first of the folios to appear has the unappetising title of *The Unedited Antiquities of Attica*. A stern resolution on the urgency of publishing the Attica sites was passed in 1814, because the Society was worried that, Eleusis being so close to Athens, the main tourist centre, a foreign competitor would get in first, as Le Roy had done with Stuart and Revett.[12] Work was put in hand immediately, and a series of projected essays planned, most of which were never completed. In March 1816, Wilkins reported to the Society that the plates were all ready, but the booksellers were not. They thereupon resolved to be their own publishers and announced the appearance of a limited edition of 200 copies 'early in May.' It did not appear until the following year.

In spite of its title, the *Unedited Antiquities* is as edited as any of the Society's publications. It follows the format established in Chandler's volumes, and repeated in all the subsequent Ionian volumes — for each site, first an essay on its history and topography, then copious notes on the plates, and then the plates themselves. The maps and general scenes were drawn by Gell, the architectural plans and drawings by Bedford or Gandy, except in the case of Sunion, where the new material was mixed with older drawings from the Chandler mission. Only Gell's drawings give us any idea of what they could actually see: the architectural plans and drawings are reconstructions which often owe more to Vitruvius than to archaeology. But it was a significant book. At Eleusis they actually excavated the two propylaea and produced a very complete plan of the Telesterion, in spite of the houses standing on the site. Gandy went alone to Rhamnous, which he was the first to survey, not without some difficulty as Gell was later to relate:

> I shall not easily forget how I was scouted in a literary society at Paris, for having broken not only marbles but statues at Rhamnus, where by chance I never went. The fact was that my friend Mr. Gandy found at Rhamnus a mutilated statue and a colossal head, which he has since presented to the British Museum [...] Mr. Gandy had employed himself in making a drawing of the

---

[12] Cust and Colvin, *ibid.*, 159; J.D. Le Roy, *Les Ruines des plus beaux monuments de la Grèce* (Paris: Guerin and Delatour, 1758); James Stuart and Nicholas Revett, *The Antiquities of Athens* (London: E. Stuart; John Nichols, 1787–1794).

statue, and having no intention of removing so mutilated a fragment, yet anxious for its preservation, returned it together with two ancient marble inscribed chairs: having finished his excavations and dismissed his labourers, he found the whole the next day dug up again, and broken in pieces; he immediately resolved to convey away the fragments of the statue, which he has since adjusted and presented to the British Museum.[13]

Gell himself was not as enthusiastic a 'marble' collector as many of his contemporaries, though unlike Byron he had no moral objections to the game.[14] He had visited Eleusis twice before, without disturbing the damaged statue which appears in his 1801 sketch, and which was carried off later in that year by E.D. Clarke. (Clarke, like all marbles collectors, wanted his find to be important, claiming that it was the statue of Ceres herself from the temple, though some scholars had suggested that it was a caryatid. Gell reassured Clarke that it was not a caryatid. He was wrong: Clarke's prize, now in the Fitzwilliam Museum, Cambridge, can now be compared with its fellow-caryatid in the Eleusis museum.) But Gell did succumb once in a while, and in a subsequent volume he relates an instance on Samos:

> There are many inscriptions in the island; one of which, consisting of ten verse [sic], alternately hexameters and pentameters was on so thin a slab of marble, and so perfect, that it was brought away by the Dilettanti mission, and presented to the University of Cambridge, through the Earl of Hardwicke.[15]

The *Unedited Antiquities* was a publishing triumph compared with what was to follow. The clutch of volumes entitled *Antiquities of Ionia* constitute a bibliographical nightmare. Although all the volumes are often catalogued as *Ionian Antiquities*, only the first, Chandler's book of 1769 actually has that title: the longer title was used for the 1797 book. Now,

---

[13] William Gell, *Narrative of a Journey in the Morea* (London: Longman, 1823), 57–58.

[14] Byron's attitudes are clear from 'English Bards and Scotch Reviewers', lines 1027-1032, J.J. McGann, ed., *Lord Byron. The Complete Poetical Works* (Oxford: Clarendon Press, 1980), I, 227-264 (261) and 'Childe Harold's Pilgrimage', Canto II, lines 91-108, J.J. McGann, ed. *Lord Byron. The Complete Poetical Works* (Oxford: Clarendon Press, 1980), II, 47-48, 190-191. On Gell see Stonehouse, *op. cit.*, 174.

[15] *Antiquities of Ionia*, Part the First (London: Bulmer, 1821), 64.

instead of an entirely new book, the Society opted to produce in 1821 a revised version of the 1769 volume. The original authors' names have been dropped from the title page which now reads: *Antiquities of Ionia published by the Society of Dilettanti. Part the First*. There is no indication here that this is a second edition, although the following page is obscurely headed *Preface to the First Edition*; this is followed by an *Introduction* which at last reveals that this volume is a conflation of the findings of the two missions. It still requires some painstaking detective work to find out which parts relate to which mission.

Following the formula of its predecessors, the 1821 book is arranged in five chapters, each devoted to a separate site. Only three of these — those on Samos, Priene and Miletus — contain results from the second mission; reports on Teos and Labranda are reprinted from the first edition, while Sigeum and Scio are omitted entirely.

Today, the book is redeemed by including one of the rare bits of eyewitness reporting in the volumes, unmistakeably written by Gell. In the notes on the temple of Apollo at Didyma, near Miletus, he gives us a vivid picture of contemporary conditions. Gell had no great liking for peasants whether they were Greek or Turkish, and was at some pains to show his readers that what the missions were doing was to save the ruins of civilisation from the barbarians:

> When Chandler visited the temple, there were no habitations nearer than Ura, about two miles distant on the road towards Miletus ... the modern village surrounding the temple having been deserted. It appears to be reviving; and the diminution of the ancient materials is unfortunately the consequence of its encreasing [sic] prosperity. In the interval of a few months which occurred between the two visits made by the gentlemen of the mission, a manifest dilapidation had taken place. Part of the wall of the pronaos had been destroyed, and a beautiful terebinth tree, the boast of the village, cut down. A windmill usurped the place of this sacred object; in the construction of which many of the less massive blocks, particularly those enriched with sculpture, were employed, and some converted into cement used in building it. The two Corinthian capitals were totally destroyed, and some of the statues had been grievously defaced.[16]

---

[16] *Ibid.*, 48.

Gell died in 1836, but the long-awaited third volume devoted entirely to his mission did not see the light until 1840. The delay was attributed to the illness of the editor, William Wilkins, and his death in 1839, but since the volume had been anticipated for 1832, with another soon after, there may have been other reasons. We know that the original material had been lent to Leake as early as 1822, and so was presumably not required for publication. We also know that engraved plates for the projected fourth volume had been made by 1840. We know, too, that Wilkins had quarrelled with Gell, Gandy and Bedford over the temple at Magnesia, resulting in the redrawing of the plans and elevations. And already the Society was under pressure from new men, like Fellows and Penrose, with plans for new missions.[17]

The volume called Part the Third is a thick book, though it covers only Cnidus, Aphrodisias and Patara. The established formula is followed, and at both Cnidus and Patara there are site plans and general views by Gell, with the bulk of the measured drawings being signed by Gandy. But a new confusion has arisen in the chapter on Aphrodisias, which is credited to a mission on behalf of the Society carried out in 1813 by one J.P. Deering. In fact, this was Gandy who had changed his name to Deering on receipt of an inheritance in 1828, and had been elected in that name as a member of the Society in 1830. The absence of any Gell or Bedford drawing of Aphrodisias suggests that Gandy may have gone there alone.

Part the Fourth of *Antiquities of Ionia*, published in 1881, really does belong to another mission, and another age. It is devoted entirely to a series of excavations made by R.P. Pullan in the 1860s, and although it pays a small tribute to Gell and the mission of 1812, it is the product of a far more sophisticated archaeology.

So the Gell mission became forgotten and thanks to the *Gentleman's Magazine*, its very date mis-remembered. Then, in 1912, the Society of Dilettanti presented the Royal Institute of British Architects with a set of proofs of engravings made, it is supposed, between 1820 and 1840 for a companion volume to Part III, together with many of the original finished drawings. Further enquiry revealed that the copper plates were still with

---

[17]   *Antiquities of Ionia*, Part the Fifth (London: Macmillan, 1915), xi–xii.

Messrs. Rees, the plate makers. And so, in 1915, a hundred and two years after the mission ended, the Society of Dilettanti published *Antiquities of Ionia, Part the Fifth being a supplement to Part III*. It was edited by the architect, W.R. Lethaby, who devotes much of his introduction to explaining why these already historic drawings should now be published. He argues not only that the drawings themselves are of a quality which justifies publication, but that they serve as a reminder that the Society had been the first to excavate sites mostly by this time being excavated by others: he is careful not to mention the Germans, but in 1915 the implication was plain.

The brief text of thirty-six pages is chiefly concerned to relate the plates to the subsequent discoveries and conclusions of a self-consciously more scientific age, but the first chapter gives a useful account of the role of the Society of Dilettanti and of its two Ionian missions. There are forty-five plates, six of them views redrawn from sketches by Gell all at Magnesia or Myra, the others architectural drawings by Bedford or Gandy, mostly of the same two sites, but also of tombs at Telmessus, Antiphellus, Phellus and Lindos.

Antiquities of Ionia did not become one of the architectural classics of the nineteenth century. Probably none of the volumes was printed in a large edition, and because of the confused publication few libraries have a complete set which includes all the editions, and it has been well-nigh impossible to catalogue them in a way which makes sense. The British Library has four copies of the 1769 volume, but only one of the 1915, and only the dogged pertinacity of a library assistant there dug that one out for me. Yet the mission's achievements were important, and it is little short of astonishing that it still manages to rate two entries in the current *Blue Guide* for Turkey, and four in that for Greece.

If the Society of Dilettanti had published properly and promptly, if the original documentation had not been lost, and if the *Gentleman's Magazine* had got his obituary correct, Gell's reputation might have been considerably better than that of an amusing coxcomb. Even if he did exceed the budget, he organised the tour efficiently and brought it to a successful completion. And although his own sketches often left a lot to be desired (and were redrawn for publication), they were accurate, and his maps were excellent for their date. But it must be remembered that, as the authors of the 1915 volume emphasise, 'most of the earlier engraved plates of Greek architecture rest on hurried and confused notes, which were interpreted at home sometimes after a long interval of time. It was on data so untrustworthy that commentators built up their elaborate theories of architectural proportions.'[18]

The Ionian Mission was to be Gell's last journey to the east. Ironically, he received his knighthood at the hands of the Prince Regent in Carlton House on 14 May 1814, and within three months he and Keppel Craven left England as joint chamberlains to the Prince's hated wife, Caroline. After helping her to plan her own ill-fated tour of the Mediterranean, he quitted her service and settled in Rome and Naples, returning to Britain for only a few months in 1820 to attend Caroline (by now an unwanted queen) again, and to give evidence at her trial. He planned to visit Egypt, but arthritis cut short his travelling days, and he died in Naples, nursed by the faithful Keppel Craven, on 14 April 1836.

Bibliography

Publications by the Society of Dilettanti, relating to the Ionian Mission:

Report of the Committee of the Society of Dilettanti, appointed by the Society to superintend the expedition lately sent by them to Greece and Ionia (London: W. Bulmer, 1814).

The Unedited Antiquities of Attica, comprising the architectural remains of Eleusis, Rhamnus, Sunium and Thoricus (London: Longman, Hurst, 1817).

Antiquities of Ionia published by the Society of Dilettanti. Part the First (London: W. Bulmer and W. Nichol, 1821).

Antiquities of Ionia [...] Part the Third (London: W. Nichol, 1840).

Antiquities of Ionia [...] Part the Fifth, being a supplement to Part III (London: Macmillan, 1915).

---

[18] *Ibid.*, 16n.

Other sources:

Blue Guides to Greece and Turkey. (London: A. & C. Black, various dates).

Clay, Edith (ed.), *Sir William Gell in Italy, Letters to the Society of Dilettanti, 1831–1835* (London: Hamish Hamilton, 1976).

Colvin, H.M., *A Biographical Dictionary of English Architects, 1660-1840* (London: John Murray, 1954).

Cust, Lionel, and Sidney Colvin, *History of the Society of Dilettanti* (London: Macmillan, 1898).

Gell, William, *Narrative of a Journey in the Morea* (London: Longman, Hurst, 1823).

Gentleman's Magazine, new series, 5 (1836).

Lascarides, A.C., *The Search for Troy 1553–1874* (Bloomington: Indiana University Press, 1997).

McGann, J.J. (ed.), *Lord Byron. The Complete Poetical Works*, 7 vols (Oxford: Clarendon Press, 1980–1989).

Schapp, Alain, *The Discovery of the Past* (London: British Museum, 1996).

Stoneman, Richard, *Land of Lost Gods* (London: Hutchinson, 1987).

Thompson, Jason, *Sir Gardner Wilkinson and His Circle* (Austin, Texas, University of Texas Press, 1992).

The Anger of Lady Hester Stanhope: some letters of Lady Hester Stanhope, John Lewis Burckhardt and William John Bankes

Norman N. Lewis

In the following pages I intend to draw attention to one and only one aspect of Lady Hester Stanhope's complicated and peculiar psychology — her malicious temper, as evidenced by her dealing with two other people, John Lewis Burckhardt and William John Bankes. This might be thought unfair because it highlights an unfavourable aspect of her behaviour at the expense of all others, but on the other hand this particular characteristic, which is surely worth a mention, has hardly been noticed in the many biographies which have been written about her. That it has attracted little comment is due in part to the fact that much of our information about it is derived from hitherto unpublished correspondence on which this paper is largely based. As I will make clear, Lady Hester had reason enough to be annoyed with Burckhardt and to be seriously angry with Bankes, but the vindictive attacks she directed at each of them in retaliation were absurdly disproportionate. The weapon she employed might best be described as character assassination. What was most remarkable was that as time went on her anger seems to have fed upon itself and to have become even more extravagant and obsessive.

Lady Hester and Burckhardt met only once, on 28 June 1812, at Nazareth, soon after her arrival in Palestine. Burckhardt had been travelling in the area for nearly three years. The meeting was brief and after it she made clear that she did not like him, remarking to Michael Bruce, her lover, that she would not be surprised if he were a French spy. On a later occasion she said to Charles Meryon, her physician (and later her biographer) 'Ah! No one can deceive me. The moment I saw him at Nazareth I knew what he was. A man with such teeth as he has is always malicious (Meryon adds a note at this point: 'Sheykh Ibrahim had very uneven teeth') and I am sure that he is dissolute.'¹

Lady Hester's first opinion of Burckhardt was, then, grounded in prejudice, but a few years later Burckhardt himself provided ample reasons for her to dislike him. He was a gregarious and chatty fellow when he found agreeable company in Cairo or Alexandria; he, himself, used the phrase 'my loquacious merriness'² and he was a prolific and not always judicious letter writer: it did not occur to him that some of what he said or wrote about 'her travelling Ladyship' might find its way back to Lady Hester who was now living near Sidon in Lebanon. He really blundered in summer of 1815 when Meryon visited Egypt and met Burckhardt for the second time. The two men became temporarily good friends. Burckhardt was not particularly careful in what he said, and he admitted later to his friend, George Renouard, that he had been 'very free in his remarks' to Meryon and had spoken of Lady Hester's 'ridiculous vanity and unwarrantable pretensions'. He also told Renouard, though presumably not Meryon, that he thought she exhibited 'more foibles than a lady in man's clothes should be guilty of.'³ He told another friend that when Lady Hester had visited Cairo in 1812 the women there had composed a song about her, the refrain of which ran 'O England poor in beauties, O Lady why do you show yourself abroad?'⁴

We do not know how much of all this Meryon reported to Lady Hester when he returned to Lebanon in the autumn of 1815, but it was enough to make her very angry. She also resented the fact that Burckhardt had asked Meryon questions about her, which, she pronounced, was very impertinent and vulgar of him, and she took great offence at a letter which

[1] Wellcome Institute, Western European Mss (hereinafter Wellcome), Ms. 7116, cxxi-cxxii. See also page 60 and n.13 below, and Appendix, pages 68-69 below.

[2] Burckhardt to Meryon, 29 November 1815, in C.E. Bosworth 'Some correspondence in the John Rylands University Library of Manchester concerning John Lewis Burckhardt and Lady Hester Stanhope's physician', *Bulletin of the John Rylands University Library of Manchester*, 55:1 (1972), 33-59 (hereinafter Bosworth).

[3] The quoted phrases above are from Burckhardt's letter to Renouard, 25 June 1816, British Library (hereinafter BL), Add. Ms. 27620.

[4] Burckhardt to Fiott, 5 July 1816, BL Add. Ms. 47490.

Meryon brought from Burckhardt because it contained criticisms of Asselin de Cherville, of whom she thought highly. Of this she wrote to Col. Missett, the British consul general in Egypt, and read the letter aloud to Meryon:

> I have been dissuaded by a certain person, whom you know, from writing to M. Aslyn, because he had debased himself (Meryon noted here that Asselin was reported to have put money entrusted to his care out to interest at 15%) ... Had I to choose, I would give the preference to a savant and an élève of Volney's over an adventurer whom chance had made an Englishman and who was for sale to any country that would buy him. Nor is it less criminal in my eyes to trifle with one's God for a purpose (Meryon noted that she alluded to Burckhardt's pretended conversion to the Mahometan faith in order to get to Mecca and Medina) than with other people's money'.

Lady Hester interrupted her reading at this point and asked Meryon 'What do you think of that, Doctor? Oh! I'll give it to him for all his spite'.[5]

She did indeed 'give it to him.' First she wrote to Burckhardt himself what he termed a 'very angry and extremely pointed' letter,[6] and followed that with 'a kind of circular letter to all my friends in the Levant, designed (?) to lessen the esteem in which they might hold me'.[7] Besides general denunciation of Burckhardt's character, this or later letters also apparently referred to gossip about Burckhardt's rumoured sex life in Cairo, passed on to Meryon by acquaintances there.[8] Burckhardt and Lady Hester then seem to have indulged in a bad-tempered exchange of letters; Burckhardt called hers 'quite intemperate' and said that they demonstrated 'a most selfish and unruly temper and unbounded arrogance, added I must say to a deal of wit and very vigorous understanding'.[9] He also confessed that he

---

[5] Wellcome, Ms. 7116.
[6] Burckhardt to Renouard, BL Add Ms. 27620.
[7] Burckhardt to Bankes, 16 June 1816, County Record Office, Dorchester, W.J. Bankes correspondence (hereinafter Dorchester) D/BKL, HJI/51.
[8] Letters from Thurburn and Asselin in Bosworth; Burckhardt's letter to his mother, 22 December 1816 in Carl Burckhardt-Sarasin and Hansrudolf Schwabe-Burckhardt, *Sheik Ibrahim (Johann Ludwig Burckhardt) Briefe an Eltern und Geschwister* (Basel: Helbing und Lichtenhaln, 1956) (hereinafter *Briefe*), 176.
[9] Burckhardt to Renouard, BL Add. Ms. 27620.

could not fairly find fault with Lady Hester after the reports that Meryon had made to her, but he did 'blame her for writing everywhere incendiary letters against me, putting me up as an impertinent perjured black—d'.[10]

As time went on Lady Hester's letters came to relate less to the original causes of her anger and became more wildly malicious. In January 1817, writing to Sir Joseph Banks, she described Burckhardt as 'full of envy and malice and very insincere'.[11] In August of the same year she told the second Earl of Belmore, who was about to start his eastern journeys, that she thought 'vastly ill' of Burckhardt. He was, she wrote, 'very plausible, but very false, very envious ... with the mask of sentiment and high feeling ... full of low intrigue, who wears half a dozen faces as he thinks best suit for his purpose'.[12]

Lady Hester was pleased with the results of her campaign against Burckhardt. Even as early as 31 March 1816 she wrote to Michael Bruce that 'I have converted him into an object flattened, I told you always his serpent teeth denoted him spiteful, which he is to the greatest degree'.[13] A year later she told Meryon, who was then in England, that 'Burckhardt is set down finely and is unmasked: he is now nothing'.[14]

Nothing could have been further from the truth than that last statement. It showed that in some respects Lady Hester lived in a world of fantasy. She had no first hand knowledge about Burckhardt's doings while he was in Egypt — all was hearsay. With his great journeys in

---

[10] Burckhardt to Bankes, 16 June 1816, Dorchester HJ1/51; Burckhardt's letters to his mother, 4 October and 22 December 1816, in *Briefe*, 172-3, 176.

[11] Lady Hester to Sir Joseph Banks, 3 January 1817, British Museum (Natural History) N° 20, Dawson-Turner Collection of Banks' Correspondence.

[12] Lady Hester to Lord Belmore, 25 August 1817, Archives of Castle Coole, Ulster. I am grateful to Deborah Manley for providing me with a copy of this letter, to the present Lord Belmore for permitting me to publish the above quotation from it, and to Peter Marson, the archivist at Castle Coole, for his help on this and related matters.

[13] Bodleian Library, Bruce family papers, Ms. Eng. C5758. The passage in which these words occur is in a part of Lady Hester's letter which, as Ian Bruce points out on page 376 of his *The Nun of Lebanon: The love affair of Lady Hester Stanhope and Michael Bruce: their newly discovered letters*. (London: Collins, 1951) (hereinafter *Nun*) is difficult to follow. It therefore does not appear with the rest of the letter on pages 376–79 of *Nun*.

[14] Lady Hester to Meryon, 19 May 1877, in Wellcome Ms. 7116, clxxvi.

Egypt, Nubia, Sinai and Arabia accomplished, he was in fact now both celebrated and respected. Lady Hester's slanders probably did more to add to her reputation as an eccentric than to damage Burckhardt's well-deserved renown.

Burckhardt died on 15 October 1817.

Lady Hester and William Bankes had acquaintances in common and when she heard that he was coming from Egypt to Syria she invited him to stay for a time in her house near Sidon.[15] He arrived on the 23 February 1816 and had an enjoyable and productive time there, working on an ancient tomb with fine frescoes of which he made copies.[16] She, however, quickly became irritated and 'bored' with him; he did not defer to her, as practically everyone she had met for several years had done, his conversation irritated her (almost any conversation irritated her; her guests were expected to listen rather than to talk), and worst of all he was, she said, very mean: he wanted to see everything and for it to cost him nothing.[17] Then, when he left after three weeks or so, he resumed his usual independent and wayward habits and instead of going to Baalbek, as she understood that he intended to do, took a leisurely course through the mountains to Damascus, thereby, she said, 'making himself ridiculous and occasioning great uneasiness to those who wished him well'.[18]

It would seem that in the next few weeks Lady Hester and Bankes corresponded while he travelled and that she said a few hard words to him, for the only letter which has survived of this period starts abruptly

---

[15] Lady Hester to Bankes, n.d., Dorchester HJI/40; C.L. Meryon, *Travels of Lady Hester Stanhope, forming the completion of her memoirs, narrated by her Physician* (London: H. Colburn, 1846), (hereinafter *Travels*), III, 281. A recent study of the tomb and of Bankes' work, with reproductions of his watercolours, by A. Barbet, P.-L. Gatier and N.N. Lewis appeared in *Syria*, 74 (1997).

[16] Some description of Bankes' visit and of the tomb is given by Meryon in *Travels II*, 338-53 and 380 and *III*, 281 and 293-300 and by G. Finati, in *Narrative of the Life and Adventures of Giovanni Finati*, trans. and ed. by W.J. Bankes, 2 vols (London: Murray, 1830) II, 156-9.

[17] Lady Hester to Bruce in P.S. dated 21 March to letter dated 5 March 1816, *Nun*, 379.

[18] Lady Hester to J.S. Buckingham, 23 March 1816. The original of this letter is in a private collection, an incomplete transcription among the Bankes correspondence at Dorchester, no ref. number.

with the words 'I have scolded you a great deal'. The letter was, however, a kindly and helpful one, evidently meant to improve relations. Written on 14 May, it was sent by express messenger who had orders to find Bankes wherever he might be because Lady Hester had just seen in a newspaper that Bankes' uncle had died and she thought he might wish to return home immediately. The letter continued in friendly and valedictory fashion. Unfortunately, the paper is torn and most of the last six lines is missing, but the word 'peace', underlined, has survived.[19]

A month later Bankes reciprocated appropriately with a letter almost the last words of which were: 'You desire in one of your letters to have my word that we part in peace. In peace my dear Lady Hester! In friendship I hope so long as we live'.[20] Earlier in the same letter he told her that he had been in the mountains above Tripoli to see the famous cedar grove there and had brought back cones and seeds which he would plant in the grounds of his house at Kingston Lacy in Dorset. 'By & bye' he continued, 'when we are both respectable old people, we will sit at Kingston Hall under the shade of our cedars and fancy ourselves, in spite of the difference of climate, upon Libanus'. (The seeds were sown and the cedars still flourish but needless to say Lady Hester never joined Bankes there.)

These pleasantries, however, sorted ill with the rest of the letter, in which Bankes made an extraordinary and unwelcome suggestion. He knew that Meryon was thinking of leaving Lady Hester's service and also that Lady Hester had been taking about leaving Syria and, perhaps, going to France.[21] He clearly thought that matters were much further advanced

---

[19] Lady Hester to Bankes, 14 May 1816, Dorchester HJI/47.
[20] Bankes to Lady Hester, 17 June 1816. The original of this letter and transcriptions of those cited in notes 22, 23 and 24 below are at Wellcome, Mss 5687–5689, Correspondence of Dr. C. L. Meryon. They were published, with some errors and omissions, by Frank Hamel, *Lady Hester Lucy Stanhope* (London: Cassell, 1913).
[21] Lady Hester's letters in *Nun* passim and Meryon's *Travels* passim contain frequent references to possible departures and changes of plan. Lady Hester even wrote farewell letters to a number of Syrian notables, although she may not have sent them all; translations of some of them are in the Stanhope Collection at the Centre for Kentish Studies at Maidstone, U590C247A. None of the plans under discussion in 1816 were adhered to; Meryon did not

than in fact they were and that Meryon intended to leave in the immediate future. Bankes was himself about to leave Syria and to make his way back to Italy via Constantinople and Greece, and he wondered if Meryon would like to go with him. As he put it in his letter, 'I am in real and almost daily need of an amanuensis and if you and the doctor could make the arrangement suit you I should be very glad to engage him nominally as my physician but really in the capacity rather as secretary'. If Lady Hester could spare Meryon so soon, Bankes continued, 'I should wish him to set out immediately bag and baggage for Latikieh where I hope to embark quite in the beginning of next month.' He enclosed a note making the proposal to Meryon and asked Lady Hester to give it to him if she had no objection; he hastened to add and to repeat that if she did not like the idea she should burn the note and say nothing about it. In the note to Meryon Bankes outlined his proposal, and added 'Now, if you like to be my companion in this route, leaving me to pay all your expenses whatsoever, I shall think myself fortunate'.[22] He said nothing about salary.

As if this suggestion were not enough, Bankes asked another favour: he was very anxious to get his watercolours of the Sidon tomb, and other material from there, back to England. Could, perhaps, one of Lady Hester's servants, who (Bankes apparently thought) was going back to England, take them with him? Alternatively, if Meryon accepted his offer, he could probably take them, he thought.

Exasperated by all this Lady Hester told Meryon that he could do what he liked about Bankes' proposal, but she made it clear that she thought it a poor offer, 'very impertinent and very mean', which he should refuse. As for Bankes' belongings, she ordered Meryon to pack them off to Latakia (the inference being that Bankes could then take them with him or get someone else to look after them). She continued 'I have done with him ... I will not keep one of his things another day in my house — impertinent fellow that he is! But he will learn who I am. I am not an angel of kindness like Mr. Pitt, or to be talked over at pleasure — so off

---

leave until February 1817, Bankes returned to Syria in October 1817 and Lady Hester remained in Syria until her death.

[22] Bankes to Meryon, 17 June 1816.

with frescos, drawings and packages!'[23] Meryon, of course, did what he was told and sent everything off, including the cedar cones, and he wrote Bankes a dignified letter refusing his offer.[24]

Bankes' letter was silent on another matter which would have interested Lady Hester more than anything else, and it was discourteous and deceitful of him not to mention it. Only eight days before writing the letter of 17 June 1816 he had returned from a journey to Palmyra that he had performed in a manner which he well knew would infuriate her.[25] Lady Hester, the first European woman ever to reach Palmyra, to which she had made her triumphant processional entry in 1813, had been determined that if Bankes went there he should go under her aegis. She had given him instructions as to how he should proceed and had provided him with letters of introduction, notably to Shaikh Muhanna al Fadil, ('the King of the Desert') in whose care she had travelled in 1813. Muhanna or his sons would provide him with guides and an escort.

Bankes, however, did not want to travel in grand style or to pay lavishly; he preferred to make his own way, not to follow Lady Hester's dictates. He did not use her letters of introduction, possibly out of pique because they did not carry the two seals which would have indicated that she considered him a very important person, worthy of special treatment.[26] After several setbacks he was fortunate enough to meet the newly appointed Pasha of Damascus, an official 'with a great reputation for severity' who ordered Nasir, Muhanna's eldest son, to get Bankes to and from Palmyra for a reasonable consideration. Nasir had to agree, but

[23] Lady Hester to Meryon, 23 June 1816.
[24] Meryon to Bankes, 24 June 1816.
[25] The main sources of information on Bankes' Palmyra journey are Finati, *Narrative*, II, 168–77, Meryon, *Travels* III, 301–303, and the letters from Muhanna and Razak mentioned on page (010) below. The three sources tell three different but not altogether incompatible stories: it is hoped that the summary below may approximate to the truth.
[26] The 'one or two seals' story is given by Meryon and its truth is partially attested by Barker's letter to Bankes of 1 July 1816 (Dorchester HJ1/55), in which, in mock-official style, Barker undertakes to 'keep silent on the subject of the letters of recommendation of you to Prince Muhanna and the Deribach Chief Mil Ismail, of which I solemnly acknowledge the receipt and accept the deposit.'

he and his brothers were bitterly disappointed that they had to accept a far smaller remuneration than they had hoped for.[27] They gave Bankes a hard time, one of them even imprisoning him for a day inside the great temple of Palmyra. Bankes appears to have taken this in his stride and came back with a fine harvest of inscriptions.

The news of Bankes' adventures must have reached Lady Hester very soon after she received his letter of 17 June and at about the same time as his departure from Syria on 26 June. She received confirmation of the story a few weeks later by a letter from Nasir dated 8 July and one from Razak, another of Muhanna's clan, a month later.[28] The latter described Bankes as the meanest of men: his very beard smelled of avarice. They had told him that he couldn't go to Palmyra without letters from the Lady, however much he paid. He had replied, 'I am one of the great men of the English — do you want me to take a letter from a woman?' Whether or not Bankes really said what they reported we do not know, but Lady Hester of course believed them. One can readily imagine her reaction: how could he dare to spurn her advice, to insult her and her friends? Above all, he had been *mean*, paying derisory sums to *her* shaykhs who were forced to accept because the wretched man had somehow persuaded the Governor of Damascus to help him.

The news of all this soon reached Burckhardt in Cairo, and on 15 July 1816 he wrote to warn Bankes (who was by this time in Constantinople, Asia Minor or Greece) that Lady Hester 'is dreadfully angry with you for having slighted her advice and is making very free with your name, almost as free as she does with mine, alleging as ostensible reason your little liberality to Bedouins'.[29] Burckhardt was right; Lady Hester's letters at

---

[27] By standards other than those of Lady Hester Bankes seems to have paid reasonable amounts; two years later Irby and Mangles paid only half as much for their visit to Palmyra. See their *Travels in Egypt and Nubia, Syria and Asia Minor during the years 1817 and 1818* (London: printed for Private Distribution, 1823), 249–53.

[28] Lady Hester sent translations of these letters to General Richard Grenville with her letter referred to in n.31 below so that he could see 'how little Bankes was esteemed by the Bedoweens'. Another copy of the translation of Razak's letter is at Maidstone, U1590 C247A.

[29] Burckhardt to Bankes, 15 July 1816, Dorchester HJ1/57.

this period abounded with references to Bankes. Some of these were merely facetious; in a letter to Sir Joseph Banks, for example, she remarks 'as for your namesake, Wm. Bankes, I cannot endure him and I wish I could pass a *bill* for him to be obliged to change a name which such a character can have no right to.'[30] Others were abusive. A great part of a letter to Sir Richard Grenville, nearly 5,000 words long, consisted of a diatribe against Bankes; she wrote that 'he is clever, but with the cleverness of a swindler, devoid of sincerity and liberality though he affects both; cunning to the greatest degree ... attending very little to truth, using all sorts of dirty means to accomplish his ends.' 'Although he gave himself out as a grandee of England,' she continued, his behaviour on his travels aroused 'the astonishment, contempt and ridicule of every rank of society'.[31] On 11 February 1817, she wrote triumphantly to John Barker 'I have so humbled that fellow B. he shall kiss the earth before I have done with him ... his flattery I despise as I do his vices: for a liar is the most odious of beings'.[32] On 12 October 1820, she wrote to Meryon, 'Bankes has got home, I find. What an animal!'[33] None of the other people who met Bankes on his travels and have left a written record (except J.S. Buckingham) have anything to say which remotely resembles Lady Hester's calumnies; he was generally popular and highly thought of. As we have seen, however, he had certainly been inconsiderate and rude to her, and he continued unrepentant to the end. In a letter from Cyprus dated 15 October 1817, he told Burckhardt that he had decided to return to Syria in the near future, but would not go near Lady Hester; she was, he said, 'highly irritated against me owing to a conversation which was repeated to her by some of her spies in which I simply asserted my

---

[30] Lady Hester to Bankes, 3 January 1817, Dawson-Taylor Collection, British Museum (Natural History), mo20.
[31] Lady Hester to Grenville, undated, BL Add. Ms. 42057.
[32] E.B.B. Barker (ed.), *Syria and Egypt under the last Five Sultans of Turkey: being experiences during fifty years of Mr. Consul-General Barker, chiefly from his letters and journals* (London: S. Tinsley, 1876), 270.
[33] Maidstone, U1590 S6/1/6.

conviction of her not being at all a woman of talent, an offence that is never to be forgiven'.[34]

In thus suggesting that Lady Hester would never forgive him Bankes wrote more truly than he knew. Some eighteen years later, and five years before Lady Hester's death, A.W. Kinglake visited her and listened to her talking, hour after hour. In his account of the conversation he wrote, 'one man above all others (he is now uprooted from society) she blasted with her wrath; you would have thought that, in the scornfulness of her nature, she must have sprung upon her foe with more of fierceness than of skill; but this was not so, for, with all the force and vehemence of her invective, she displayed a sober, patient and minute attention to the details of vituperation, which contributed to its success a thousand times more than mere violence'.[35]

The words ' he is now uprooted from society' must surely identify the man about whom she was talking as Bankes. Lady Hester died in 1839; *Eothen* was not published until 1844. In 1841 Bankes had been arrested by a policeman in Green Park as he was about to commit a homosexual act. Rather than face trial and risk condign punishment, he left England and never returned.[36] He was, indeed, uprooted from society, disgraced and exiled. How justified and how triumphant Lady Hester would have felt if she had lived to hear this!

---

[34] Bankes to Burckhardt, 15 October 1817, Dorchester HJ1/75. (This letter remains amongst Bankes' papers and so presumably was never despatched to Burckhardt. It seems likely that Bankes heard of Burckhardt's death, which occurred on the day the letter was written, before he was able to find a means of sending it from Cyprus to Cairo.)

[35] A.W. Kinglake, *Eothen* (1st ed., London: John Murray, 1844; repr. London: Humphrey Milford, 1919).

[36] Dorchester, HJ1/627ff.

Appendix : Source Material relating to the meeting of Lady Hester Stanhope and J.L. Burckhardt

The document from which an extract is quoted on page 60 above and which is cited in footnote 1 is a manuscript in Meryon's hand which is gummed into a copy of Volume 2, Part 2, of Meryon's *Travels*. Other notes are intercalated throughout the pages of the original printed text; it seems that Meryon was contemplating a second, revised, edition of the book, but this never materialised. The book, with its insertions and loose papers, was acquired by the Wellcome Institute in 1995.

Other source material relating to the meeting of Lady Hester, Bruce and Meryon with Burckhardt at Nazareth on 28 June 1812 (Meryon makes mistakes here and elsewhere about dates) includes an account by Burckhardt on pages 335 and 337 of his *Travels in Syria*, a letter from Burckhardt to Fiott of 10 October (BL Add. Ms. 47,490) and another to his mother of 15 October 1812 (*Briefe*, 139-40), and Meryon's account on pages 269-71 of his *Travels*. No mention of the meeting by Bruce has survived, and the only surviving indirect reference to it by Lady Hester seems to be that quoted on pages 57-58 above.

Meryon, on page 269 of his *Travels*, writes that they met 'the celebrated Burckhardt'. He wrote his book thirty years or so after the event, and may have allowed his knowledge of the fame Burckhardt eventually acquired to colour his description. Burckhardt was not, in 1812, 'celebrated'; he had not as yet travelled beyond the bounds of Syria and nothing had been published about him. Certain twentieth century biographers of Lady Hester and of Burckhardt have used the same adjective and have built on it, stating rather than suggesting that Burckhardt's fame, and the near adulation with which they say Meryon and Bruce treated him, aroused Lady Hester's jealousy and that this was the chief reason she disliked him. They may be right, but there is no such suggestion in any contemporary account which I have seen. Nor do I know from what source the lengthy and interesting details in their descriptions of the meeting were derived. They evidently did not have access to Meryon's note, referred to above, now in the Wellcome Institute.

One other document should be mentioned here. It was written by John Barker, who knew Burckhardt well: they had been friends ever since Burckhardt first came to Syria in 1809, and Burckhardt had lived in Barker's house in Aleppo for part of the time since then. In a gossipy letter to John Fiott, a mutual friend, Barker wrote on 18 July 1812 that Burckhardt had left Damascus for Jerusalem and as Lady Hester was also on the point of arriving there they would probably meet. 'Before he makes himself known' Barker continued, ' he will afford them a good deal of fun. I should like to see him perform in that Drama: what an idiot-stance he will give to his great round Eyes, while he sits squat smoking his short pipe!'[37] Presumably, Burckhardt did not choose to behave in this way when he met Lady Hester; we would surely have heard of it if he had. This description of Burckhardt's appearance, or of the appearance he could assume, combined with Meryon's reference to his 'very uneven' teeth, leaves one with the feeling that, in reality, he looked rather less impressive and more 'human' than he appears in some of the portraits which adorn his books.

Bibliography

Barker, E.B.B. (ed.), *Syria and Egypt Under the last Five Sultans of Turkey: being experiences during fifty years of Mr. Consul-General Barker, chiefly from his letters and journals.* (London: S. Tinsley, 1876).

Bosworth, C.E., 'Some correspondence in the John Rylands University Library of Manchester concerning John Lewis Burckhardt and Lady Hester Stanhope's physician', *Bulletin of the John Rylands University Library of Manchester*, 55:1 (1972), 33–59.

Bruce, I., *The Nun of Lebanon: The love affair of Lady Hester Stanhope and Michael Bruce: their newly discovered letters* (London: Collins, 1951).

Burckhardt-Sarasin, C. and H., Schwabe-Burckhardt, *Sheik Ibrahim (Johann Ludwig Burckhardt) Briefe an Eltern und Geschwister* (Basel: Helbing und Lichtenhaln, 1956).

---

[37] St John's College, Cambridge, Library, Ref. U30 W1.

Finati, G., *Narrative of the Life and Adventures of Giovanni Finati*, trans. and ed. by W.J. Bankes, 2 vols (London: Murray, 1830).

Hamel, F., *Lady Hester Lucy Stanhope* (London: Cassell, 1913).

Irby, C. L. and J. Mangles, *Travels in Egypt and Nubia, Syria and Asia Minor during the years 1817 and 1818* (London; printed for Private Distribution, 1823), 249–53.

Kinglake, A.W., *Eothen* (1st edn, London: Murray, 1844; repr. London: Humphey Milford, 1919).

Meryon, C.L., *Travels of Lady Hester Stanhope, forming the completion of her memoirs, narrated by her Physician* (London: H. Colburn, 1846).

Jacob Jonas Björnståhl and his Travels in Thessaly

Berit Wells

In 1779 the Swedish orientalist Jacob Jonas Björnståhl made a scholarly journey in Thessaly in order to study manuscripts in the Meteora and other monasteries. He had been commissioned by the Swedish king Gustav III to travel to the Orient in order to 'seek, copy, and if possible to acquire new and important variants of Hebrew and Greek manuscripts of the Bible and of the oldest biblical codices, also of other ancient sources, above all biblical.'[1] The journey was intended to include what is Greece today. However, after Björnståhl had waited in vain for three years in Constantinople for his travel companion, he determined, while waiting, to make a journey to Mount Athos and then continue to Palestine to fulfill his instructions.

For a Swede to travel beyond Italy was very unusual in those days. And for a non-aristocrat like Björnståhl to travel at all even more so. Members of the aristocracy made the Grand Tour but it went only to western Europe; Greece was considered to be the Orient. Those who did venture that far east, did so for very special reasons. To mention but one example from the seventeenth century. Anna Åkerhielm, was the travel companion of Catharina Charlotta de la Gardie, the wife of Otto

---

[1] From the instructions by the King of 27 November 1778, cited in Christian Callmer, 'Jacob Johan Björnståhls thessaliska resa, hans död och hans litterära kvarlåtenskaps öden' [Jacob Johan Björnståhl's Thessalian Travel, his death and the fate of his literary legacy], *Lychnos,* 1946-1947, (1947), 151-96 (with a summary in French) (hereinafter Callmer), at 152, n.6. The instructions exist in a copied version in the Björnståhl Papers in the Lund University Library, Sweden.

Fig. 10. Plaster cast of medallion of Jacob Jonas Björnståhl made by Johan Tobias Sergel in Rome in 1772. The cast was presumably one of the eight original medallions made in the early 1950s and now hangs in the entrance hall of the Swedish Institute at Athens. Photo by Marie Mauzy.

Wilhelm von Königsmarck, commander of the Venetian land forces in the Turko-Venetian war of the 1680s. Anna watched the Parthenon blow up in 1687 and wrote about it in a letter to her brother in Sweden.[2]

Jacob Johan Björnståhl was born in 1731. As his father was a low-ranking military officer and could not afford to send his son to university Jacob Jonas had to earn his own living after he finished school. He became a tutor to finance his studies at the University of Uppsala. When, in 1767, he left Sweden never to return he had written two dissertations, one in Hebrew and another in Arabic. He was appointed Professor of Oriental and Greek literature at Uppsala University in 1776, a position he never took up, and in February of 1779 he was appointed to the chair of Oriental and Greek languages at Lund. The news of the latter appointment never reached him, for he died of typhoid fever in Thessaloniki on 12 July of that year.

As a tutor for two sons of the aristocratic family Rudbeck he spent nearly nine years travelling through France, Italy, Switzerland, Germany, Holland and England. He hungered for knowledge and actively sought it, discoursing with the leading authorities in his field wherever he went. He made a reputation for himself as a scholar. We know that the Crown Prince Gustav, later King Gustav III, encountered Björnståhl in Paris in the late 1760s and there heard French orientalists speak very highly of him. When the second Rudbeck son, Carl Fredrik, went back to Sweden from England in 1775, Björnståhl happened to have the means to stay on in England, as he had received a lower academic position at Uppsala University. He left England in March of 1776 after he had learnt of his

---

[2] Her letter is dated 18 October 1687. Five letters by her hand to her brother Samuel were printed in Carl Christoffer Gjörwell, *Det svenska biblioteket* [The Swedish Library], part 3 (1759), 25–66, which also includes her personal diary. In his *Athens Alive* (Athens: Hermes, 1979), 105–106, Kevin Andrews translates from French parts of two of Anna's letters from L.-E. de Laborde, *Athènes aux XVe, XVIe et XVIIe siècles* (Paris: Jules Renouard, 1854), II, 274–9. In an appendix to Vol. II, 256–349, Laborde, obviously from Gjörwell, with a translation into French, reprints Anna's letters to her brother and her journal together with her biography by Gjörwell. The passage pertinent to the destruction of the Parthenon is at pages 276–9 in Laborde.

appointment to the chair at Uppsala, apparently feeling that he could now afford to extend his travels to the Orient.

Björnståhl did not himself produce an account of his travels for the press. However, during the twelve years he spent travelling he kept a journal and also wrote a large number of letters. Most of the preserved letters were addressed to Carl Christoffer Gjörwell, a devoted friend and admirer of his scholarly work. The understanding was that he would print the letters in his periodicals, of which he had several,[3] and thus Björnståhl would be able to finance further travels. Some of Björnståhl's letters were published in this way but most of them, together with a comprised version of Björnståhl's travel journal came out posthumously. This was due to several factors. Apparently Björnståhl sometimes did not quite live up to the agreement of regular communications. Björnståhl's untimely death and the ensuing convoluted history of his legacy delayed publication.

When Björnståhl died his papers, including the Thessalian journal, were sent from Thessaloniki to the Swedish legation in Constantinople. Before setting off for Mount Athos, Björnståhl had spent nearly three years there and had made many friends. One of them was the Swedish envoy to the Sublime Porte, Ulric Celsing, and another one was the legation priest, Carl Peter Blomberg. Gjörwell and Blomberg agreed that the journal was of importance to a general public and should be published but it needed translation, as it was written in French, and editing in order not to offend people in Constantinople. Blomberg undertook to do both. He not only left out the unprintable comments but also almost all of the inscriptions which Björnståhl had copied during his journey. He then left the final editing to Gjörwell, who decided that whatever events were already

---

[3] Jac. Jon. Björnståhl, *Resa till Frankrike, Italien, Sweitz, Tyskland, Holland, Ängland, Turkiet och Grekeland* [Journey to France, Italy, Switzerland, Germany, Holland, England, Turkey and Greece], posthumously published by Carl Christof. Gjörwell in six volumes, 1780–1784 (hereinafter Björnståhl with the relevant volume); in the preface of vol. I (Stockholm, 1780), 5, Gjörwell mentions the earliest letters and the names of his periodicals where they were printed. In this preface he also sets out the conditions of their agreement.

covered in the letters did not merit printing. Thus it was an abbreviated version of the Thesssalian journal that was printed by Gjörwell in 1783.[4]

The original journal was among the books and manuscripts that Björnståhl left in his will to the most devoted of his two former students, Carl Fredrik Rudbeck. After the latter's death this part of the legacy was soon scattered. Most of it was sold at an auction in 1815 but part of it had most likely been sold previously to the Russian minister to Sweden in Stockholm, Jan Pieter van Suchtelen, an avid collector. Amongst the papers bought by him was the travel journal covering the journey to the Orient, that is to say Björnståhl's sojourn in Constantinople and Thessaly. Suchtelen died in Stockholm in 1836 and his library probably ended up in Tambov in Russia. It was later divided between two libraries in St. Petersburg.[5] The journal is still among the Suchtelen papers but now in the National Library in that same city.[6]

Björnståhl's journey to the Orient was sanctioned by King Gustav III. Certainly their meeting in Paris, already mentioned, and above all the international recognition Björnståhl had received on the continent had influenced the royal decision also to award Björnståhl a stipend to support his undertaking. In addition, several of his friends interfered to bring about a positive answer to a letter drafted by Gjörwell in support of Björnståhl's further travels. The instructions for the journey mentioned at the beginning of this paper, arrived in Constantinople at the end of November 1778. Gustav III had commissioned a new translation of the Bible in 1773 and Björnståhl's scientific task was to collect material to aid the translation.[7]

Of his departure from Constantinople, his adventurous voyage in snow, sleet and ice through the Dardanelles and his arrival in Volos on 3

---

[4] Björnståhl, *op. cit.*, (1783), V, 91–158. In his preface to vol. I, Gjörwell briefly accounts for these circumstance.

[5] C. Callmer, 'Jacob Jonas Björnståhls thessaliska resa, hans död och hans litterära kvarlåtenskaps öden' [Jacob Jonas Björnståhl, his death and the fate of his literary legacy], *Lychnos*, 1946–1947, (1947), 192–3.

[6] This has been confirmed by Dr Alexander Sapozhnikov, Head of Collection Division of the National Library at St Petersburg.

[7] Callmer, *op. cit.*, 152–3.

February 1779, we learn from his letter to Gjörwell written on 1 March.[8] Volos was to have been the point of departure for Mount Athos. While in Volos he learnt about the Meteora monasteries and their libraries, and immediately decided to change his itinerary. He was aware of the fact that nobody had previously visited them for a scholarly purpose and was excited by the potential prospects of furthering his knowledge.

Although the number of travellers visiting Greece increased through the seventeenth century, it was always southern Greece, and especially Athens with its great monuments, that attracted the attention. Thessaly had little to offer in that respect. Most travellers to Greece never even contemplated a journey to the north and before Björnståhl, those who did, made few comments about life there. Richard Chandler, whom Björnståhl had met in London, did not visit Thessaly. One who did was Edward Wortley Montagu, Lady Mary's son. In a letter to the envoy, Ulric Celsing, in Constantinople Björnståhl vividly describes his visit to the Meteora monasteries and how to anyone who cannot fly, the ascent is 'the worst in the world'. He remarks that many who have travelled there out of curiosity had not dared ascend to the heights. One of them, he says, is the well-known Montagu, who despite his adventurous mind, had to view them from below.[9] Montagu was in Thessaly some ten years before Björnståhl, who refers to him in his previously cited letter to Gjörwell from 1 March.[10]

For information on the history of Thessaly Björnståhl had to consult mainly the ancient authors and a more recent Greek geographer, Meletios, whom he found not too reliable. Actually Björnståhl is the first in a line of scholars, much more renowned than him, such as Edward Daniel Clarke, Edward Dodwell, William Martin Leake, F.C.H.L. Pouqueville

---

[8] Björnståhl, *op. cit.* (1780), III, 235–63. This letter also tells us of the extremely cold winter in Thessaly with deep snow — no winter since 1709 had been so cold–and in it Björnståhl at length discusses the Greek language and Greek toponyms. The last letter to Gjörwell is dated 10 March and is also printed in *op. cit.*, III, 264–71.

[9] This letter is in the Björnståhl Papers in the Lund University Library and is cited by Callmer, *op. cit.*, 168–72.

[10] Björnståhl, *op. cit.* (1780), III, 250.

and the Dane, J.L. Ussing, to make a scientific journey in Thessaly.[11] Of these, Pouqueville alone points out the pioneering feat of Björnståhl.

Travelling in Thessaly was a dangerous undertaking but Björnståhl took such precautions as he could. He procured a *firman*, let his beard and moustache grow and sometimes assumed Turkish dress to look less like a foreigner. He was also accompanied by a Janissary who was a Turk. Björnståhl spoke both Turkish and Greek himself and learnt some Albanian. He realised, of course, that if he did not dare anything he would not learn anything.[12] He tells us all this in his letter to Gjörwell of 10 March, and he then remarks:

> First of all, all Turks and Greeks always look upon every traveller as a strange animal and believe that nobody wants to travel unless they can profit, either as a merchant or through searching for hidden treasures in the ground, which they believe are everywhere where there are any ruins; yes, that every stone which has an old, and for them illegible inscription, has in it gold, silver, coins and precious stones. They further believe that the writing reveals how to find them. Now in these perilous times it is even worse, for every traveller is immediately taken for a Russian spy, which has happened to me here. [13]

The concern about Russian spies is easily explained since the Russo-Turkish war of 1768–1774 had recently ended. The Albanians, he says, 'constitute a hoard, just like the old Goths, Herulians, Vandals etc. They plunder and roam both the countryside and the seas'.[14] Actually Björnståhl did very well in Thessaly. He was well received by Greeks, Turks and Albanians alike.

---

[11] Edward Daniel Clarke, *Travels in Various Countries in Europe, Asia and Africa, 2: Greece, Egypt and the Holy Land* (London: J. Cadell and W. Davies, 1816); Edward Dodwell, *A Classical and Topographical Tour through Greece during the years 1801, 1805 and 1806* (London: 1819); W.M. Leake, *Travels in Northern Greece* (London: J. Rodwell, 1835), III-IV; F.C.H.L. Pouqueville, *Voyage de la Grèce* (Paris: Didot, 1820-1822); and J.L. Ussing, *Reisebilleder fra Syden* (Kjöbenhavn: C.A. Reitzel, 1847).

[12] Björnståhl, *op. cit.* (1780), III, 264-71. All translations from Swedish into English are the author's.

[13] Björnståhl, *op. cit.* (1780), III, 268.

[14] *Ibid.*, 270.

Map 3. Björnståhl's route through Thessaly, from Callmer, 161.

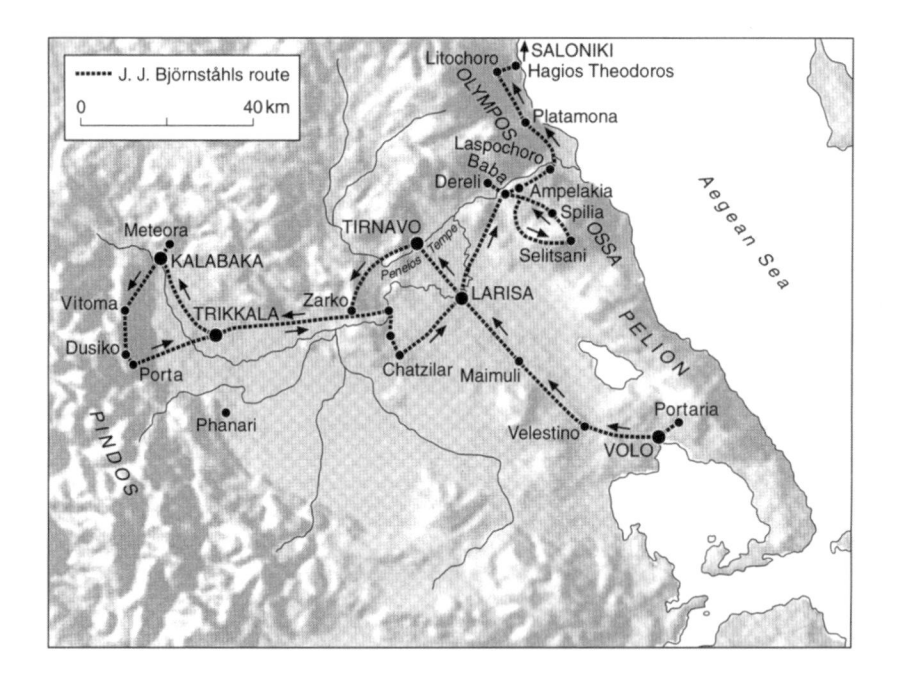

On 17 March Björnståhl finally left Volos. This is also the day his Thessalian journal begins.[15] His route went northwest to Larissa and Tirnavos, then southwest via Trikkala to Kalambaka and the Meteora, where he spent more than a month doing research in several of the monastic libraries. Thereafter he visited the monasteries of Vitoma and Dusiko to the south before returning to Larissa via Trikkala. He then travelled northeast, making a stop at Ambelakia and continuing to the Tempe Valley. On 27 June he reached the village of Laspochori at the eastern end of the Tempe pass, and here his travel journal ends. His notes[16] takes us to Lithochori the next day, but there he fell ill. Against his protest, his friends secretly sent to Thessaloniki for the Swedish sea captain on whose ship he had travelled to Volos from Constantinople. He came with a small caïque in order to bring Björnståhl to Thessaloniki, but during the voyage his condition deteriorated rapidly and he died on 12 July.[17] He was buried to the east of Thessaloniki and in 1781 a tombstone was placed on his grave during an elaborate ceremony described by Gjörwell.[18] Neither grave nor stone are to be found today.[19]

Björnståhl is an astute observer, meticulously recording whatever he sees and learns during his travel through Thessaly. For each village and town he passes through he states the number of churches and mosques. Trikkala, for instance, had six large mosques with minarets, which he calls *cami*, and ten small mosques; the Greeks had seven churches. In the diocese of Trikkala lived more Turks than Greeks, but the latter, he says, 'govern the area through their money. With this money they appoint or dispose of the agahs or chieftains'. There was also a small Jewish community, but the Jews were poor. There, were almost no Franks, that is, Europeans.[20] In many places the churches had been destroyed by the

---

[15] Björnståhl, *op. cit.* (1783), V, 91–158 comprise the whole Thessalian journal in its edited version as reported above.
[16] The Björnståhl Papers in the Lund University Library referred to by Callmer, *op. cit.*, 181.
[17] Callmer, *op. cit.*, 182–3.
[18] Björnståhl, *op. cit.*, IV, in the preface, where also the Latin inscription on the stone is cited.
[19] Callmer, *op. cit.*, 191–2.
[20] Björnståhl, *op. cit.* (1783), V, 97–98.

Turks and the law forbade the Greeks to rebuild them unless they paid large sums of money to the Ottoman authorities; regular maintenance could be carried out for the payment of a smaller sum.[21]

Greeks were generally not allowed to carry arms, but there were exceptions. The village of Ambelakia, on the slopes of Kissavo (Ossa), was one. This was a very wealthy village and the prices were high, also because of the shortage of food caused by the severe winter. Most of the inhabitants were dyers, producing red cotton thread, which was exported to Vienna and Leipzig, where the villagers had also established agencies. There were many well-to-do merchants and many spoke German. Björnståhl tried to get them interested in exporting goods to Sweden and also translated a letter from a Swedish merchant to one of the villagers.[22]

On the night before Björnståhl's arrival in Ambelakia in June 1779, the Greeks had killed nine Albanians in a village close to Olympos and sent their heads to the Kapudan Pasha, who, with a seat in Trikkala, seems to have been newly appointed governor of all of Thessaly. Björnståhl noted in his diary for 11 June. *Arnautian* is Albanian in Turkish, a word often used by Björnståhl:

> for he (Kapudan Pasha) had given the Greeks permission to arm themselves against the Albanians and to kill all whom they come upon. He has further promised to pay 4 piasters for every Arnautian head sent to him. This is the first time that Greeks here in the country may carry arms and kill Moslems. They have also hastened to profit from this liberty. In all villages there are now Greek soldiers, in the area as many as seven hundred armed men. The village of Ambelakia has equipped fifty soldiers. Five years ago Volos was given a similar permission.[23]

Björnståhl lived in the Meteora for five weeks. With an introductory letter from the metropolitan of Larissa the doors were opened to him almost everywhere and as a rule he was very well received. From his descriptions of the landscape, the trees that grew in the monastic gardens on the pinnacles, the flowers and the birds he obviously was at ease in the monasteries. In some of them he found learned men to discourse with, as

[21] *Ibid.*, 138.
[22] Callmer, *op. cit.*, 176–7.
[23] Björnståhl, *op. cit.* (1783), V, 149–50.

at Agios Stephanos where he met the bishop of Kalambaka who had escaped from the roving hoards of Albanians who had nearly stopped Björnstråhl's own journey. An Italian doctor from Trikkala had sought refuge at the Great Meteora and with him Björnståhl could discuss, among other things, the writings of Carl von Linné (Linnaeus).[24]

In the Agia Triada monastery Björnståhl found nothing of interest, although some manuscipts, 'lay in the church thrown aside without care or organisation'.[25] On the whole the monastic libraries were in a sad state of organisation. Everything was covered in dust and nobody seemed really to care. At Agios Stephanos Björnståhl learnt from the bishop of Kalambaka that a certain Athanasios from Cyprus, pretending that he was an Orthodox monk, had come from Rome two hundred years previously and he had, on Mount Athos, at the Meteora and at other monasteries, not only bought but also stolen as many manuscripts as he had been able to lay his hands on. He paid according to how much the manuscripts weighed. Other disasters had befallen the Agios Stephanos monastery. Also about two hundred years ago there had been a devastating fire destroying many manuscripts and not so long ago the Prince of Moldavia had borrowed some manuscripts under the pretext that he wanted to print them with his own money and then immediately return them. They were never returned. Björnståhl writes: 'These are the learned repugnancies that these places have encountered'.[26]

At the Great Meteora he found Hesiod and Sophocles in the same volume, with *scholia* in the margins and commentaries between the lines in red ink. But the manuscript was modern and on paper.[27] Robert Curzon mentions in his *Visits to the Monasteries in the Levant*, which appeared in London in 1849, that he searched for this volume mentioned by Biornstern (he got the spelling of Björnståhl's name totally wrong) but it was no longer to be found. His comment is: 'some later antiquarian

---

[24] Björnståhl, *op. cit.* (1783), V, 102–106.
[25] *Ibid.*, 109; pages 106–109 deal with the Agia Triada monastery.
[26] *Ibid.*, 103-104.
[27] *Ibid.*, 112.

may, perhaps, have got possession of them and taken them to some country where they will be more appreciated than they were here.'[28]

At the Great Meteora Björnståhl also read a vellum manuscript of Josephus, 'The History of the Jewish People until the Roman Conquest' (περὶ ἁλώσεως (λόγοι). He estimated it at being four hundred years old and he spent much time over it.[29]

After having visited the Varlaam monastery as well, Björnståhl left the Meteora and travelled south to visit two other monasteries, Vitoma and Dusiko (Map. 3). There were no manuscripts at Vitoma. 'The monks,' says Björnståhl, 'live in abysmal ignorance; they do not even know how to read a book.'[30] Dusiko had been plundered by the Albanians but there was still a large manuscript of the four gospels with annotations in the margins. In a room which had been destroyed Björnståhl found manuscripts thrown away as garbage. The monks defended themselves by saying that they had enough books as it was. There was no room for more. Despite the devastated buildings the library was richer than the one at the Great Meteora. Björnståhl made excerpts and a list of the extant manuscripts, but some of the monks jeered at him for his zeal.[31]

Although Björnståhl had been instructed to buy manuscripts he apparently did not do so in the Meteora, nor anywhere else in Thessaly. He read copiously and copied whatever he found of interest. I have found no information about what happened after his death to the great quantity of excerpts that he made.

Jacob Jonas Björnståhl was an astute observer also of the landscape through which he travelled. This, I believe, can best be exemplified by an incident at the end of his Thessalian journey. Scholars had previously not been able to agree on where exactly to locate Tempe. Björnståhl is the first traveller to give a true description of it.[32] He was enthralled by the valley, the nightingales singing and the abundant waters pouring out of the

[28] Robert Curzon, *Visits to the Monasteries in the Levant* (London: John Murray, 1849), 279.
[29] Björnståhl, *op. cit.* (1783), V, 112–14.
[30] *Ibid.*, 129–30.
[31] *Ibid.*, 131-4.
[32] Callmer, *op. cit.*, 178–81.

mountains. As he reached the eastern end of the Tempe Valley he comments on Olympos and Ossa, and on his right hand above the valley on a smoothed surface discovered a rock-cut inscription in Latin. He traced the partly effaced letters with his fingers. He could make out three lines but deciphered only part of the inscription:

— CASSIVS
— COS
TIMPE MVNIVIT

He was convinced that, once he had access to a list of consuls, he would be able to supply the rest of the words. Locally a story was told of how the inscription was either Frankish or Venetian and established the cost of salt given to the workmen building the road.[33] Later several travellers were to claim the discovery of the inscription. Among them was the previously mentioned Edward Daniel Clarke. He, however, was able to read the whole of the text which celebrates L. Cassius Longinus, Caesar's *legatus* who built the military road through the pass before the battle of Pharsalos in 48 BC.[34]

The printed Swedish version of Björnståhl's travels started to appear in 1780. It was immediately translated into German and Dutch and an Italian translation was made of the German edition. Excerpts were also translated into Danish. This maybe explains why Jacob Jonas Björnståhl was almost unknown to the English travellers at the end of the eighteenth and the

---

[33] Björnståhl, *op. cit.* (1783), V, 156–8.

[34] Edward Daniel Clarke in his *Travels in Various Countries of Europe* (London: J. Cadwell and W. Davies, 1818), VII, 373–80, discusses the location of the Tempe Valley. Clarke travelled through Greece in 1801–1802. In a footnote on pages 349–50 he lets a Mr John Palmer attribute the identification of Tempe to himself; see also Callmer, *op. cit.*, 180–1. See also Dodwell, *op. cit.*, I-II; vol. II gives a depiction not only of the narrow pass cut in the rock but also of the inscription facing page 113. Here the inscription is given as L CASSIUS LONGIN PROCOS TEMPE MVNIVIT. The question is, did it read TEMPE or TIMPE, as Björnståhl maintains. It may be impossible to verify this today. I recently passed through the Tempe Valley. The inscription, together with the cliff it was on, and a fortification on top of it were obliterated when the road was built through the valley.

beginning of the nineteenth centuries. It is my hope that this paper will draw attention to a remarkable Swedish traveller.

Bibliography

Andrews, Kevin, *Athens Alive* (Athens: Hermes, 1979).

Björnståhl, Jacob Jonas, *Resa till Frankrike, Italien, Sweitz, Tyskland, Holland, Ängland, Turkiet och Grekeland* [Journey to France, Italy, Switzerland, Germany, Holland, England, Turkey and Greece], posthumously published by Carl Christoffer Gjörwell (Stockholm, 1780–1784), I–VI.

Callmer, Christian, 'Jacob Jonas Björnståhls thessaliska resa, hans död och hans litterära kvarlåtenskaps öden' [Jacob Jonas Björnståhl, his death and the fate of his literary legacy], *Lychnos*, 1946–1947, (1947), 151–96 (with a summary in French).

Clarke, Edward Daniel, *Travels in Various Countries in Europe, Asia and Africa, 2: Greece, Egypt and the Holy Land* (London: J. Cadwell and W. Davies, 1818).

Curzon, Robert, *Visits to the Monasteries in the Levant* (London: John Murray, 1849).

Dodwell, Edward, *A Classical and Topographical Tour through Greece during the Years 1801, 1805 and 1806*, London: Rodwell and Martin, 1819).

Gjörwell, Carl Christoffer, *Det svenska biblioteket* [The Swedish Library] (Stockholm, 1759), part 3.

Laborde, L.-E. de, *Athènes aux XVe, XVIe et XVIIe siècles* (Paris: Jules Renouard, 1854).

Leake, William M., *Travels in Northern Greece* (London: J. Rodwell, 1835), III–IV.

Pouqueville, F.C.H.L., *Voyage de la Grèce* (Paris: Didot, 1820–1822).

Ussing, J.L., *Reisebilleder fra Syden* (Kjöbenhavn: C.A. Reitzel, 1847).

Pilgrimage to Tourism

Pilgrimage has always been a powerful spur to travel and the papers in this section demonstrate that as a constantly recurring theme in travels within and to the Levant. The ultimate goal was Jerusalem but other sites in the Near East — Damascus, Hebron, Bethlehem, the River Jordan — also had attracted the pilgrim. From the mid-nineteenth century the development of tourism, with its ramifications of guides, hostelries, provisioning, added to the ancient rites of pilgrimage. In the sanctified lands of Syria and Palestine there should in fact be little distinction between the pilgrim and the tourist, the latter as much a pilgrim as the former was and is a tourist, albeit more single-minded. The tourism under consideration here, for instance, the development of Thomas Cook's enterprise in Palestine described by Kark, was focussed almost exclusively on the enduring magnet of Jerusalem, mainly its Christian sites in the case of Cook's clients, but their visit introducing them to the fervour of other faiths, Jewish and Islamic. That introduction was also an important element in the experiences of the Italian visitors described by Codacci.

This cultural interchange between 'east' and 'west', one religious outlook with another is a major aspect of the research encouraged by ASTENE, described here in Frankopan's paper on ninth-to-tenth century pilgrims to Constantinople and Palestine. These pre-Crusade pilgrims were travelling mainly by land but never far from the shores of a culturally harmonious Mediterranean world that tended to blur the political and economic distinctions that have played a more destructive role in recent years. We learn about the diplomatic, Byzantine setting from the Christian travellers, while Frenkel's thirteenth-to-sixteenth century post-Crusade Muslim pilgrims are more concerned in their accounts, a particular genre of medieval Arabic literature, to justify their journeys, their reprehensible absence from home, by describing the network of religious scholars met on the way, accentuating an orthodox Islamic world view. Neither Frankopan's nor Frenkel's pilgrims tell us much about the physical environment of the region through which they travelled, often in considerable hardship. It was axiomatic that both Christian and Muslim enhanced their reputations by the difficulty of their journeys, to the extent occasionally of emphasising the hazards to highlight the miracle of reaching the goal.

The nineteenth century Italian visitors to Palestine whose accounts are outlined by Codacci tell us more about the physical and political environment but are also more partisan. They expose the problems of accommodating the three monotheistic religions occupying the region, the local Orthodox Christianity often seeming as alien to Roman Catholic visitors as Islam and Judaism; towards the end of the century there are some interesting comments on the growing Jewish population, especially in Jerusalem. In mid-century Marianne North, in the manuscript autobiography located by Moon, describes the visit she and her father made in 1865–1866 to Palestine and Syria, an account typical of so many written by those attracted to the region at this time by travel literature, dioramas, museum acquisitions, topographical painting and so on. But she also throws light on contemporary society in Syria, Palestine and Mount Lebanon, both local and expatriate at a time when Ottoman control of the region was being challenged by local unrest. In exploring the experiences of mid-Victorian tourists in the Levant, with all their worries and prejudices and enthusiasms, the stage is set for the arrival in the latter part of the century (his first visit in 1869 was just prior to the inauguration of the Suez Canal) of Thomas Cook. Kark traces the development of the company and organisation in Palestine, and its role in assisting not only pilgrims and tourists (virtual pilgrims after all) but also some more politically motivated visitors such as Kaiser Wilhelm II.

None of these contemporary accounts is objective; these travellers, medieval as much as nineteenth century, come with pre-packed religious and cultural baggage which they are unlikely to change. There is a risk here that we may learn more about the pilgrim's domestic context than we do about his experience of the Near East. Cultural interchange in the nineteenth century is much less apparent; the pilgrim is too focussed on his holy agenda, the tourist on his sense of superiority. The seeds are being sown of today's mass tourism, with even less regard for the Near Eastern world beyond the coach window.

Levels of Contact between West and East: pilgrims and visitors to Constantinople and Jerusalem from the ninth to twelfth centuries

Peter Frankopan

The relationships between different cultures forms one of the key themes in the history of the modern world. Even without defining or delineating precisely what we mean by broad terms such as 'East' and 'West', there is, of course, an obvious, intrinsic value in studying political, economic and cultural interchange between peoples. The ways in which individuals and groups of individuals viewed and undertook travel, the means by which they communicated with, and learnt from others from different geographical, cultural and religious backgrounds inevitably yields interesting insights: for it not only tells us how the 'other' is perceived from without; it also tells us a great deal about the perceptions people have about themselves, about the way in which they deal with concepts with which they are unfamiliar, and about what it is that they find important in life.

There can be few better places to look for evidence of interchange than in the Mediterranean basin in the late antique and early medieval periods, a time of profound change in this region. In the centuries which followed the decline and the fall of Rome, the Mediterranean world provided the arena for a series of extraordinary geo-political developments which were to shape the history not only of western and eastern Europe, but of the world around it, from northern Africa to Scandinavia, from Spain to the Holy Land. From the great migrations of the Goths and the Slavs in the fifth to seventy centuries to the Norman conquest of Britain in the eleventh, from the great Arab conquests which followed the death of Muhammad to the arrival of the first crusaders by Jerusalem in 1099, the late antique and early medieval Mediterranean was characterised by the movement of large numbers of peoples which served, with a few exceptions, to give the region the cultural and religious — if not the political — shape which it has today.

Of course, there are many avenues where the study of the post-Roman world could lead us (and by post-Roman, I mean from the fifth century onwards): we could, for example, look at the influences which the Goths had on central and eastern Europe — or on Spain and northern Africa for that matter;[1] we could examine the extent and nature of the relationship between Christian and Muslim concepts of Holy War;[2] or we could perhaps assess the impact of the adoption of the Cyrillic alphabet by the Slavic peoples at the end of the ninth century.[3] Analysis of the various forms of political and cultural interchange between different peoples and between different regions in the Mediterranean in the centuries after the sack of Rome provides an extraordinarily rich seam of material and evidence to interpret.

This essay, however, seeks to assess levels of contact between West and East in the early medieval period. But first this topic should be more clearly defined. It is the interchange within what can be justifiably called — at least in the period in question — the Christian world, which is the subject of this inquiry. It is the contact between the western and eastern halves, and specifically the Latin West and the eastern Christian Roman Empire, known since the Middle Ages as the Byzantine empire, which

---

[1] H. Wolfram, *History of the Goths* (London: University of California Press, 1990); P. Heather, *Goths and Romans 332–489* (Oxford: Clarendon Press, 1991).

[2] For example, T. Kolbaba, 'Fighting for Christianity: holy war in the Byzantine empire,' *Byzantion*, 68 (1998), 194–221.

[3] A. Vlasto, *The Entry of the Slavs into Christendom* (Cambridge: Cambridge University Press, 1978).

will be examined here. Although there were many levels to, and stages of, the relationship between East and West in this period, the most prominent was perhaps the religious schism of the eleventh century, the aspect on which attention will be focussed is the growing familiarity of the people living in various parts of the Christian world with the Holy Land and with Constantinople and Jerusalem in particular.

From the end of the ninth century to the start of the twelfth, the Christian world shrank rapidly. Rather like the latter part of the twentieth century, a sharp rise in the numbers of people who were able and prepared to travel long distances, meant that ideas and cultural influences from one side of the known world could be brought back to the other. It meant that individuals who had travelled on pilgrimages to the great holy sites brought home personal bonds and friendships which they had made *en route*, and which could even be maintained through correspondence. The Mediterranean basin was the setting for an explosion in communication and travel in the early medieval period.

Although many factors contributed to the context of people wanting and being able to travel from the end of the ninth century onwards, the most important were the growing power of the Church and the formation of what has become known as Christian knighthood.[4] Of course, political formalisation and the early feudal system, particularly in northern France and in Germany, helped to facilitate exchange, as did the growth of the maritime city states like Venice and Genoa, which made travel that much easier.[5] Increasing levels of literacy and education, which bred a seemingly insatiable intellectual curiosity, also played a vital part

---

[4] H. Cowdrey, 'Cluny and the First Crusade', *Revue Bénédictine*, 83 (1983), 287-308; C. Morris, 'Equestris Ordo: chivalry as a vocation in the 12th century', *Studies in Church History*, 15 (1978), 87-96; and M. Bull, *Knightly Piety and the Lay Response to the First Crusade: the Limousin and Gascony* (Oxford: Clarendon Press, 1993).

[5] See, for example, R. Bartlett, *The Making of Europe: conquest, colonization and cultural change 950-1350* (London: Allen Lane, 1993); B. Arnold, *Medieval Germany 500-1300* (Basingstoke: Macmillan, 1997); D. Nicol, *Byzantium and Venice* (Cambridge: Cambridge University Press, 1988).

in encouraging members of both the ecclesiastical and secular worlds to cast their physical and mental horizons ever further afield.[6]

But it was the lure of the East which proved to be decisive. Christianity had, at the start at any rate, been an Eastern religion. With the exception of Rome itself, the other sees which made up the ecclesiastical Pentarchy — Jerusalem, Antioch, Alexandria and Constantinople — were located in the East, or, to be more precise, in the eastern half of the Roman Empire. And it had not taken long for pilgrims to want to travel eastwards, as St Jerome put it, 'to follow in the footsteps of Christ'.[7] Indeed, by the early part of the third century AD, pilgrims had already begun to arrive in the Holy Land in the belief that divine sustenance could be found at the graves of the early Christian saints and martyrs, and that their bodies would, or certainly could, work miracles for those in need.[8]

The Emperor Constantine's adoption of Christianity, coupled with imperial sponsorship of the Holy Places, particularly of Jerusalem, and, above all, of the Holy Sepulchre itself, meant that the Levant became increasingly accessible to those with the resolve and the resources to go there. By the late fourth century, St Jerome was living in Palestine, recommending visits to places which featured prominently in the Scriptures, not only to close personal friends but also to a wider audience. The evidence we have suggests that the numbers of pilgrims rose steadily around this time.[9]

---

[6] R. Southern, *Medieval Humanism* (Oxford: Blackwell, 1970). See also D. Luscombe and G. Evans, 'The 12th century Renaissance', in *The Cambridge History of Medieval Political Thought c.350-1450*, edited by J. Burns (Cambridge: Cambridge University Press, 1988), 252-305.

[7] *In Joannem*, VI, xxix, in *Patroligiae cursus completus, Series graeca*, edited by J.-P. Migne 161 vols (Paris, 1857-1866), XIV, col. 269.

[8] S. Runciman, *A History of the Crusades*, 3 vols (Cambridge: Cambridge University Press, 1952-1955), I, 38-41.

[9] See the correspondence of and relating to St Jerome, especially letters 46 and 47, in *Patroligiae cursus completus. Series latina*, 221 vols (Paris, 1844-1890), XXII, cols. 483ff. See also *Liber Paralipumenon*, in *ibid*, LVIII, cols. 1325-6.

The Arab conquests of the seventh century therefore had important practical and theological consequences. In the first place, it became much harder to reach Jerusalem. The few travellers who did succeed in reaching the city over the course of the next 250 years made it clear that it was only those with the greatest determination, patience, and above all, luck, who were able to visit the Holy Sepulchre.[10]

By the end of the ninth century, however, the passage eastwards had become marginally easier. In addition to the more common route along the Via Egnatia, which ran from Rome to Brindisi, and then from Dyrrakhion to Constantinople via Thessaloniki, it had become possible, though not risk-free, to reach Byzantium by passing through Hungary and Bulgaria, or to travel by sea from Venice.[11] But these routes could only take the aspiring pilgrim as far as Constantinople, and there were still great dangers to be faced in crossing Asia Minor by land, or by attempting to sail around the southern coast and then on to one of the coastal ports that led on to Jerusalem. It was only after the Byzantine reconquests of vast swathes of Anatolia from the early tenth century, and above all, with the recapture of Crete in 961, which robbed the Arabs of their principal raiding base in the eastern Mediterranean, that the flow of pilgrims began to swell.[12]

We know, for example that leading magnates from France made the journey to Jerusalem in the last decades of the tenth century. Many important members of clergy also reached the Holy Land at this time,

---

[10] Note, for example, the cases of Vulphy of Rue in Picardy, in *Acta Sanctorum quotquot tote orbe coluntur*, 70 vols so far (Antwerp, Brussels, Tongerloe, 1643-), *Junii*, II, 30-31; or of Willibald, who late became Bishop of Eichstadt, *Hodoeporicon*, trans. W. Brownlow, 13 vols (London: Palestine Pilgrims' Text Society, 1896-1897), III, *passim*.

[11] For information about Via Egnatia see G. Skrivanic, 'Roman Roads and Settlements', in *An Historical Geography of the Balkans*, edited by F. Carter (London: Academic Press, 1977), 122-6.

[12] Runciman, *op. cit.*, I, 43. For the Byzantine reconquest of Asia Minor and Crete, see M. Whittow, *The Making of Orthodox Byzantium 600-1025* (Basingstoke: Macmillan, 1996), 310ff.

often on repeat visits. Bishop, later Saint, Conrad of Constance visited Jerusalem on at least three occasions. Another bishop, John, Bishop of Parma, succeeded in getting there no less than six times. The extent to which the objective of setting out for, and reaching, the Holy Land had became both popular and realistic can be shown from the fact that, by 970, Judith of Bavaria, sister of Otto I, was able to undertake a pilgrimage along with several of her retinue which, while easier than it had been in earlier times, was still evidently arduous and ambitious.[13]

That travel to Jerusalem was precipitous and strenuous explains why so much *kudos* was accorded to those who had managed to achieve their goal. For example, this is how Adhemar of Chabannes, a well-known chronicler of the eleventh century describes the return of William Taillefer of Angoulême, who had reached the Holy Land in the spring of 1027: 'When the rumour of his approach reached Angoulême, all the magnates, not only from Angoulême, but also from Perigord, and Saintonge, and of both sexes and all ages, rushed joyfully to meet him, eager to see him. The monks of Saint Cybard, in white vestments and ecclesiastical panoply, processed rejoiced with a large crowds of people to meet him a mile outside the city, singing praises and antiphons. And they led him in, singing the *Te Deum* loudly, as is usual.'[14] The example of William of Angoulême is not exceptional, and the sources make it clear that considerable prestige was derived from a successful journey to Jerusalem and back.[15]

Needless to say, there were times when travel to and from the Holy Land were harder than others. For example, the destruction of the Holy Sepulchre in 1009, apparently on the instructions of the Fatimid Caliph al-Hakim, was followed by several years of sustained persecution of Christians, which appears to have had a telling effect on travel at this

[13] L. Bréhier, *L'Église et l'Orient au Moyen Age: les Croisades* (Paris, 1928), 32-33; J. Ebersolt, *Orient et Occident*, 2 vols (Paris, 1928-1929), I, 72-73.
[14] Adhémar of Chabannes, *Chronicon*, edited by J. Chavanon (Paris, 1897), 190.
[15] J. Riley-Smith, *The First Crusaders 1095-1131* (Cambridge: Cambridge University Press, 1997), 23-39.

time.[16] Similarly, in the mid-1050s, as the Seljuks were establishing political control over Baghdad, conditions in Asia Minor deteriorated sharply as the Seljuk sultan, Tughril, and quasi-independent Türkmen raiders launched a series of surprise attacks on several targets in Anatolia.[17] To make matters worse, around the same time, the Muslim authorities in Jerusalem closed the compound around the Holy Sepulchre and attempted to prevent pilgrim traffic altogether.[18] The effect seems to have been devastating. To the dismay of Lietbert, bishop of Cambrai, the disruption meant that he was prevented from leaving Laodicea (Lattaqia) on the western cost of Syria in 1055, and, in spite of eventually leaving for Cyprus and waiting patiently there for over two months, was unable to complete his journey.[19] Such turbulence was unusual, however, and in the eleventh century the greatest threat to pilgrims seems to have been more standard problems experienced by any and every traveller: disease and exhaustion could pose serious dangers; the inability to communicate with locals could also, on occasion, prove fatal.

One counterbalance to the problems which could be experienced on the journey to Jerusalem came from the existence of hostels and inns where pilgrims could stay.[20] Some of these were foundations set up and run by Westerners — although these tend to have appeared from the

---

[16] *Ibid.*, 25; Runciman, *op. cit.*, I, 35-36.

[17] C. Cahen, 'La première pénétration turque en Asia Mineure', *Byzantion*, 18 (1948), 16-23; V. Stepanenko, *Vizantia v mezhdunarodnykh otnosheniyakh na blizhnem vostoke 1071-1176* (Sverdlovsk, 1988), 25-27.

[18] *Acta Sanctorum. Junii*, IV, 597-9, *Miracula Sancti Wolframni Senonensis* in *Acta Sanctorum ordinis Sancti Benedicti*, edited by J. Mabillon and L. d'Archéry, 9 vols (Paris, 1668-1685), III, 381-2.

[19] *Vita Lietberti*, in Migne, *Patrologia Latina*, CXLVI, cols. 1466-7. See also S. Runciman, 'The Pilgrimage to Palestine before 1095', in *History of the Crusades*, edited by K. Setton *et al*, 6 vols (Philadelphia: University of Pennsylvania Press, 1955-), I, 76.

[20] K. Ciggaar, *Western Travellers to Constantinople; the West and Byzantium 962-1204* (Leiden: Brill, 1996), 36-44.

twelfth century onwards.²¹ There were a few institutions set up before this, such as the monastery established near Nicaea by the Byzantine Emperor Alexios I Komnenos in the 1080s, which were manned by Western monks.²² For the most part, however, pilgrims and travellers would stay in one of the many specially built Byzantine inns, set up to cater for pilgrim traffic, which were called *xenodochia*, or places for foreigners.²³

If such inns could provide at least some consolation for the long-distance visitor, lists of basic words in Greek which are known to have circulated in Europe provided another. Although there is the occasional piece of evidence to suggest that there were officials to help and even to interpret for pilgrims, these word lists may have gone some of the way towards averting the inevitable quarrels which would accompany a tiring and disorientating journey.²⁴ Some lists simply gave the equivalent for

---

21   A European settlement near Philippopolis existed by the middle of the twelfth century, Odo of Deuil, *De profectione Ludovici VII in orientem*, edited by H. Waquet, *La Croisade de Louis VII, roi de France* (Paris, 1949), 35-36. There were Latin monasteries in Adrianople, and in the Peloponnese, at Corinth and Sparta, by the end of the 1170s, P. Schreiner, 'Untersuchungen zu den Niederlassungen westlicher Kaufleute im byzantinischen Reich des 11 und 12 Jahrhunderts', *Byzantinische Forschungen*, 7 (1979), 178-9; R.-J. Lilie, 'Die lateinische Kirche in Romania vor dem vierten Kreuzzug', *Byzantinische Zeitschrift*, 82 (1989), 202ff, and Ciggaar, *op. cit.*, 40-41.

22   *Letters of Peter the Venerable*, edited by G. Constable, 2 vols (Cambridge, Mass.: Harvard University Press, 1967), I, 208-10; J. Gay, 'L'abbaye de Cluny et Byzance au début du XII siècle', *Echos d'Orient*, 30 (1931), 86-87.

23   *Jerusalem Pilgrimage 1099-1185*, edited by J. Wilkinson *et al* (London: Hakluyt Society, 1988), 200; B. Kaczynski, 'Some St. Gall glosses on Greek philanthropic nomenclature', *Speculum*, 58 (1983), 1008-17.

24   There are, for example, a handful of seals belonging to individuals who were evidently official interpreters, For these and other references see D. Miller, 'The Logothete of the Drome in the Middle Byzantine period: the corps of interpreters', *Byzantinische Zeitschrift*, 36 (1966), 449-58; see also W. Aerts, 'The Knowledge of Greek in Western Europe at the time of Theophano and the Greek fragment in Vindob. 114', in *Byzantium and the Low Countries: aspects of War and History in the Ottonian era* (Hernen, 1986), 78-103.

basic foodstuffs (such as bread, water, and wine), clothes, bed, horses, and so on.[25] Others had more colloquial sentences, suggesting appropriate greetings, requests for directions, and questions which could be asked of a concierge.[26] Such lists, which are perhaps understandably uncommon, provide a precious insight into how people communicated when on their travels, and it is interesting to find that there are also a few instances in Byzantine sources where Greek and Latin phrases appear next to each other, which again provides important evidence for the extent of bilinguality in the early medieval period.[27]

These then were the mechanics of travel to and from the Levant. There were essentially three routes by which travellers and pilgrims could reach Constantinople; Asia Minor could be crossed by land. Although there were times when the journey to Jerusalem was particularly dangerous, completion of this journey always required a certain determination, as well as the ability to overcome hardship — regardless of the various inns and other facilities which could make travel less problematic. But the picture of travel in the early medieval world is not without its defects. In the first place, the sources often prove frustrating. As a general rule, for example, the chronicles recording the various pilgrimages to Jerusalem rarely say much about the actual journey itself. Indeed, even the route which was taken is often not even mentioned — and if it is, then only the briefest of details are given. It was the end goal which was important to record and commemorate, rather than anything else. Accounts, such as those by Daniel, an abbot who travelled to Jerusalem from Russia in the first decade of the twelfth century, where the itinerary, as well as comments about the various places which he passed on his way to the

---

[25] W. Aerts, 'The Latin-Greek wordlist in MS 236 of the Municipal Library of Avranches, Fol. 97ᵛ', *Anglo-Norman Studies*, 9 (1986), 64-69.

[26] M. Triantaphyllidis, *Neollenike grammatike*, 2 vols (Athens, 1938), I, 195-6; Ciggaar, *op. cit.*, 33.

[27] N. Wilson, *Scholars of Byzantium* (London: Duckworth, 1983), *passim*, but especially pages 151, 192; H. Hunger, 'Zum Epilog der Theogonie des Johannes Tzetzes', *Byzantinische Zeitschrift*, 46 (1953), 305.

Holy Land, are few and far between and, consequently, are valuable indeed.[28]

In recent years, the study of charters, grants and similar documents has proved to be of great value to historians seeking to establish the motivations behind pilgrimages. This evidence has been exceptionally useful in allowing us to reach some conclusions about what the First Crusaders, in particular, were seeking to achieve when they set out from all over Europe in the last decade of the eleventh century.[29] But because this kind of evidence normally refers to the preparations for travel, and for the provisions made before the journey had begun, they too often prove to be frustrating. Greek sources are even less helpful: even those pilgrimages where the number of participants appear to have been exceptional — such as the expedition led by Robert of Normandy in 1035, or that of the 1064-1065 which was led (amongst others) by the Bishop of Bamberg and the Archbishop of Mainz — do not even appear in the Byzantine chronicles of this period.[30] But is it the examination of the Byzantine background to travel and pilgrimage which proves highly revealing, for although the Greek sources do not tell us much about pilgrims and travel to the Holy Land, they do allow us to assemble a picture of the level of contact between East and West between the ninth and twelfth centuries. This has important implications for our understanding of the extent, and even the nature of, political and cultural interchange in the early medieval Christian world.

Visitors to Constantinople can be broadly divided into three categories: those passing through on their way to the Holy Land; official embassies; and those who came to settle in Byzantium. As we have seen, the pilgrims on their way east rarely make an appearance in the sources. Curiously, official embassies often fare no better. For example, we know of two

---

[28] Wilkinson, *op cit.*, 120-71.
[29] For example, Bull, *op. cit.*
[30] Cf. Ralph Glaber, *Historiarum libri quinque*, edited and revised by J. France (Milan: Jaca Books, 1983; repr., Oxford, 1989), 198-205; Lambert of Hersefeld, *Opera*, edited by O. Holder-Eggar (Leipzig, 1894), 94-98.

Ottonian missions to Constantinople in the middle of the tenth century which were led by Liudprand of Cremona. Although both were evidently high-level delegations, we know of these, and of the business which Liudprand was charged with only from his own accounts of the missions.[31] Nor is this exceptional: in fact, when material on and information concerning Byzantine diplomatic relations with the West is compiled, the striking common feature is that such evidence is often drawn from the obscurest of sources.[32]

However, this is not to say that the Byzantines neglected foreign affairs, that they considered diplomatic relations to be unimportant, or that it was not worth recording these. On the contrary, as two handbooks from the tenth century make absolutely clear, officials in Constantinople knew exactly how to deal with embassies and how to play the game of foreign affairs: there were set formulae which were used when receiving and addressing an envoy, which depended not only on his status, but on that of the country which had sent him.[33] In other words, strict hierarchical orders were observed;[34] set answers were kept at the ready to fend off the two requests most commonly made by foreigners — namely an imperial bride, and Greek fire.[35] And, in a wonderful set-play, the emperor's throne was specially designed to elevate him towards the

---

[31] For Liudprand's accounts see *Liudprandi episcopalis Cremonensis: Opera*, in *Monumenta Germanicae Historica, Scriptores* (Hannover, 1872–), III. A more modern edition of Liudprand's second visit to Byzantium, which took place in 968, appears with an excellent commentary and translation by B. Scott, *Relatio de legatione Constantinopolitana* (Bristol: Bristol Classical Press, 1993).

[32] For example, J. Shepard and S. Franklin (eds), *Byzantine Diplomacy* (Aldershot: Variorum, 1992), *passim*.

[33] Note, for example, Liudprand's indignation at being ranked lower than a Bulgarian envoy who was in Constantinople at the same time, Scott, *op. cit.*, chapter 19, 7–8.

[34] *De Cerimoniis aulae Byzantinae libri duo*, edited by J. Reiske, 2 vols (Bonn, 1829–1830), especially vol. II, chapter 48, 688–90.

[35] *De Administrando Imperio*, edited and translated by G. Moravcsik and R. Jenkins (Washington, D.C., 1967), especially chapter 12, 64–76.

ceiling and out of polite speaking distance, if and when that was necessary.[36]

By the end of the eleventh century, the sheer numbers of those who were coming into contact with Constantinople had become so great that large parts of this ceremonial appear to have been replaced. In 1097, for example, confronted with a huge contingent of armed pilgrims (including a substantial number of experienced Frankish knights) who had made their way east following Pope Urban II's appeal for a crusade to liberate the Holy Places from Muslim control the Byzantine Emperor Alexios Komnenos seems to have had a much more informal set-up when some of the crusade leaders came to his palace. Indeed, it is not clear if the emperor even sat on his throne during this interview: one of the more confident knights had to be rebuked — not by a Byzantine, but, rather significantly by another European — for daring to sit on the imperial throne.[37] Certainly, although ceremonial was still rigorously enforced when the occasion was appropriate, it is no coincidence that there is clear evidence that this emperor was careful to play down the magnificence of Constantinople and of Byzantium when needed.[38]

The example of Alexios' care with the crusaders is chosen deliberately here, for it fits in neatly with what we can piece together from a wide range of sources about the numbers of those who were being drawn to settle in Constantinople between the ninth and twelfth centuries. Constantinople had been, after all, the largest and grandest city in the

---

[36] *De Cerimoniis*, II, 597.
[37] Anna Comnena, *Alexiade*, edited by B. Leib (Paris, 1937–1945), III, bk 10, chapter 10, 229; for an English translation see *The Alexiad of Anna Comnena*, translated by E. Sewter (Harmondsworth: Penguin, 1988), 325.
[38] For an excellent analysis of the ways in which Byzantine methods of diplomacy changed between the tenth and eleventh centuries see J. Shepard, '"Father" or "scorpion"? Style and substance of Alexios' diplomacy', in *Alexios I Komnenos* edited by M. Mullett and D. Smythe (Belfast, 1996), I, *Belfast Papers*, 68–132.

Christian world in the centuries which followed the sack of Rome.[39] As such, it had always attracted visitors from far afield who were keen to experience its glory. The lure of the city proved particularly strong, for example, for the Scandinavians and the Rus' in the ninth century, who were drawn in increasing numbers along the great rivers stretching south towards the Black Sea.[40] With its physical splendour, its great churches, enormous cisterns and its other impressive monuments, such as a zoo filled with exotic animals not far from the city centre, it was with no irony that a tenth-century visitor wrote of the 'Seven Wonders of Constantinople'.[41]

In the ninth and tenth centuries, however, visitors to Constantinople had largely remained as that: visitors. Numbers of those allowed into the city were carefully monitored. For example, no more than ten Rus' were allowed in at any one time;[42] traders from outside Byzantium were subjected to stringent controls;[43] marriage alliances between the imperial

---

[39] For example, D. Jacoby, 'La Population de Constantinople à l'époque Byzantine: un problème de démographie urbaine', *Byzantion*, 31 (1961), 81–109.

[40] J. Shepard and S. Franklin, *The Emergence of Rus' 750–1200* (London: Longman, 1996; repr. Aldershot, 1998), 112–38.

[41] For the various and many attractions of Constantinople, see Ciggaar, *op. cit.*, 45–77. For the wonders of Constantinople, see E. Legrand, 'Constantin le Rhodien: description des œuvres d'art et de l'église des Saints Âpotres', *Revue des Etudes Grecques*, 9 (1896), 32–65; G. Downey, 'Constantine the Rhodian: his life and writing', in *Late Classical and Medieval Studies in honor of A.M. Friend* (Princeton, 1950), 212–21.

[42] *The Russian Primary Chronicle*, translated by S. Cross and O. Sherbowitz-Wetzor (Cambridge, Mass.: Mediaeval Academy of America, 1953), 65–66. Similar controls were effective towards the end of the eleventh century, for example, *Saxo Grammaticus: Gesta Danorum*, edited by A. Holder (Strasbourg, 1886), 407–408. See also the care taken by the Byzantines at the time of the First Crusade which resulted in large numbers of knights and armed pilgrims living in close proximity to the city, J. France, *Victory in the East* (Cambridge: Cambridge University Press, 1994), 108ff.

[43] For example, J. Freshfield (ed. and trans.), *The Book of the Eparch* (Cambridge: Cambridge University Press, 1938), chapter 5, 30–31.

family and foreigners were only made on two occasions in this period;[44] and it is extremely rare to find foreigners holding important positions in the Byzantine armed forces or at the imperial court at this time.[45]

However, this policy of exclusion based, effectively, on Byzantium's strong sense of supremacy over other nations, was to undergo a fundamental re-orientation after the death of Basil II in 1025, and particularly in the later part of the eleventh century. Byzantium was simply coming into contact with more and more outsiders, whether in the form of pilgrims who were passing through imperial territory, or in the form of traders from the city states of Venice, Pisa, Genoa, and Amalfi, who had begun to establish colonies not only in the capital but in secondary, though still important, towns such as Dyrrakhion on the western flank of the empire.[46]

Moreover, faced with extraordinary pressure on three sides — with major invasions on an almost annual basis from the 1070s in the northern territories by Pecheneg nomads, with the Seljuk Turks driving ever deeper into Asia Minor following the battle of Manzikert in 1071, and with the Normans establishing hegemony over the Byzantine territories in southern Italy and threatening to expose yet more of the western flank

---

[44] The exceptions came with the marriage of the daughter of the Emperor Romanus I Lecapenus to the Emperor Peter of Bulgaria soon after 927, and with the marriage of Theophani and Otto II in 972 (Whittow, *op. cit.*, 292, 372). See also R. Macrides, 'Dynastic marriages and political kinship', in Shepard and Franklin, *op. cit.* (1992), 263–80.

[45] R. Guilland, *Recherches sur les institutions byzantines*, 2 vols (Berlin: Akademie-Verlag in Arbeitsgemeinschaft mit Adolf M. Hakkert, Amsterdam, 1967), I, 380ff.

[46] A. Pertusi, 'Venezia e Bisanzio nel secolo XI', in *Storia della civiltà veneziana*, edited by V. Branca, 2 vols (Florence, 1965), I, 184–7, and, above all, R.-J. Lilie, *Handel und Politik zwischen dem byzantinischen Reich und den italienischen Kommunen Venedig, Pisa und Genua in der Epoche der Komnenen und der Angeloi (1081–1204)* (Amsterdam, 1984).

of the empire. There was an increasing demand to find mercenaries and for experienced knights in imperial service.[47]

The result was a dramatic increase in the numbers of foreigners not only being deliberately attracted to Byzantium by the promise of service and reward, but also of being accepted into the imperial system. We know, for example, of several Normans whose families assumed considerable standing within the court soon after their arrival in Byzantium and we know of others who were given the very highest of all the titles at the emperor's disposal.[48] And foreigners were drawn to Constantinople from far and wide. By the 1090s, and before the arrival of the First Crusade, we know of Greeks, Bulgarians, Germans, Hungarians, Russians, Danes, Swedes, Venetians, Amalfitans, Turks, Pechenegs, Cumans, Jews and Arabs living in the city.[49] Foreign visitors, perhaps understandably, speak of their amazement at the cosmopolitan nature of Constantinople at the end of the eleventh century.[50] Contingents passing through Constantinople could often cross paths with fellow countrymen by chance. For example, an English monk from Canterbury wrote of his astonishment at meeting old friends from home who were serving in the imperial bodyguard whom he met on his way

---

[47] For the Pecheneg raids on Byzantium in this period, see P. Diaconu, *Les Pétchénègues au Bas-Danube* (Bucharest, 1970); for the Turks in Asia Minor see C. Cahen, 'La première pénétration turque en Asia Mineure', *Byzantion*, 18 (1948), 5–67; for the situation in southern Italy, and for the Normans' relations with Byzantium, the best survey is still F. Chalandon, *Histoire de la domination normande en Italie et Sicilie*, 2 vols (Paris, 1907).

[48] M. de la Force, 'Les Conseillers Latins du basileus Alexis Comnène', *Byzantion*, 11 (1936), 153–65; D. Nicol, 'Symbiosis and integration: some Greco-Latin families in Byzantium in the 11th–13th centuries', *Byzantinische Forschungen*, 7 (1979), 129–32.

[49] K. Ciggaar, 'Une description de Constantinople dans le Tarragonensis 55', *Revue des Etudes Byzantines*, 53 (1995), 117–40.

[50] Bartulf of Nangis, *Gesta Francorum Hierusalem expugnantium*, in *Recueil des historiens des croisades: Historiens Occidentaux*, 5 vols (Paris, 1844–1855), III, 494.

back from Jerusalem in the 1080s and 1090s;[51] Icelandic visitors had similar experiences around the same time.[52]

But, as is often the case in many modern societies, the sudden and rapid influx of foreigners came at a price. While Byzantium was able to draw much that was positive from the outsiders with whom it was coming into increasing contact from the middle of the eleventh century onwards — not least an important reservoir of outsiders and mercenaries at a critical point in its history, as well as a vital stimulation of the economy brought about by an upsurge of trade with the West — the reaction within Byzantium had started as early as the 1070s, by which time disgruntled local magnates had begun to complain that they were losing out to the newcomers.[53] By the end of the twelfth century outbreaks of violent hostility and racial tension in Constantinople itself had become features if not of daily life, then at least they had manifested themselves with unpleasant regularity.[54] Certainly, this was not an unimportant factor in the sack of the city by the westerners in 1204.[55]

My aim here has not been to consider the influences which the East had on the West or that the West had on the East in the period between the ninth and twelfth centuries. That very broad, nebulous question is one which has seen considerable debate in recent years, and is one which requires no little diplomatic skill. My objective has been to chart the ways in which Jerusalem and Constantinople, or the Christian East, became

---

[51] C. Haskins, 'A Canterbury monk at Constantinople c. 1090', *English Historical Review*, 25 (1910), 293-5.

[52] K. Ciggaar, 'L'émigration anglaise à Byzance après 1066: un nouveau texte en latin sur les Varangues à Constantinople', *Revue des Études Byzantines*, 32 (1974), 340-2.

[53] A. Vasiliev, 'The opening stages of the Anglo-Saxon immigration to Byzantium in the 11th century', *Seminarium Kondakovianum*, 9 (1937), especially pages 65–66.

[54] C. Brand, *Byzantium Confronts the West, 1180-1204* (Cambridge, Mass.: Harvard University Press, 1968).

[55] J. Gill, *Byzantium and the Papacy, 1198-1400* (New Brunswick, N.J.: Rutgers University Press, 1979), 1ff.

increasingly accessible to those in the West, particularly from the mid-eleventh century onwards. In part, this can be shown by the numbers of those prepared to travel to the Holy Land and succeeded in reaching it at this time. The picture which we can assemble from contemporary Constantinople gives an indication not only of when the levels of contact between West and East rose sharply, but also just how much contact there was between the two halves of the Christian world in this period.

Bibliography

Adhémar of Chabannes, *Chronicon*, edited by J. Chavanon (Paris, 1897).

Aerts, W., 'The Knowledge of Greek in Western Europe at the time of Theophano and the Greek fragment in Vindob. 114', in *Byzantium and the Low Countries: aspects of War and History in the Ottonian era*, edited by V. van Aalst and K. Ciggaar (Hernen: Brediusstichting, 1986), 78–103.

Aerts, W., 'The Latin-Greek wordlist in MS 236 of the Municipal Library of Avranches, Fol. 97^v', *Anglo-Norman Studies*, 9 (1986), 64–69.

Arnold, B., *Medieval Germany 500–1300* (Basingstoke: Macmillan, 1997).

Bartlett, R., *The Making of Europe: conquest, colonization and cultural change 950–1350* (London: Allen Lane, 1993).

Bartulf of Nangis, *Gesta Francorum Hierusalem expugnantium*, in *Recueil des historiens des croisades: Historiens Occidentaux*, 5 vols (Paris, 1844–1855), III.

Brand, C., *Byzantium Confronts the West, 1180–1204* (Cambridge, Mass.: Harvard University Press, 1968).

Bréhier, L., *L'Église et l'Orient au Moyen Age: les Croisades* (Paris, 1928).

Bull, M., *Knightly Piety and the Lay Response to the First Crusade: the Limousin and Gascony* (Oxford: Clarendon Press, 1993).

Cahen, C., 'La première pénétration turque en Asia Mineure', *Byzantion*, 18 (1948), 5–67.

Chalandon, F., *Histoire de la domination normande en Italie et Sicilie*, 2 vols (Paris, 1907).

Ciggaar, K., 'L'émigration anglaise à Byzance après 1066: un nouveau texte en latin sur les Varangues à Constantinople', *Revue des Études Byzantines*, 32 (1974), 301-42.

——, *Western Travellers to Constantinople: the West and Byzantium 962-1204* (Leiden: Brill, 1996).

——, 'Une description de Constantinople dans le Tarragonensis 55', *Revue des Etudes Byzantines*, 53 (1995), 117-40.

Comnena, Anna, *Alexiade*, edited by B. Leib (Paris, 1937-1945).

Constable, G., *Letters of Peter the Venerable*, 2 vols (Cambridge, Mass: Harvard University Press, 1967).

Cowdrey, H., 'Cluny and the First Crusade', *Revue Bénédictine*, 83 (1983), 287-308.

Cross, S. and O. Sherbowitz-Wetzor (trans.), *The Russian Primary Chronicle* (Cambridge, Mass.: Mediaeval Academy of America, 1953).

Diaconu, P., *Les Pétchénègues au Bas-Danube* (Bucharest, 1970).

Downey, G., 'Constantine the Rhodian: his life and writing', in *Late Classical and Medieval Studies in honor of A.M. Friend* (Princeton, 1950), 212-21.

Ebersolt, J., *Orient et Occident*, 2 vols (Paris, 1928-1929).

Force, M. de la, 'Les Conseillers Latins du Basileus Alexis Comnène', *Byzantion*, 11 (1936), 153-65.

France, J., *Victory in the East* (Cambridge: Cambridge University Press, 1994).

Freshfield, J. (ed. and trans.), *The Book of the Eparch* (Cambridge: Cambridge University Press, 1938).

Glaber, Ralph, *Historiarum libri quinque*, edited and revised by J. France (Milano Jaca Book, 1983: repr. Oxford, 1989).

Gay, J., 'L'abbaye de Cluny et Byzance au début du XII siècle', *Echos d'Orient*, 30 (1931), 84-90.

Gill, J., *Byzantium and the Papacy, 1198-1400* (New Brunswick: Rutgers University Press, 1979).

Guilland, R., *Recherches sur les institutions byzantines*, 2 vols (Berlin: Akademie-Verlag in Arbeitsgemeinschaft mit Adolf M. Hakkert, Amsterdam, 1967).

Haskins, C., 'A Canterbury monk at Constantinople c. 1090', *English Historical Review*, 25 (1910), 293-5.

Heather, P., *Goths and Romans 332-489* (Oxford: Clarendon Press, 1991).

Holder, A. (ed.), *Saxonix Grammaticus: Gesta Danorum* (Strasbourg, 1886).

Hunger, H., 'Zum Epilog der Theogonie des Johannes Tzetzes', *Byzantinische Zeitschrift*, 46 (1953), 302-307.

Jacoby, D., 'La Population de Constantinople à l'époque byzantien: un problème de démographie urbaine', *Byantion*, 31 (1961), 81-109.

St Jerome, *In Joannem*, VI, xxix, in *Patroligiae cursus completus, Series graeca*, edited by J.-P. Migne 161 vols (Paris, 1857-1866).

Kaczynski, B., 'Some St. Gall glosses on Greek philanthropic nomenclature', *Speculum*, 58 (1983), 1008-17.

Kolbaba, T., 'Fighting for Christianity: holy war in the Byzantine empire,' *Byzantion*, 68 (1998), 194-221.

Lambert of Hersefeld, *Opera*, edited by O. Holder-Eggar (Leipzig, 1894).

Legrand, E., 'Constantin le Rhodien: description des œuvres d'art et de l'église des Saints Âpotres', *Revue des Études Grecques*, 9 (1896), 32-65.

Lilie, R.-J., *Handel und Politik zwischen dem byzantinischen Reich und den italienischen Kommunen Venedig, Pisa und Genua in der Epoche der Komnenen und der Angeloi (1081-1204)* (Amsterdam: Hakkert, 1984).

——, 'Die lateinische Kirche in Romania vor dem vierten Kreuzzug', *Byzantinische Zeitschrift*, 82 (1989), 202-20.

Liudprand of Cremona, *Liudprandi episcopalis Cremonensis: Opera*, in *Monumenta Germanicae Historica, Scriptores* (Hannover, 1872-), III.

——, *Relatio de legatione Constantinopolitana*, edited and translated by B. Scott (Bristol: Bristol Classical Press, 1993).

Luscombe, D. and G. Evans, 'The 12th century Renaissance', in *The Cambridge History of Medieval Political Thought c.350–1450*, edited by J. Burns (Cambridge: Cambridge University Press, 1988), 252–305.

Migne, J.-P. (ed.), *Patroligiae cursus completus. Series latina*, 221 vols (Paris, 1844–1890).

——, *Patroligiae cursus completus, Series graeca*, 161 vols (Paris, 1857–1866).

Miller, D., 'The Logothete of the Drome in the Middle Byzantine period: the corps of interpreters', *Byzantinische Zeitschrift*, 36 (1966), 449–58.

Moravcsik, G., and R. Jenkins (eds and trans.), *De Administrando Imperio* (Budapest, 1949: reprint, Washington, D.C., 1967).

Morris, C., 'Equestris Ordo: chivalry as a vocation in the 12th century', *Studies in Church History*, 15 (1978), 87–96.

Nicol, D., *Byzantium and Venice* (Cambridge: Cambridge University Press, 1988).

——, 'Symbiosis and integration: some Greco-Latin families in Byzantium in the 11th–13th centuries', *Byzantinische Forschungen*, 7 (1979), 113–36.

Odo of Deuil, *De profectione Ludovici VII in orientem*, edited by H. Waquet, *La Croisade de Louis VII, roi de France* (Paris, 1949).

Pertusi, A., 'Venezia e Bisanzio nel secoilo XI', in *Storia della civiltà veneziana*, edited by V. Branca, 2 vols (Florence, 1965), I, 175–98

Reiske, J. (ed.), *De Cerimoniis aulae Byzantinae libri duo*, 2 vols (Bonn, 1829–1830).

Riley-Smith, J., *The First Crusaders 1095–1131* (Cambridge: Cambridge University Press, 1997).

Runciman, S., 'The Pilgrimage to Palestine before 1095', in *History of the Crusades*, edited by K. Setton *et al*, 6 vols (Philadelphia: University of Pennsylvania Press, 1955-), I, 68–80.

——, *A History of the Crusades*, 3 vols (Cambridge: Cambridge University Press, 1952–1955).

Schreiner, P., 'Untersuchungen zu den Niederlassungen westlicher Kaufleute im byzantinischen Reich des 11 und 12 Jahrhunderts', *Byzantinische Forschungen*, 7 (1979), 175-92.

Sewter, E (trans.),*The Alexiad of Anna Comnena* (Harmondsworth: Penguin, 1988).

Shepard, J. '"Father" or "scorpion"? Style and substance of Alexios' diplomacy', in *Alexios I Komnenos*, edited by M. Mullett and D. Smythe (Belfast, 1996), I, *Belfast Papers*, 68-132.

Shepard, J. and S. Franklin (eds), *Byzantine Diplomacy* (Aldershot: Variorum 1992).

——— , *The Emergence of Rus' 750-1200* (London: Longman 1996; reprint, Aldershot, 1998).

Skrivanic, G., 'Roman Roads and Settlements', in *An Historical Geography of the Balkans*, edited by F. Carter (London: Academic Press, 1977), 115-45.

Southern, R., *Medieval Humanism* (Oxford: Blackwell, 1970).

Stepanenko, V., *Vizantia v mezhdunarodnykh otnosheniyakh na blizhnem vostoke 1071-1176* (Sverdlovsk, 1988).

Triantaphyllidis, M., *Neoellenike grammatike*, 2 vols (Athens, 1938).

Vasiliev, A., 'The opening stages of the Anglo-Saxon immigration to Byzantium in the 11th century', *Seminarium Kondakovianum*, 9 (1937), 39-70.

Vasto, A., *The Entry of the Slavs into Christendom* (Cambridge, 1978).

Vulphy of Rue in Picardy, in *Acta Sanctorum quotquot tote orbe coluntur*, 70 vols so far (Antwerp, Brussels, Tongerloe, 1643-).

Whittow, M., *The Making of Orthodox Byzantium 600-1025* (Basingstoke: Macmillan, 1996).

Wilkinson, J. et al (eds), *Jerusalem Pilgrimage 1099-1185* (London: Hakluyt Society, 1988).

Wilson, N.G., *Scholars of Byzantium* (London: Duckworth, 1983).

Wolfram, H., *History of the Goths* (London: University of California Press, 1990).

Muslim Travellers to *Bilad al-Sham* (Syria and Palestine) from the thirteenth to the sixteenth centuries: Maghribi travel accounts

Yehoshu'a Frenkel

Introduction

This paper discusses travel narratives (*rihla*) written in Arabic by North African and Spanish travellers to *Bilad al-Sham* during the later Middle Ages (c. 1200–1500).[1] Were these accounts unique and in what way do they differ from European accounts of the same period? For the Muslim traveller, unlike the European, a voyage to the Levant was a *rite de passage*. He was not motivated by the desire to explore new territory, nor to report on local geography. On the contrary, most Muslim travellers were writing of journeys over territory familiar to their readers.

It seems appropriate, therefore, to suggest two working hypotheses. In the first place medieval *rihla* literature is a stylistic genre rather than a formal geographical or ethnographical account.[2] Secondly, the writers' aim was to present an exclusively orthodox Islamic view of the world rather than depicting other cultures and religions met on the road. Hence the impression created by several of the *rihla* accounts that the aim of the

---

[1] That is, the land of Palestine (*filastin wa-al-urdunn* of the Islamic Caliphate) and Syria (the provinces of Aleppo, Homs and Damascus).

[2] I.R. Netton, 'Myth, miracle and magic in the *rihla* of Ibn Battuta', *Journal of Semitic Studies*, 29 (1984), 131.

journey was a search for religious blessing (*baraka*) rather than for worldly adventure.³

Several use a literary formula that recites the particular merits of places they visited, a genre of literature that became widespread in the medieval Arab world. They tend, for instance, to describe the interior of the mostly religious institutions in which they stayed, which were mainly concerned with ritual and learning. Travel was largely restricted to the Islamic world though a few went further afield; those who did, such as Ibn Baṭṭuṭa travelling as far as Central Asia, India and China, included ethnographical and geographical material missing from the exclusively Islamic environment.

Bilad al-Sham as an Islamic Holy Land

From as early as the Umayyad dynasty (AD 660–750) *Bilad al-Sham* was considered a holy land (*al-arḍ al-muqaddasa*). In following centuries this was influenced by three factors: the duty of *hajj*, the establishment of the Islamic Caliphate (*c.* 660),⁴ and the ancient, pre-Islamic status of southern *Bilad al-Sham*, the territory surrounding Jerusalem, as a blessed land (*al-arḍ al-mubaraka*),⁵ identified in the Qur'anic verse: 'O people go into the holy land (*al-arḍ al-muqaddasa*) which Allah had ordained for you.'⁶

During the Mamluk period (1260–1516) a growing number of Muslim visitors came to Damascus, Jerusalem, Hebron as well as other Syrian cities. Most came overland rather than by sea. They came from near and far: Spain and North Africa in the west, Iraq and Iran in the east, Anatolia

---

3   See C.F. Beckingham, 'In search of Ibn Battuta', *Asian Affairs,* 8 (1978), 267, reprinted as Study 7 in his *Between Islam and Christendom* (London: Variorum Reprints, 1983).

4   Y. Frenkel, 'Roads and Station in Southern Bilad al-Sham in the 7th and 8th centuries', *Aram,* 8 (1996), 177–88.

5   Qur'an XVII: 1. I use the translation by M. Pickthall, *The Glorious Koran* (1936; London Fine Books (Oriental): Allen and Unwin 1976).

6   Qur'an V: 21. See also the exegesis of al-Muqatil b. Sulayman to this version.

in the north, northern Arabia in the south after completing the *hajj*; others came from Egypt.

The few Maghribi travellers coming by sea generally landed in Alexandria,[7] crossing the western branch of the Nile and spending some time in Cairo before continuing their journey; if to Syria they used the road along the Mediterranean coast to Gaza.[8] Among them were Muḥammad b. Rushayd al-Fihri (travelled 683–686/1284–1287); Abu ʿAbd Allah Muḥammad al-ʿAbdari (travelled 688–689/1289–1290); Muḥammad b. Jabr al-Wadi Ashi (d.749/ 1338); Jamal al-Din b. Nubata (d.768/1366); Khalid b. ʿIsa al-Balawi (travelled 736–740/1336–1339).[9]

In contrast, Christian visitors, including an impressive number of Russians, generally came to the region via Italy and the Aegean. A sizeable number among the Europeans who stopped in Cairo opted for an excursion to St Catherine's monastery in southern Sinai.

The general impression from these accounts is that travelling was far from pleasurable. Conditions on board boat and in caravans were harsh; soldiers and governors extracted illicit payments; the sense of separation

---

[7] Ibn Jubayr, *al-Riḥla. Tadhkirat al-akhbar ʿan ittifaqat al-asfar* [Relation of events that Beffal upon certain Journeys ...], ed. W. Wright (1852); second revised edition by M.J. de Goeje (Leiden and London: Luzac, 1907; reprinted New York: AMS Press, 1973), 39–40, 303. *The Travels of Ibn Jubayr*, English translation by R.J.C. Broadhurst (London: Jonathan Cape, 1952), 31, 324.

[8] A partial list of Maghribian travellers, that is, from Spain and North Africa, was prepared by M. al-Ḥabib al-Haila, 'Al-Quds wa-shʿaʿuha al-thaqafi fi al-maghrib', in the proceedings of the third *Al-Muʾtamar al-duwali li-taʾrikh bilad al-sham 1980* (Amman: al-Jamiʿah al-Urdunniyya, 1983), I, 'al-Quds', 291–301; ʿAli Ahmad, *al-Andalusiyyun wa-al-maghariba fi bilad al-sham min nihayat al-qarn al-khamis wa-hatta nihayat al-qarn al-tasiʿ al-hijri* (Damascus: Dar Talas, 1989), 262–6.

[9] A partial description of the sources is provided by Kamil Jamil Asali (compiler), *Muqaddimah fi tarikh al-tibb fi al-Quds mundhu aqdam al-azminah hatta sanat 1918 [Jerusalem in Travel Books (Arabic and Islamic)]* (Amman: private edition, 1992); and A.N. Ibesch and K. Shihabi (compilers), *Damascus in the works of Arab and Muslim Travellers and Geographers*, 2 vols (Damascus: Ministry of Education, 1998).

from family and friends is described as oppressive.¹⁰ Travellers were sometimes away from their loved ones for long periods; al-Balawi, for example started his journey on Saturday 18 *Safar* 736 and returned home on Monday 1 *Dhu al-Hijja* 740, thus wandering for nearly five years between Spain and Arabia.¹¹ Ibn al-Arabi was away from his home town for ten years, spending these years travelling in North Africa and the Near East before returning to Spain.¹²

The medieval Muslim intelligentsia was well versed in a range of Islamic works: exegeses of the Qur'an, sayings of the Prophet Muhammad (*hadith*), commentaries on the *hadith*, the Companions' histories (*sira*), histories of Islamic conquests (*futuhat*) and other genres of Arabic literature, all containing details of sites within *Bilad al-Sham*. To both travellers and readers of their narratives, whether in North Africa and Spain or in Iraq and Iran or further east, the places in *Bilad al-Sham* and the Hijaz mentioned in the texts were well known. Muslims arriving in Gaza or Damascus found themselves in a familiar landscape, also recognised as such by readers who never left home. The narratives familiarised them even further with place names: al-'Abdari for instance, on his way from Jerusalem to Gaza, identified Wadi al-Naml (the valley of the ants) with the Qur'anic verse XXVII: 17.¹³

In *Bilad al-Sham* Muslim travellers stayed in hospices and inns (*funduq*) erected by local rulers. Most of these foundations were financed by religious endowments (*waqf*), providing funds for both construction and maintenance. Under endowment regulations travellers were to be

---

10   Ibn Battuta, *Voyages*, eds and trans. C. Defremery and B.R. Sanguinette (1858; Paris: l'Imprimerie Nationale, 1893; repr. F. Maspero, 1982), I, 112 (Arabic and French); *The Travels of Ibn Battuta*, AD *1325–54*, trans. H.A.R. Gibb (Cambridge: Hakluyt Society, 1958), I, 72.
11   Al-Khalid b. 'Isa, *Taj al-mafriq fi 'ulama' al-mashriq* ed. Hasan al-Sa'ih, I, 144 and II, 154, 156.
12   Ihsan 'Abbas, 'Rihlat Ibn al-'Arabi ila al-mashriq kama sawwaraha qanun al-ta'wil', *Al-Abhath*, 21 (Beirut: American University in Beirut, 1968), 71.
13   Abu 'Abd Allah Muhammad al-'Abdari, *Rihlat al-'Abdari*, ed. M al-Fasi (Rabat, 1968), 232.

provided with a place to stay, food, water and other provisions for those far from home.[14] Contact between the Muslim visitor and the local population was restricted to these Islamic institutions.

Motives for travel as expressed in *riḥla*

How did these travellers rationalise their wanderings? Some outlined their motives in introductions to their books, as a desire to fulfil religious obligations, the only socially acceptable reason; medieval Islamic public opinion would not favour other reasons for leaving home. While travel might be a sort of self-imposed exile or migration, travellers preferred to present religious duty as the sole reason behind their decision to leave their place of birth (*masqat al-ra's*) and endure hardship in an alien environment;[15] this may explain the limited expression of personal experience.[16] Wanderlust, rites of passage, or any other individual motive were not seen as legitimate justification, nor was migration or exile.

Religious obligation included the following: the Meccan *ḥajj*, a visit to the holy places of Jerusalem, the search for religious knowledge (*ṭalab al-'ilm*). The first of these precepts, noted by many in their introductory paragraphs, is the Qur'anic command to make the pilgrimage to Mecca at least once in a lifetime.[17] A second religious motivation was Jerusalem's unique religious merit.[18] As early as the second quarter of the eighth

[14] Y. Frenkel, 'Muslim Pilgrimage to Jerusalem in the Mamluk Period', in *Pilgrims and Travellers to the Holy Land*, edited by B.F. Le Beau and M. Mor (Omaha, Nebraska: Creighton University, 1996), 63-88.

[15] Ibn Baṭṭuṭa (eds, Defremey and Sanguinette), I, 12; (trans. Gibb) I, 8.

[16] For an opposite evaluation see Abderrahmane El Moudden, 'The ambivalence of *riḥla*: community integration and self definition in Moroccan travel accounts, 1300-1800', in *Muslim Travellers: pilgrimage, migration and the religious imagination*, edited by Dale F. Eickelman and James Piscatori (London: Routledge, 1990), 73.

[17] Ibn Baṭṭuṭa, *op. cit.*

[18] M.J. Kister, 'You shall not set out for three mosques', *Le Museon*, 82 (1969), 173-96 (repr. In his *Studies in Jahiliyya and Early Islam* (London: Variorum,

century the Umayyad Caliphs were urging their followers to visit the city. There was some objection to the rituals practised by certain visitors but in general Islamic Jerusalem was regarded as a holy site (*haram*) and was soon recognised in Muslim eyes as a legitimate goal for pilgrims seeking to pray in holy places. Large numbers of pilgrims were noted at the time of the Frank capture of the city in 1099: 'In the al-Aqsa Mosque the Franks slaughtered more than 70,000 people, among them a large number of imams and scholars, devotees and ascetics, Muslim men who had left their homelands to live lives of pious seclusion in the noble place.'[19] Successive governments provided suitable accommodation for visitors to spend days or weeks close to the Dome of the Rock and al-Aqsa Mosque.

The third religious motive for travel was stimulated by the prophetic recommendation of travel to acquire religious knowledge (*talab al-'ilm*).[20] This led many Muslims to spend time even in remote cities that were perhaps less religiously hallowed but which boasted renowned religious teachers and institutions of learning. Travel in search of such knowledge, publicised by certain individuals, unified Islamic society, creating networks between cities and lands otherwise separated by days and even months of travel. In Syria, from the Zangid to the Mamluk period (c. 1050–1516), Damascus and Aleppo were such centres of scholarship; Cairo from the time of Salah al-Din al-Ayyubi (d. 1193) was another. The Spanish al-Balawi (d. 765/1364 or 767/1366), from Cantoria in Almeria, stated in his narrative that he hoped to achieve two targets in his journey

---

1980), art. 13); F.E. Peters, *Jerusalem* (Princeton: Princeton University Press, 1985), 176–250, 379–426; *Distant Shrine: the Islamic centuries in Jerusalem* (New York: AMS Press, 1983); *Jerusalem and Mecca: the typology of the Holy City in the Near East* (New York: New York University Press, 1986).

[19] 'Izz al-Din al-Athir (555–630/1160–1233), *Al-kamil fi al-ta'rikh* (Beirut: Dar Sadir, 1966), X, 283; English translation by Fr. Gabrieli, *Arab Historians of the Crusades* (London: Routledge Kegan Paul, 1969; repr. 1984), 11.

[20] S.E. Gellens, 'The search for knowledge in medieval Muslim societies: a comparative approach', in D. Eickelman and J. Piscatori, *op. cit.*, 50, 53–55, 58.

east, namely to fulfil the *hajj* and to study in Islamic institutions.²¹ Similar features of *rihla* literature were demonstrated by al-Sabti (d. 721/1321 in Fez), who wrote of 'the filling up of the leather bag with what was collected during the long period of absence in the direction of the high-standing nobility, the two holy cities of Mecca and Madina.'²²

Al-Qalsadi, another Spaniard who wandered in North Africa, Egypt and the Holy Places in Arabia during the years 1439–1451, opens his *rihla* with a long passage on the merits of *talab al-'ilm*, followed by quotations from the Qur'an on the duty of *hajj* and including a list of schools he attended and scholars he met during his journey.²³ Religious duties were in fact the most commonly stated reason for travellers deciding to leave home.

General features of *rihla* narratives

From the narratives under investigation, several general characteristics can be detected, of which four are highlighted here. The first relates to the extent to which the accounts serve as data sources for a variety of subjects. Information on what the travellers did, the people they met and the places they visited is limited as is that on political and military events. Usually the accounts revolve around scholastic activity. Ibn al-'Arabi for instance describes communal discussion and his victory over his scholarly

---

21 Al-Balawi, *op. cit.*, I, 142–4.
22 Abu 'Abd Allah Muhammad b. 'Umar b. Rashid al-Fihri al-Sabti, *Mal'al-'aiba bima jumi'a bi-tul al-ghaiba fi al-wijha al-wajiha ila al-haramaini makka wa-taiba*, ed Muhammad al-Habib b. al-Khuja (Beirut, 1988), V, 3 (l.5, 'and we did not meet there any scholar'), 5, 7.
23 Abu al-Hasan 'Ali al-Qalsadi, *Al-Rihla (tamhid al-talib wa-muntaha al-raghib ila a'la al-manazil wa-al-manaqib)* ed. Muhammad Abu al-Ajfan (Tunis, 1978), 81–82, 115. Ahmad al-Balawi al-Wadi Ashi, *Thabat*, ed. A. al-'Imrani (Beirut, 1983). This work is a long list of teachers and their works. Jerusalem is named in several chains of knowledge transmission.

adversaries ('we used to hold conferences and argue with them').[24] The Moroccan Abu Salim al-'Ayyashi (1037–1090/1628–1679) meets the Tunisian *ḥajj* caravan on his way to Jerusalem via Tripoli and describes its scholarly members and their families.[25]

As we have seen plenty of space is devoted to scholars and saints met *en route*, thereby fulfilling a perceived duty to depict centres of learning and scholarly networks of teachers and disciples. The information could then be used by other students of religious knowledge. Naming teachers and texts studied is like a disciple's report, showing off his credentials, but also showing the involvement in a unified Islamic world, emphasising a contemporary and ubiquitous culture. There is nothing that might be regarded as unorthodox in the narratives; nor were they journeys of self-discovery; they were a means of strengthening existing beliefs.[26] This is underlined by a short note by Ibn Khaldun.[27] According to his story he left Cairo to pay a visit (*ziyara*) to the holy shrines in Jerusalem. Arriving in the city he went to the al-Aqsa Mosque to ask for blessing. Not content, however, with describing only the merits of pilgrimage, he adds: 'I refrained from entering the church of the resurrection [the Holy Sepulchre], since by doing so it would mean upholding falsehood denials of the Qur'an. Because it is the construction of Christian people, built, according to what they claim, on the site of the cross. My soul denies it and I disavow to enter it. I carried out my visit according to the custom

[24] Abu Bakr ibn al-'Arabi (d. 342/1148), *Qanun al-ta'wil*, ed. M. Slimani (Beirut: Dar al-Gharb, 1990), 95–96.
[25] Abu Salim al-'Ayyashi, *Ma' al-mawa'id* (section on Libya), edited by Sa'ad Zaghlul *et al* (Alexandria: al-Ma'arif, 1996), 195–6.
[26] See H.T. Norris (ed. and trans.), *The Pilgrimage of Ahmad Son of the Little Bird of Paradise* (Warminster: Aris and Phillips Press, 1977), 2–3.
[27] On *Al-ta'rif bi-Ibn Khaldun*, cf. W.J. Fischel, *Ibn Khaldun in Egypt, his Public Fuctions and his Historical Research (1382–1406)* (Berkeley: University of California Press, 1967), 159–63.

of Islamic tradition.'[28] None of the writers refers to non-Muslims or their institutions.

There are, however, other explanations for the readiness to face the hardships of travel and long years away from home.[29] These include the desire to escape from the burden of society; to wander in remote places (although, as we have seen, generally within the bounds of Islam); to escape changing political conditions at home. The desire to flee political problems explains the large number of travellers from the Iberian peninsula, compared to the total arriving in Cairo and Damascus. With the *Reconquista* armies advancing on Islamic Andalucia, travel to Arabia and *Bilad al-Sham* was a way of escaping from the floundering Islamic state and from participation in holy war (*jihad*), acceptable as temporary migration rather than flight from the Christians. Ibn al-'Arabi for instance states clearly that he set out to escape the unrest that accompanied the arrival of the Almoravids (1056-1147) in his home town of Seville on 20 *Rajab* 484.[30] Al-Qalsadi did not return to his home town, but preferred to settle in Granada.[31]

An important feature of these narratives is their style, a major contribution to the history of Arab literature. The language is often sophisticated, poetic, with lavish quotations from the Qur'an and *hadith*. Some authors even use rhyming prose.[32] They quote freely from predecessors, including passages from the Merits of Places literature (*fada'il*). Some name their sources, others prefer to create an impression of originality. This last point obscures the large amount of copying, declared or disguised, in these narratives that should caution us in using

[28] Ibn Khaldun, *Al-ta'rif bi-Ibn Khaldun wa-rihlatihi gharban wa sharqan,* ed. M. ben Ta'wit al-Tanji (Cairo and Beirut: Dar al-Kitab al-Lubnani, 1951), 349, l.18-350, l. 5; A. Cheddadi (trans.), *Ibn Khaldun, Le Voyage d'Occident et d'Orient: autobiographie* (Paris: Sindbad, 1980; repr. 1995), 215.
[29] Al-Qalsadi, *op. cit.*, 83, 92-93.
[30] Ibn al-'Arabi, *op. cit.*, 74.
[31] Al-Balawi, *op. cit.*, 74; al-Qalsadi, *op. cit.*, 162; al-'Abdari, *op. cit.*, 4.
[32] Al-Balawi, *op. cit.*, I, 346.

them to reconstruct the topography or history of sites they describe. The story of the alleged visit to Syria of Ibn Baṭṭuṭa is an example: the track which he describes as following is virtually impassible.[33] However, while geographical information is of little value, the Muslim traveller, fluent in Arabic and able to read inscriptions, could sometimes gain greater insight into local society than was possible for European visitors.[34]

The travellers investigated in this paper focussed on places where Islamic beliefs and civilisation were dominant. By claiming that he was leaving for Mecca and Jerusalem, the traveller could be seen as an erudite and devout Muslim; in the quest for religious fulfilment the traveller could seek adventure in places that were new but not alien to him. The European pilgrim, in contrast, was traversing remote and alien lands, his adventures resulting in a much less conformist account than that of the orthodox Muslim.

Bibliography

Abderrahmane El Moudden, 'The ambivalence of *riḥla*: community integration and self definition in Moroccan travel accounts, 1300–1800', in

Abu 'Abd Allah Muḥammad al-'Abdari, *Riḥlat al-'Abdari*, ed. M al-Fasi (Rabat, 1968).

Abu 'Abd Allah Muḥammad b. 'Umar b. Rashid al-Fihri al-Sabti, *Mal'al-'aiba bima jumi'a bi-tul al-ghaiba fi al-wijha al-wajiha ila al-haramaini makka wa-taiba*, ed Muḥammad al-Ḥabib b. al-Khuja (Beirut, 1988).

Abu Bakr ibn al-'Arabi (d. 342/1148), *Qanun al-ta'wil*, ed. M. Slimani (Beirut: Dar al-Gharb, 1990).

Abu al-Ḥasan 'Ali al-Qalṣadi, *Al-Riḥla (tamhid al-talib wa-muntaha al-raghib ila a'la al-manazil wa-al-manaqib)* ed. Muḥammad Abu al-Ajfan (Tunis, 1978).

Abu Salim al-'Ayyashi, *Ma' al-mawa'id* (section on Libya), edited by Sa'ad Zaghlul *et al* (Alexandria: al-Ma'arif, 1996).

Aḥmad al-Balawi al-Wadi Ashi, *Thabat*, ed. A. al-'Imrani (Beirut, 1983).

---

[33] 'Amikan El'ad, 'The description of the travels of Ibn Battuta in Palestine: is it original?', *Journal of the Royal Asiatic Society* (1987), 256–72.

[34] Al-Balawi, *op. cit.*, I, 247.

ʿAli Ahmad, *al-Andalusiyyun wa-al-maghariba fi bilad al-sham min nihayat al-qarn al-khamis wa-hatta nihayat al-qarn al-tasiʿ al-hijri* (Damascus: Dar Talas, 1989).

ʿAmikan Elʾad, 'The description of the travels of Ibn Battuta in Palestine: is it original?' *Journal of the Royal Asiatic Society* (1987), 256–72.

Beckingham, C.F., 'In search of Ibn Battuta', *Asian Affairs*, 8 (1978), 267, reprinted as Study 7 in his *Between Islam and Christendom* (London: Variorum Reprints, 1983).

Broadhurst, R.J.C. (trans.), *The Travels of Ibn Jubayr* (London: Jonathan Cape, 1952).

Cheddadi, A. (trans.), *Ibn Khaldun, Le Voyage d'Occident et d'Orient: autobiographie* (Paris: Sindbad, 1980; repr. 1995).

Eickelman, Dale F. and James Piscatori (eds), *Muslim Travellers: pilgrimage, migration and the religious imagination* (London: Routledge, 1990).

Fischel, W.J., *Ibn Khaldun in Egypt, his Public Functions and his Historical Research (1382–1406)* (Berkeley: University of California Press, 1967).

Frenkel, Y., 'Roads and Station in Southern Bilad al-Sham in the 7th and 8th centuries', *Aram*, 8 (1996), 177–88.

——, 'Muslim Pilgrimage to Jerusalem in the Mamluk Period', in *Pilgrims and Travellers to the Holy Land*, edited by B.F. Le Beau and M. Mor (Omaha, Nebraska: Creighton University, 1996).

Gibb, H.A.R (trans.), *The Travels of Ibn Battuta*, AD *1325–54* (Cambridge: Hakluyt Society, 1958).

Ibesch, A.N. and K. Shihabi (compilers), *Damascus in the Works of Arab and Muslim Travellers and Geographers*, 2 vols (Damascus: Ministry of Education, 1998).

Ibn Battuta, *Voyages*, eds and trans. C. Defremery and B.R. Sanguinette (1858; Paris: l'Imprimerie Nationale, 1893; repr. F. Maspero, 1982) (Arabic and French).

Ibn Jubayr, *al-Rihla. Tadhkirat al-akhbar ʿan ittifaqat al-asfar* [Relation of events that Beffal upon certain Journeys ...], ed. W. Wright (1852); second revised edition by M.J. de Goeje (Leiden and London: Luzac, 1907; reprinted New York: AMS Press, 1973).

Ibn Khaldun, *Al-taʿrif bi-Ibn Khaldun wa-rihlatihi gharban wa sharqan* ed. M. ben Taʾwit al-Tanji (Cairo and Beirut: Dar al-Kitab al-Lubnani, 1951)

Ihsan ʿAbbas, 'Rihlat Ibn al-ʿArabi ila al-mashriq kama sawwaraha qanun al-taʾwil', *Al-Abhath*, 21 (Beirut: American University in Beirut, 1968).

ʿIzz al-Din al-Athir (555–630/1160–1233), *Al-kamil fi al-taʾrikh* (Beirut: Dar Sadir, 1966); English translation by Fr. Gabrieli, *Arab Historians of the Crusades* (London: Routledge Kegan Paul, 1969; repr. 1984).

Kamil Jamil Asali (compiler), *Muqaddimah fi tarikh al-tibb fi al-Quds mundhu aqdam al-azminah hatta sanat 1918 [Jerusalem in Travel Books (Arabic and Islamic)]* (Amman: private edition, 1992).

Al-Khalid b. 'Isa, *Taj al-mafriq fi 'ulama' al-mashriq* ed. Hasan al-Sa'ih.

Kister, M.J., 'You shall not set out for three mosques', *Le Museon*, 82 (1969), 173–96 (repr. In his *Studies in Jahiliyya and Early Islam* (London: Variorum, 1980), art. 13);

M. al-Habib al-Haila, 'Al-Quds wa-shʿaʿuha al-thaqafī fī al-maghrib', in the proceedings of the third *Al-Muʾtamar al-duwali li-taʾrikh bilad al-sham 1980* (Amman: al-Jamiʿah al-Urdunniyya, 1983).

Netton, I.R., 'Myth, miracle and magic in the *riḥla* of Ibn Battuta', *Journal of Semitic Studies*, 29 (1984).

Norris, H.T. (ed. and trans.), *The Pilgrimage of Ahmad Son of the Little Bird of Paradise* (Warminster: Aris and Phillips Press, 1977).

Peters, F.E., *Distant Shrine: the Islamic centuries in Jerusalem* (New York: AMS Press, 1983).

——— , *Jerusalem and Mecca: the typology of the Holy City in the Near East* (New York: New York University Press, 1986).

——— , *Jerusalem* (Princeton University Press, 1985)

Pickthall, M., *The Glorious Koran* (1936; London Fine Books (Oriental): Allen and Unwin 1976).

Italian Travellers in Palestine: Retracing the Bible in a World of Muslims and Jews

Barbara Codacci

Introduction

A significant aspect of reports by nineteenth-century Italian travellers to the Middle East is that at least half of them visited Palestine, either exclusively, or completing a Grand Tour with short or longer excursions to Lower Egypt or rapid calls to other Eastern Mediterranean ports. Travellers to Palestine therefore constitute the largest if not the only kind of Italian travellers to the Mediterranean area of the Ottoman Empire. The common feature linking them was a widespread desire to go to the places mentioned in the Old and New Testaments, thus making their journey a pilgrimage.

The literature examined in this paper comprises about forty texts and documents. There are only two women among the authors, indicating that questions of faith or writing about such topics were not generally considered women's business during the Italian Risorgimento and at the turn of the century.

The period considered ranges from the Congress of Vienna in 1814–1815 to the beginning of the First World War. Most of the travels took place in the second half of the nineteenth century, when it still seemed an adventure to sail from Italy to Palestine.[1] A significant increase took place from the 1870s to the 1890s, when groups of pilgrims organised by dioceses or other religious associations began to travel to Palestine.

Most of the authors are unknown and nowadays it is difficult to obtain even simple information about their lives. The few exceptions concern

---

[1] Some dates are only presumed, because of the vagueness of temporal references in the texts.

those travellers who, not by chance, had their accounts printed or reprinted in the last decade. Their renown owes less to the journey or the report they wrote, than to personal matters that will be briefly mentioned.

The first three names probably belong to the best lay Italian writers of travels in Palestine, all of whom visited the Holy Land as part of a longer tour. Princess Cristina Trivulzio from Belgioioso, who travelled to Palestine leading a convoy through the southern Anatolian mountains and through Syria before leaving the Middle East in 1852, was a heroine of Italian Romanticism and her oriental memoirs probably made her the most famous Italian female traveller in the Levant.[2] Another excellent traveller and writer was the young Giuseppe Salvago Raggi.[3] His trip to Palestine constitutes just one part of the entire tour of the Levant that he made in 1888, before starting his brilliant diplomatic career. The third name is that of Luigi Barzini.[4] He travelled throughout Palestine in 1902, at the beginning of his career as a journalist. Barzini soon became famous in Italy as a special foreign correspondent for the newspaper *Il Corriere della Sera*, but also for his numerous travel books.

The fourth author is a real curiosity. In 1993 a slim book appeared containing articles written by Angelo Roncalli, who is better known throughout the world as Pope John XXIII.[5] In 1906 Don Angelo was twenty-five years old and had been a priest for two years. As a secretary to Bishop Radini Tedeschi, he accompanied him on his pilgrimage to the holy places in 1906.[6]

A few other notable names are worth mentioning, such as Angelo De Gubernatis who visited Palestine, Beirut and Damascus in 1889[7] and Matilde Seraoa, writer and journalist who travelled throughout Palestine

---

[2] Cristina di Belgioioso, *Asie Mineur et Syrie: souvenirs de voyage* (Paris: Lévy, 1858).
[3] Giuseppe Salvago Raggi, *Lettere dall'Oriente* (Genova: ECIG, 1992).
[4] Luigi Barzini, *Viaggio in Terrasanta* (Padova: Franco Muzzio Editore, 1996).
[5] Angelo Roncalli, *1906: viaggio in Terra Santa. Articoli di un giornalista diventato Papa* (Bergamo-Milano: Ferruccio Arnoldi Editore, Editrice Massimo, 1993).
[6] From 18 September to 22 October.
[7] Angelo De Gubernatis, *In Terrasanta* (Milano: Treves, 1889).

at the end of the century, also staying for a short time in Egypt.[8] She wrote of her pilgrimage in various journals and in a monumental volume.[9]

Retracing the Bible ... in a world of Muslims and Jews

The kind of journeys undertaken by lay people or clergy as well as their accounts, differ considerably from the classic, fashionable oriental tours. Accounts are full of biblical traces, in the descriptions of glimpses of Jerusalem or the evangelical evidence found in villages, as well as in the depiction of faces and features.

A journey though Palestine was a profession of faith in God: 'We are travelling trough the heart of the Old Testament ... . The ancient kingdom of Israel is like an enormous open Bible, on which we wander around like library mice', Barzini observes acutely.[10] His is, however, one of the few lay accounts we have of the Holy Land.

It is easy to agree with Perpetuo Dionigi Damonte (in charge of scholastic and religious institutions in Greater Syria between 1858 and 1895) when he says: 'If a lay man visits those places, he will describe them in one way; if a secular priest visits them, he will represent them in a different way; if it is a friar, he will talk about it in yet another way.'[11] The attitude of the accounts cannot surprise us, as they are full of religious references and long religious reports on the origins and the history of each place visited. Angelo De Gubernatis well sums it up: 'The Gospel has been my never-ending guide.'[12]

---

[8] Matilde Serao, *Nel paese di Gesù: ricordi di un viaggio in Palestina* (Napoli: Tip. cav. Aurelio Tocco, 1899); Matilde Serao, 'Il Mar Morto', *In giro pel mondo*, 21:1 (1899), 166–7; Matilde Serao, 'Nel paese di Gesù: Magdala', *Flegrea*, 3:I, fasc. IV (1899), 299–306.

[9] I do not refer to the number of pages (only 366, not really above average), but to their density.

[10] Barzini, *Viaggio*, 71.

[11] Perpetuo Dionigi Damonte, *La Siria. Lettere, 1858–1895* (Torino: Tip. San Giuseppe degli Artigianelli, 1896).

[12] Angelo De Gubernatis, *In Terrasanta* (Milano: Fratelli Treves Editori, 1899), Prefazione.

A religious feeling so imbues the writing that it even obscures the Orientalist discourse and the *topoi* that colour European travel literature about the Levant. In the descriptions of Palestine no *harem* or veiled women appear, no *kief, dervish, cibuk* nor *narghilé*, all common topics in Orientalist literature. The pilgrims talk about faith and confessions, competitors in the possession and management of the places of Christian, Jewish and Muslim history. They write to satisfy their wish to offer religious testimony, using their erudition in that field to fill their pages with classical and biblical quotations, rather than the images and lexical resources which both their personal experience and the oriental culture of those times offered. They travel with the Bible in their hands, minds and pens, together with a hunger to retrace the life of Christ in just a few days. On the eve of their arrival, they imagine Palestine as the birthplace of Christianity and seem to be convinced that only accident brought Palestine into the hands of the unbelieving Muslims. The Jewish heritage usually remains at the back of their minds, or is sometimes re-considered in the light of the Messiah's arrival.

From the moment they land in Jaffa, they are immediately put under the guardianship of the Franciscan friars. The friars take care of the pilgrims, offering them hospitality and food, and accompanying them during their tour of Jerusalem or during their excursions to Judaea and Galilee. In short, they offer themselves as experienced guides and dragomans, speaking a friendly language, for most of them are native Italian, Spanish or French speakers.

They usually stay in the so-called *casanovas*. Pietro Stoppani, following his trip in 1905, explains the history of this name (which means new house), saying that the first *casanova* was built in Jerusalem by the Franciscans as a new building beside the old city.[13] The name also helps to differentiate the *casanovas* from the Franciscan monasteries to which pilgrims are not admitted, unless they are religious men who want to share the brothers' way of life for a short period. Only very few friars work in the *casanovas* all around Palestine, but they offer hospitality 'to

---

[13] Pietro Stoppani, *Dal Nilo al Giordano* (Milano: Cogliatti, 1905).

whoever arrives, from wherever he comes, to whatever confession of Christ he belongs', as Matilde Serao puts it.[14]

Every aspect of this friendly reception seems to confirm the pilgrims' expectation that they have found themselves in Jesus' homeland. But Palestine during the nineteenth century and, furthermore, at the beginning of the twentieth, presents a reality that has very little to do with Christianity. Beyond the filter of the Franciscan friars, the pilgrims travel through a land whose every stone recalls the history of the three monotheistic religions. Muslims and Jews rather than Christians populate it. And most of the Christians who are present belong to the Orthodox or Eastern Church.

Visiting the holy places, pilgrims are obliged to recognise the presence and the role of these different religious communities. In Jerusalem, all Christian confessions prostrate themselves in the Church of the Holy Sepulchre and retrace the Via Dolorosa towards Calvary, praising their Redeemer God. Not far away, in front of the Wailing Wall, the Jews read and meditate on the Old Testament. Finally, the mosques of 'Umar and al-Aqsa remind the pilgrims of the Muslim reality of the country. Depending on the scenes they observe, the pilgrims' accounts respectively show heart-felt participation, irritation or curiosity.

It is hard to describe in detail every single pilgrim's itinerary. As was said in the introduction, some travellers had no other intended destinations than Palestine, but they often had to stop off in the Egyptian ports on their way, They are, in chronological order:[15] Guglielmo Massaia;[16] Gaspero Olmi;[17] Leonardo Placereani;[18] Domenico Faijna;[19]

---

[14] Serao, *Nel paese*, 309.
[15] See appendix.
[16] Guglielmo Massaia, 'Monsig. Guglielmo Massaia a Gerusalemme, 1851', in *La Terra Santa*, 11 (1886), 25–29 and 33–36.
[17] Gaspero Olmi, *Memorie del mio pellegrinaggio in Palestina* (Modena: Tip. dell'Immacolata Concezione, 1872).
[18] Leonardo Placereani, *Un viaggio in Terra Santa* (Modena: Tip. dell'Immacolata Concezione, 1872).
[19] Domenico Faijna, *Breve viaggio pei luoghi santi della Palestina nel 1873* (Palermo: Tip. Barravecchia, 1874).

Giorgio Tornielli;[20] Giuseppe Romani;[21] Jacopo Bernardi;[22] Giuseppe Lovisolo;[23] Luigi Rossi;[24] Alessandro Strambio;[25] Giovanni Beltrame;[26] Leonida Olivari;[27] Matilde Serao; Gaetano Finco.[28]

A second group of pilgrims began their oriental adventure by sailing to Tyre (Giovanni Failoni)[29] or Beirut in Lebanon: Luigi Valiani;[30] Alessandro Bassi;[31] Francesco Cassini da Perinaldo;[32] Isidoro Giorgi;[33]

---

[20] Giorgio Tornielli, *Un viaggio in Egitto e Palestina, descritto da un giovane sedicenne colle poesie sacre estemporanee* (Novara: 1877).

[21] Giuseppe Romani, *Viaggio in Palestina e nell'Egitto, fatto dal sac. Romani Giuseppe, Prevosto di Caspano* (Como: ditta C. Pietro Ostinelli dei fratelli Giorgetti di Ant., 1879).

[22] Jacopo Bernardi, *Viaggio in Terra Santa descritto da Jacopo Bernardi* (Treviso: Tip. Pio Ist. Turrazza, 1877 and 1878).

[23] Giuseppe Lovisolo, *Il pellegrino di Terra Santa. Lettere sui santuari della Palestina del sacerdote Giuseppe Lovisolo Canonico della cattedrale d'Acqui* (Savona: A. Ricci, 1889).

[24] Luigi Rossi, *Un viaggio in T.S. e in Egitto. Set-ott 1889. Impressioni e ricordi del sac. Luigi Rossi, Parroco di Fimon nel vicentino* (Vicenza: Premiata Tip. S.Giuseppe, 1890 e 1891).

[25] Alessandro Strambio, *Dal Nilo al Giordano. Note di Viaggio* (Torino: Candeletti, 1892).

[26] Giovanni Beltrame, *In Palestina. L'ultimo mio viaggio con alcuni ricordi della terra Santa premessi dal prof. A.Conti* (Firenze: Barbera, 1895).

[27] Leonida Olivari, *Terra Santa: note di Viaggo* (Genova: Tip. Pagano, 1896).

[28] Gaetano Finco, *Il mio ritorno nella Giudea. Diario, 12apr–14mag 1902* (Torino: Manetti, 1903).

[29] Giovanni Failoni, *Viaggio in Siria, e nella Terra Santa preceduto da alcune notizie geografiche e d'alcuni cenni sulle diverse religioni che professano gli abitanti di quelle contrade. Coi piani dell'antica e nuova Gerusalemme e colla pianta del gran tempio del San Sepolcro, 1826–1828* (Verona: coi tipi di Pietro Bisesti, 1833).

[30] Luigi Valiani, *Viaggio a Gerusalemme per l'Asia e Soria ove si descrivono tutti i luoghi santi della Palestina, Giudea, Galilea ed altre provincie* (Firenze: Stamperia Granducale, 1828).

[31] Alessandro Bassi, *Pellegrinaggio storico e descrittivo di Terra Santa (1847), con bibliografia dei viaggi in Palestina* (Torino: Tip. Subalpina, 1856–1857 and 1858).

[32] Francesco Cassini da Perinaldo, *La Terra Santa descritta dal padre Cassini da Perinaldo visitante in Terra Santa* (Genova: Ferrando, 1855).

[33] Isidoro Giorgi, *Viaggio in Terra Santa* (Firenze: Tip. Ducci, 1865).

Filippo Cardona;[34] Giuseppe Vigoni;[35] De Gubernatis; Bonomelli;[36] Barzini; Bonaventura Buselli;[37] Pietro Stoppani; Angelo Roncalli.

Not all of them stayed in Lebanon or in Syria, however. After a period of quarantine and after a brief look at Beirut, Giorgi and Buselli sailed on to Haifa. Valiani, Bassi and Cardona turned towards the south, only visiting coastal towns, such as Sidon, Tyre and St. Jean d'Acre. Vigoni went from Beirut to Damascus via ruins of Baalbek. A few years after his first visit, Cassini went back to Syria to stay in Damascus. Lastly De Gubernatis, Bonomelli and Stoppani first visited Beirut and Damascus but devoting the main part of their trip to Palestine.

Other travellers inserted their Palestine visit in a longer journey. We have already introduced the Princess of Belgioioso, who came from Anatolia along the Lebanese coast, to reach Jerusalem; Damonte, whose mission led him all over Syria, Lebanon and Palestine; Giuseppe Salvago Raggi and Luigi Barzini. Further names include: Narciso Ghislanzoni, who stayed in Egypt and Anatolia as well as Palestine;[38] Vittorio Del Corona, who briefly visited Beirut and Damascus;[39] Giovanni Genocchi, who visited the Nile delta and stayed in Beirut, Damascus, Cyprus, Rhodes, Smyrna and Ephesus;[40] Adriano Colocci, who, together with the Prince of Naples's retinue, visited Egypt and Damascus;[41] Enrico Zunini, who spent a part of his journey in Beirut and Damascus;[42] Alfonso Maria

---

[34] Filippo Cardona, 'Mio viaggio in Palestina', *Nuova Antologia Italiana*, 4:1 (February–April 1867), 298–347, 480–509, 690–709.
[35] Giuseppe Vigoni, *Viaggi* (Milano: Ariel, 1935).
[36] Geremia Bonomelli, *Un autunno in Oriente* (Milano: Tip. ed. L.F. Cogliati, 1895).
[37] Bonaventura Buselli, *Attraverso la Palestina. Impressioni e ricordi* (Firenze: Barbèra, Alfani, Venturi, 1904).
[38] Narciso Ghislanzoni, *Una corsa in Oriente* (Lecco: Tip. del Resegone, 1896).
[39] Vittorio Del Corona, *Una visita ai luoghi santi: lettere e appunti* (Modena-Arezzo: 1881).
[40] Giovanni Genocchi, *Il mio viaggio in Oriente nell'autunno del 1885: lettere familiari*, tip. S. Apollinare, Ravenna 1886; *Carteggio, 1877-1900* (Roma: 1978).
[41] Adriano Colocci, *In Oriente: ricordi di viaggio di S.A.R., il principe di Napoli* (Roma: Stab. Tip. Della Tribuna, 1887).
[42] Enrico Zunini, *In Palestina e in Siria (1885). Impressioni di viaggio* (Milano: Galli, 1892).

Minghelli, who travelled through Egypt and Anatolia;[43] Stefano Marescotti, who visited Beirut, Smyrna, Istanbul and Athens.[44]

Religious Topography of the Holy Places

The pilgrimage to the Holy Places usually starts from Jaffa, whose 'proximity to Jerusalem made it its natural port', in Olivari's words.[45] Landing there is always difficult but gives pilgrims the chance to see Jaffa. 'From afar, the town seems beautiful, but when you arrive inside it is dirty, with irregular and very narrow streets and worse than all our villages,' Tornielli states.[46] In a gloomy, dark atmosphere, everyone sees the same dirty streets. Lovisolo says that the streets are 'covered with mud and puddles.'[47] In Ghislanzoni's accounts, the same streets become 'filthy, full of mud, rubbish and even worse.'[48] Olivari talks of 'a horrible agglomeration of ugly houses, a labyrinth of dirty and absurd streets.'[49]

The pilgrims' remarks are almost unanimous: often, they even use the same words. To this catalogue of adjectives, Luigi Rossi adds the fact that 'anyway, this is one of the oldest cities in the world, and although nothing remains of its past, it aroused beautiful memories in me.'[50] The only writer who wholly defends Jaffa is Matilde Serao, who, surprisingly, describes a city 'splendid in his hundred gardens', with picturesque streets and comfortable beautiful houses![51]

---

[43] Alfonso Maria Minghelli, *Impressioni e memorie del viaggio in Terra Santa, nell'Egitto e Costantinopoli, aprile e maggio 1894* (Modena: Antica tip. Soliani, 1899).
[44] Stefano Marescotti, *Un pellegrinaggio in Terra Santa ed una visita a Beirut ed a Smirne, a Costantinopoli, ad Atene ed a Napoli* (Alessandria: Tip. Jacquemod, 1895).
[45] Olivari, *Terra Santa*, 6.
[46] Tornielli, *Un viaggio*, 26.
[47] Lovisolo, *Il pellegrino*, 35.
[48] Ghislanzoni, *Una corsa*, 87.
[49] Olivari, *Terra Santa*, 6.
[50] Rossi, *Un viaggio*, 1.
[51] Serao, *Nel paese*, 53.

Such aesthetic opinions of Jaffa are symptomatic of remarks dedicated to villages and cities in Palestine. Bethlehem is the only place that stirs favourable impressions in the pilgrims, maybe because of its mainly Christian population, its benign appearance and the fact that it does not trouble European aesthetic sensitivities. In Vigoni's description, for example, it appears as 'a pleasant village, recently rebuilt, one of the cleanest in Palestine.'[52]

After Jaffa, the itineraries only differentiate in the sequence of places visited. Many pilgrims go straight to Jerusalem. Next they discover Judaea ('anything but pleasant,' Zunini writes),[53] with, in random order, the Jordan river, the Dead Sea, the villages of Bethlehem, Bethany, Jericho ('what a disappointment,' Zunini again)[54] and Hebron. Here Pietro Stoppani arrives to visit the mosque containing Abraham's tomb, but he leaves the village with his desire unfulfilled: he writes that 'the people of Hebron's fanaticism' forbid non-Muslims admittance to the famous mosque.[55]

Afterwards the pilgrims visit Galilee: Nazareth ('the *coup d'œil* was admirable,' the Princess of Belgioioso says),[56] Cafarnao, then Mount Tabor, the village and lake of Tiberias, and, finally, Mount Carmel. Travellers coming from Lebanon see Galilee first and then Judaea, but sometimes go straight to Jerusalem and return to the north of the country afterwards.

Jerusalem

Jerusalem is the chief destination and aim of a pilgrimage. Zunini writes that the city is overflowing with 'places whose tradition, more or less authentic, records the memory of various moments of Jesus' life and

---

[52] Vigoni, *Viaggi*, 37.
[53] Zunini, *In Palestina e*, 78.
[54] Ibid., 94.
[55] Stoppani P., *Dal Nilo*, 195.
[56] Belgioioso, *Vita intima*, 178.

passion.'⁵⁷ Travel literature regarding this town, beloved by Christians, Jews and Muslims, is enormously rich. The density of religious description here is in proportion to the concentration of holy places and objects sacred to the different religions present in such a small space.

For every pilgrim the moment of arrival in Jerusalem represents the fulfilment of a dream or a prophecy. Yet passing through the walls, their first impressions are filled more with melancholy than delight. 'When just arrived in Jerusalem, my first impression was of a pious sadness,' Monsignor Massaia writes.⁵⁸ He adds: 'If a foreigner were not here to follow his faith, and if he were not attracted by spiritual comfort, he would not stay here for more than one day.'⁵⁹

Other writers offer the same view. Ghislanzoni writes: 'only faith and religion can draw so many pilgrims to a place where everything is trouble, privation, danger, and where ruins, cemeteries ... death are the outcome!!.'⁶⁰ Bonomelli says: 'What squalor! What desolation! The soul feels oppressed and suffocated at such sight and one realises that a divine curse weighs on Jerusalem ... it is the town of pain and indescribable sorrow.'⁶¹ Genocchi observes that: 'Jerusalem is a town mainly dim and gloomy',⁶² whilst Lovisolo states that: 'everywhere there is the silence of death.'⁶³ Lastly, Strambio notes 'the image of an eternal sorrow.'⁶⁴

What are the reasons for such disappointment? On the one hand, the pilgrims' emotion on arriving in a place that they have so longed for, is one of bewilderment. Equally what they find does not match their expectations or dreams. Indeed, eighteen centuries had passed since Jesus Christ's era, the city marked by different periods, not to mention the consequences of Ottoman dominion. This 'profanity' (to paraphrase our authors), offends many of the pilgrims, especially the clergymen.

---

[57] Zunini, *In Palestina e*, 72.
[58] Massaia, 'Monsig Guglielmo', 26.
[59] *Ibid*.
[60] Ghislanzoni, *Una corsa*, 105.
[61] Bonomelli, *Un autunno*, 212.
[62] Genocchi, *Il mio viaggio*, 70.
[63] Lovisolo, *Il pellegrino*, 172.
[64] Strambio, *Dal Nilo*, 31.

Journalist Colocci's disappointment is of a different kind: 'I rest my vexed eye on cluttered ugly churches, monasteries, chapels, Jesuit schools, would-be charitable institutions, and all the hovels that smother modern Jerusalem.'[65]

The Church of the Holy Sepulchre is the most beloved place. Our devotee travellers describe profusely every sanctuary in the church, with the history of their different origins, a description of each ornament and painting, and all the pertinent evangelical references. This church is the highlight of their passion for biblical description; there are hundreds of pages on the subject. Giuseppe Salvago Raggi is the only one who does not care too much about it: without worrying about appearing blasphemous, he talks of the ugly interior of the Church and of its dirtiness.

After the Church of the Holy Sepulchre, the Mosque of 'Umar is the monument that receives most attention. Italian pilgrims approach the mosque, which Zunini calls a 'wonderful monument', with mixed feelings of fear and curiosity.[66] The Princess of Belgioioso was unable to visit it: 'we, the Christians,' she writes, 'are condemned to see the temple (today the Mosque of 'Umar) only from the roof of a Turkish barracks.'[67] Some years later, the Ottoman authorities slackened their rigour against non-Muslims, so that later pilgrims only had to pay *bakshish* and put on, as in every mosque, the slippers that the doorkeepers give, in order to be admitted to the celebrated Muslim building. Even here, our curious travellers alternate descriptions of architecture and art with pages on the history of the mosque.

Mount Moriah or Temple Mount on which the mosque is built is full of significance also for Jews and Christians. 'Entering the Temple area on Moriah,' De Gubernatis writes, 'my first impression was one of a great relief; ... breathing a completely biblical air, we have a sensation of peace, in which the mind lies down to contemplate a great past.'[68] Here Jews complain about the destruction of the Temple, standing in front of the

---

[65] Colocci, *In Oriente*, 87.
[66] Zunini, *In Palestina e*, 67.
[67] Belgioioso, *Vita intima*, 189.
[68] De Gubernatis, *In Terrasanta*, 149.

Wailing Wall. Here, in Barzini's words, 'every Jew who visits Jerusalem, as a votive offering, goes to drive in a nail ... to reinforce the holy and precious ruins with this symbolic action.'[69]

People and Religion

Wandering from one village to the next through Palestine, pilgrims point out the population according to its different faiths. The emphasis on Christians is undeniable, but even though the Christian East includes different confessions, most of the authors concentrate their attention on Roman Catholics, and only secondarily on Armenians and Greeks. Other communities interest pilgrims mainly for their outlandish costumes and habits.

In the streets of Jerusalem, Italian pilgrims try to understand the kaleidoscope of people and confessions. 'It is all a mess of types, idioms, habits, religions,' argues Stoppani.[70] Elsewhere he writes: 'There is not another town that offers such a complicated scene in its elements.'[71] Travellers in general are pleased to talk of biblical faces and types 'which recall the characters of the Holy Scriptures. All kinds and colours of costumes, bedouins ..., Turkish women completely covered up or Christian women with their bodies all painted.'[72]

The Muslims

The fundamental ethnic and linguistic distinction between Ottoman Turks and Arabs is not always clear and usually ignored: surely this was not why they had come to Palestine. Even if they see the differences, they often write in a confused way. Damonte, for example, who was neither in a hurry, nor uneducated, uses the adjective 'Turkish' as a synonym for

---

[69] Barzini, *Viaggio*, 92.
[70] Stoppani, *Dal Nilo*, 188.
[71] *Ibid.*, 149.
[72] Vigoni, *Viaggi*, 23.

'Muslim': 'Ramadam was celebrated by Turkish people in a strange way.'[73]

In general the real Turks are perceived as few in number, mostly living in the towns and attached to the Ottoman administration or working as guardians of mosques and other holy places. Rossi writes that they are 'lazy and labour's enemies'.[74] In the minds of visitors to the birthplace of Christianity, Turks are the usurpers of the beloved holy places.

The writers are moderately interested in the beduin, described by Giorgi as 'street murderers, ... always ready to attack, rob, despoil and even kill.'[75] Other authors are less drastic in their comments. Vigoni meets them in Damascus and on the roads of Palestine. Sometimes he argues that they 'could be compared to animals rather than to men.'[76] Elsewhere he writes that they have 'grim faces'.[77] Later he changes his first opinion completely and says: 'they are really dirty, but they can be lovely people.'[78] Barzini's attitude is quite different. He admires their costumes, finding even the poor people elegant, and he notes that 'the noble charm of the gestures is enough to reveal the nobility of their race.'[79]

Another pilgrim, Padre Genocchi, tells how he offered coffee to a group of friendly beduin near the Jordan River. He alternates personal impressions, for example describing their attitude during the meeting, with arid information on costumes and habits. Throughout his account, *Il mio viaggio in Oriente nell'autunno del 1885: lettere familiari*, the different regard he has for the beduin on the one hand, and the Arabs and Turks on the other, is remarkable. The beduin appear bold and friendly, and worthy of European respect. On the other hand, his experiences of Arab or Turkish guides convinces him of their bad faith and intriguing nature, a menace to the unfortunate traveller.

---

[73] Damonte, *La Siria*, 72.
[74] Rossi, *Un viaggio*, 232.
[75] Giorgi, *Viaggio*, 7.
[76] Vigoni, *Viaggi*, 23.
[77] Ibid., 31.
[78] Ibid., 32.
[79] Barzini, *Viaggio*, 32.

The Muslim attitude towards the Christians, who increasingly crowd the holy places, is hardly discussed. The pilgrims have the impression that Muslims respect the Christian faith, even if they do not appreciate Europeans, as Cristina di Belgioioso writes. The Princess expresses her fear of Muslims, like many other Italians who travelled before or soon after her. Damonte, on the other hand, underlines the fact that, since the end of the Crimean War (he writes shortly after), Christians' safety is more or less guaranteed: 'we can come and go, alone or escorted, nobody disturbs us,'[80] Finally, Romani, travelling in 1874, observes that after having oppressed Christians for centuries, 'their tyranny has lessened; today we can affirm that it has almost disappeared.'[81]

The Jews

Throughout their pilgrimage and, more especially in Jerusalem, our authors note the Jews whose numbers grow considerably towards the turn of the century. Some pilgrims describe only prayer scenes, with the classic image of a curly-haired Jew, prostrate with grief and weeping near the Wailing Wall. Others elaborate their remarks with personal ideas concerning the appearance of the Jews, their religion and the huge new wave of immigration into the 'Kingdom of Israel'. Only a few authors explicitly write about Zionism, but the increasing Jewish presence touches the feelings of many.

It is interesting to take a look at the comments about Jerusalem's Jewish quarter. Luigi Rossi says: 'It is the most poverty-stricken and dirty I have ever seen in the world.'[82] Ghislanzoni describes 'sad dirty people sitting on the ground, in the middle of horrible rubbish.'[83] And Minghelli observes 'how pitiable are these people sad and gloomy! Everyone is badly dressed.'[84] Dirtiness and ragged clothes, desolation, melancholy,

---

[80] Damonte, *La Siria*, 62.
[81] Romani, *Viaggio*, 61.
[82] Rossi, *Un viaggio*, 99.
[83] Ghislanzoni, *Una corsa*, 164.
[84] Minghelli, *Impressioni*, 99.

humiliation and degeneration are the expressions most used to talk about the Jews. These are often accompanied by a feeling of sadness or, occasionally, by veiled contempt, sometimes by both. Bonomelli, for instance, writes of a 'nation loaded with gold and hate, owner and servant of everyone, so diffident as to become vile, so audacious as to become heroic, submissive and unconquerable.'[85]

In Zunini's pages on Jerusalem's Jews we find a respectful attitude both towards the religion and the people. He sympathises with their misfortunes and the fact that they are refugees everywhere, even in their fatherland. He admires the vigour of their faith, the noble way in which they bemoan the ruin of the ancient kingdom of Israel. But, when talking about the Jews of Tiberias, he comments on 'the fanaticism of a declining religion' and affirms that 'their race, in Palestine, is the dirtiest.'[86]

Just how difficult it is to extrapolate a general from the personal opinion is evident. One idea in particular recurs: Jews are frequently qualified as deicides. Our pilgrims fail to understand the anti-Judaic force of this concept, but without an intended anti-Semitism.

De Gubernatis, on the contrary, explicitly tries to contest 'the Jews' awful plight that was always made and still is caused by Christians in the name of religion.'[87] Troubled by the bad reputation that still follows them throughout the world, he argues the unfairness of the fact that since the time of Christ's death the Jews have been charged with deicide. All of us, he argues, 'have been the cause of this humiliation and depravation,' but he himself does not deny that they are a 'sordid and vile race'.[88]

What do Italian authors think, in particular, about the growing presence of Jews in Palestine? The pilgrim mind tends to assume a Christian Palestine. Nobody argues that the Jews are out of place, but seeing them in Bethlehem or around the Church of the Holy Sepulchre is not appreciated by many. Matilde Serao says: 'They look like an intruder who is almost stealing Jerusalem's air.'[89] She continues: 'They

---

[85] Bonomelli, *Un autunno*, 230.
[86] Zunini, *In Palestina e*, 150.
[87] De Gubernatis, *In Terrasanta*, 164.
[88] Ibid.
[89] Serao, *Nel paese*, 100.

know that they live in Jerusalem thanks to generous permission, a sovereign's inattention, and they fear that their residence is only temporary, depending on a sultan's *firman* by which they can be expelled at any moment.'[90]

Belgioioso, in 1850, and Zunini, in 1885, notice Jews coming to Palestine to die and thus to rest forever in the shadow of the ancient walls. Around 1889, De Gubernatis sees the beginning of the massive influx of new immigrants wanting to live in Palestine, although this aim is not yet declared in the Zionist agenda. The newly arrived are helped by rich Jewish families in Europe and America to find a new life, safe from the persecution they have suffered in Europe for centuries. But even in Palestine they are not received with open arms. De Gubernatis remarks how, in an attempt to stop the new immigration, 'a sultan's *firman* prevents Jews from buying new land in Palestine.'[91]

By so writing, De Gubernatis' respect for the sad destiny of the Jewish people is plain. However he notes a profound difference between the Jews who have always lived in the Orient ('the old, often splendid Jews from Syria and Jerusalem'),[92] who preserve the noblest aspects of Semitic culture, and the Jews of the Diaspora whom he describes as the 'degeneration of a great historical race'.[93] Also, he notices the problems caused by the existence of a large number of Jews in a society that until this moment has tolerated only a small number. According to his account, the Eastern Jews have just started to acquire some rights and respect in the Ottoman Empire, whereas the newly arrived can disturb delicate social and political relations.

Nearly twenty years later, in 1905, two thirds of the 80,000 inhabitants of Jerusalem are Jewish, according to Stoppani's account. Wondering whether it is possible to define Jerusalem as a Jewish city, he argues: 'We could say that Jerusalem has returned to what it used to be during the

---

[90] *Ibid.*
[91] De Gubernatis, *In Terrasanta*, 103.
[92] *Ibid.*, 101.
[93] *Ibid.*, 102.

Roman Empire.'[94] And he admits 'with an unaccountable sorrow' that Jerusalem is already a Jewish city.[95]

Appendix: dates of Italian travels in Palestine

Valiani	1826–1827	Genocchi	1885
Failoni	1826–1828	Zunini	1885
Bassi	1847	Colocci	1887
Cassini	from 1847	Salvago Raggi	1888
Massaia	1851	De Gubernatis	c. 1889
Belgioioso	1852	Marescotti	1889
Giorgi	1853	Rossi	1889
Damonte	1858–1895	Strambio	1892
Cardona	1859	Minghelli	1894
Vigoni	1869	Bonomelli	1894
Olmi	1872	Ghislanzoni	1895
Placereani	1872	Olivari	1895
Faijna	1873	Beltrame	c. 1895
Tornielli	c. 1873	Serao	c. 1899
Romani	1874	Barzini	1902
Bernardi	1877	Finco	1902
Del Corona	1879	Buselli	c. 1904
Lovisolo	1879–1888	Stoppani	c. 1905
		Roncalli	1906

Bibliographic References

Barzini, Luigi, *Viaggio in Terrasanta* (Padova: Franco Muzzio Editore, 1996).
Bassi, Alessandro, *Pellegrinaggio storico e descrittivo di Terra Santa (1847), con bibliografia dei viaggi in Palestina* (Torino: Tip. Subalpina, 1856–1857 and 1858).
Beltrame, Giovanni, *In Palestina: L'ultimo mio viaggio con alcuni ricordi della terra Santa premessi dal prof. A.Conti* (Firenze: Barbera, 1895).

[94] Stoppani, *Dal Nilo*, 166.
[95] *Ibid.*, 167.

Bernardi, Jacopo, *Viaggio in Terra Santa descritto da Jacopo Bernardi* (Treviso: Tip. Pio Ist. Turrazza, 1877 and 1878).

Bonomelli, Geremia, *Un autunno in Oriente* (Milano: Tip. ed. L.F. Cogliati, 1895).

Buselli, Bonaventura, *Attraverso la Palestina: impressioni e ricordi* (Firenze: Barbèra, Alfani, Venturi, 1904).

Cardona, Filippo, 'Mio viaggio in Palestina', *Nuova Antologia Italiana*, 4:1 (February-April 1867), 298-347, 480-509, 690-709.

Cassini, da Perinaldo, Francesco, *La Terra Santa descritta dal padre Cassini da Perinaldo visitante in Terra Santa* (Genova: Ferrando, 1855).

Colocci, Adriano, *In Oriente: ricordi di viaggio di S.A.R., il principe di Napoli* (Roma: Stab. Tip. Della Tribuna, 1887).

Damonte, Perpetuo Dionigi, *La Siria. Lettere, 1858-1895* (Torino: Tip. San Giuseppe degli Artigianelli, 1896).

De Gubernatis, Angelo, *In Terrasanta* (Milano: Fratelli Treves Editori, 1899).

Del Corona, Vittorio, *Una visita ai luoghi santi: lettere e appunti* (Modena-Arezzo: 1881).

Faijna, Domenico, *Breve viaggio pei luoghi santi della Palestina nel 1873* (Palermo: Tip. Barravecchia, 1874).

Failoni, Giovanni, *Viaggio in Siria, e nella Terra Santa preceduto da alcune notizie geografiche e d'alcuni cenni sulle diverse religioni che professano gli abitanti di quelle contrade. Coi piani dell'antica e nuova Gerusalemme e colla pianta del gran tempio del San Sepolcro, 1826-1828* (Verona: coi tipi di Pietro Bisesti, 1833).

Finco, Gaetano, *Il mio ritorno nella Giudea. Diario, 12apr-14mag 1902* (Torino: Manetti, 1903).

Genocchi, Giovanni, *Il mio viaggio in Oriente nell'autunno del 1885: lettere familiari* (Ravenna: Tip. S. Apollinare, 1886).

Genocchi, Giovanni, *Carteggio 1877-1900* (Roma: 1978).

Ghislanzoni, Narciso, *Una corsa in Oriente* (Lecco: Tip. del Resegone, 1896).

Giorgi, Isidoro, *Viaggio in Terra Santa* (Firenze: Tip. Ducci, 1865).

Lovisolo, Giuseppe, *Il pellegrino di Terra Santa: lettere sui santuari della Palestina del sacerdote Giuseppe Lovisolo Canonico della cattedrale d'Acqui* (Savona: A. Ricci, 1889).

Marescotti, Stefano, *Un pellegrinaggio in Terra Santa ed una visita a Beirut ed a Smirne, a Costantinopoli, ad Atene ed a Napoli* (Alessandria: Tip. Jacquemod, 1895).

Massaia, Guglielmo, 'Monsig. Guglielmo Massaia a Gerusalemme, 1851', in *La Terra Santa*, XI (1886), 25-29 and 33-36.

Minghelli, Alfonso Maria, *Impressioni e memorie del viaggio in Terra Santa, nell'Egitto e Costantinopoli, aprile e maggio 1894* (Modena: Antica tip. Soliani, 1899).

Olivari, Leonida, *Terra Santa: note di Viaggo* (Genova: tip. Pagano, 1896).

Olmi, Gaspero, *Memorie del mio pellegrinaggio in Palestina* (Modena: Tip. dell'Immacolata Concezione, 1872).

Placereani, Leonardo, *Un viaggio in Terra Santa* (Modena: Tip. dell'Immacolata Concezione, 1872).

Romani, Giuseppe, *Viaggio in Palestina e nell'Egitto, fatto dal sac. Romani Giuseppe, Prevosto di Caspano* (Como: ditta C. Pietro Ostinelli dei fratelli Giorgetti di Ant., 1879).

Roncalli, Angelo, *1906: viaggio in Terra Santa: articoli di un giornalista diventato Papa* (Bergamo-Milano: Ferruccio Arnoldi Editore, Editrice Massimo, 1993).

Rossi, Luigi, *Un viaggio in T.S. e in Egitto: set-ott 1889: impressioni e ricordi del sac. Luigi Rossi, Parroco di Fimon nel vicentino* (Vicenza: Premiata Tip. S.Giuseppe, 1890 e 1891).

Salvago Raggi, Giuseppe, *Lettere dall'Oriente* (Genova: Ecig, 1992).

Serao, Matilde, 'Il Mar Morto', *In giro pel mondo*, 21-I (1899), 166-167.

Serao, Matilde, 'Nel paese di Gesù: Magdala', *Flegrea*, 3-I, fasc. IV (1899), 299-306.

Serao, Matilde, *Nel paese di Gesù: ricordi di un viaggio in Palestina* (Napoli: Tip. cav. Aurelio Tocco, 1899).

Stoppani, Pietro, *Dal Nilo al Giordano* (Milano: Cogliatti, 1905).

Strambio, Alessandro, *Dal Nilo al Giordano: note di Viaggio* (Torino: Candeletti, 1892).

Tornielli, Giorgio, *Un viaggio in Egitto e Palestina, descritto da un giovane sedicenne colle poesie sacre estemporanee* (Novara: 1877).

Trivulzio, di Belgioioso, Cristina, *Asie Mineur et Syrie. Souvenirs de voyage* (Paris: Lévy, 1858).

Valiani, Luigi, *Viaggio a Gerusalemme per l'Asia e Soria ove si descrivono tutti i luoghi santi della Palestina, Giudea, Galilea ed altre provincie* (Firenze: Stamperia Granducale, 1828).

Zunini, Enrico, *In Palestina e in Siria, 1885. Impressioni di viaggio* (Milano: Galli, 1892).

Fig. 12. Frederick North, , photograph reproduced by permission of Mr Tom North.

Fig. 11. Marianne North, photograph reproduced by permission of Mr Tom North.

The Norths in Syria, Egypt and Palestine, 1865–1866

Brenda E. Moon

This is the story not of explorers nor of orientalists but of two tourists, father and daughter, Frederick and Marianne North, who went to the Levant, as many of their generation did, to see the sights of which they had read in the burgeoning travel literature, and in Marianne's case, to sketch them. They set out in the autumn of 1865, shortly after Frederick North had lost his seat in Parliament, where he had represented Hastings for thirty-five years. He had lost it by just nine votes, and it was a bitter blow. His daughter Marianne is known today for her oil paintings of plants exhibited in the gallery which she built at Kew Gardens, but her journey with her father to the Near East was made before she took up oil painting, or committed herself to the mission of painting the world's flowers. Frederick North was sixty-five years old, and Marianne thirty-five, when they left for what she calls 'our Egyptian journey'.

The chief source for their travels is Marianne's manuscript autobiography written between 1880 and 1886. It was published posthumously, much abridged by her sister Catherine, in 1892, as *Recollections of a Happy Life*, in two volumes.[1] Catherine initially omitted the journeys in Europe and the Middle East, thinking these regions more than adequately covered in travel literature already; it was the astonishing success of the two volumes of more exotic travels that persuaded her to publish the account of the earlier journeys of 1865–1866 in *Some Further*

---

[1] Marianne North, *Recollections of a Happy Life, being the autobiography of Marianne North*, edited by her sister, Mrs John Addington Symonds, two vols (London: Macmillan, 1893). Photographs in this paper reproduced by kind permission from Tom North.

Recollections of a Happy Life, in 1894.² The manuscript survives in the possession of Mr Tom North of Rougham Hall, Norfolk, as do Marianne's albums of water-colours and her father's diaries.³ I should like to record my warm thanks to Mr North for access to these documents and permission to quote from them.

Fig. 13. Frederick North in the hotel, Beirut, photograph reproduced by permission of Mr Tom North

---

2   Marianne North, *Some Further Recollections of a Happy Life, selected from the Journals of Marianne North, chiefly between the Years 1859 and 1869*, edited by her sister, Mrs John Addington Symonds (London: Macmillan, 1894). Quotations from Marianne North are from this book, 99–203.

3   Quotations from Frederick North are from his diaries for 1865 and 1866.

Frederick North and his daughter first landed on Syrian soil on 1 November 1865 at Beirut, and made for the Oriental Hotel, but they found, as Frederick North wrote, 'One double bedroom offered, but no immediate prospect of more, so Pop [that was his nickname for Marianne] solaced herself with a novel and coffee.' They were rescued by the landlord's dragoman, who took them to his own establishment, 'and very oriental it was,' Marianne writes, 'but full of men boarders.' 'Pop does not like herself in this house,' wrote her father, 'with about a dozen men only at table, ... so we shall, I think, move into the Belle Vue.' And move they did, two days later, finding 'nice rooms,' according to his daughter, 'with a long open gallery to sit in.' There were many letters waiting for them at Beirut, and she painted a picture of her father sitting on the veranda, reading them.

Frederick North was still anxious on Marianne's behalf. Mr Eldridge, the Consul General, and Mr Rogers of Damascus were, he wrote, 'very good-humoured & courteous, but neither make up to Pop, which troubles her. I rather fancy that in this country of secluded women her appearance at all in a public dining table seems contrary to "the nature of things". Certainly it is rather a commercial room society!' 'All their families being still in the hills,' Marianne explains, 'and having taken their cooks with them, the men were forced to live in the hotels.' But she loved Beirut: 'Behind the house were huge old hedges of cactus higher than myself,' she wrote, 'with palms and agaves and flat-roofed houses golden in the sunshine. ... Many picturesque people wandered about, who looked pleased to see us, and did not want to be our dragomen, or object to being drawn; women with their faces uncovered too, and glorious eyes.'

After what she calls 'a certain amount of civilization' in Beirut, they set out for Damascus on 13 November, 'Pop dying to be off with the tents, & thinking only of the Bright Side of pictures,' wrote her father, '& ignoring both fatigue & chances of weather.' In the event they went to Damascus by a new diligence road which the French had just opened, 'in a sort of omnibus, in which we were too crammed to be able to see out,' wrote Marianne, who had wanted to ride. Her father, however, had persuaded himself that 'Pop now admits that mountain travelling with tents would have been a hazardous experiment. It would have been a fearful tempting of providence to risk damp, cold nights, cholera and fever their common sequel.' The journey was enlivened by the fact that a new French consul was travelling just ahead of them, and local officials and their escorts appeared at various points to do him honour; 'the wildest creatures... galloped up and down the banks on either side of us, and had mock fights wherever there was room, ... flourishing spears twice as long as themselves. They rode in the most reckless way. ... The men were ragged enough, with scarcely a pair of stockings among a hundred,' Marianne wrote. When the diligence stopped for half an hour, she and her father took the opportunity to walk on ahead. They came upon 'a whole tribe of many hundreds of Arabs crossing the valley, gaudily dressed in red, purple, gold and silver.' She was just beginning to sketch them, when the wild escort caught up with them, and they were again packed into the 'horrid diligence ... in the midst of a perfectly good-humoured tumult which was most exciting in its novelty.'

It was dark when they reached Damascus and settled comfortably in the house of Dimitri, who had been Kinglake's dragoman when he visited the East in 1835. Frederick North wrote in his diary: 'Pop declares herself quite happy — Damascus comes up to her ideas of picturesqueness.' The next morning they were offered the choice of horses or white asses, 'any other colour being infra dig.,' to use Marianne's expression; they chose the latter. 'Pop of course delighted with everything — till she got tired & fancied her donkey had a sore back, which I dare say it had,' her father wrote, adding somewhat unkindly, '& that it was not improved by carrying so much weight.' While at Damascus they called at the house of Lady Ellenborough, or 'Madame Digby' as she was known there, but she was away in tents with her husband. Marianne comments that her garden was 'in a complete tangle'.

They had originally planned to go on to Baalbek, taking tents, but Frederick North admitted in his diary that he was 'excessively nervous about the proceeding without a good regular guide, even did the weather favour. Days are so short, & our own dependence so absolute upon the people, who all think travelling Xtian fair game for pillage. I am, too, far from well myself. Pop is in raptures with Damascus, mainly because it is so picturesque in its buildings & in its population.' So they abandoned the idea of Baalbek. After some days in Damascus they returned to Beirut, riding this time on the top of the diligence with the driver, and admiring the scenery 'as well as we could through a snowstorm ... which nearly froze us to our seats.' They turned their thoughts instead to Egypt, boarding a Russian steamer on 26 November. At Port Said they rowed out in the captain's boat to the end of the stone jetty under construction at the mouth of the Canal and watched dredgers working incessantly. They landed at Alexandria on 30 November.

Alexandria made a bad impression. 'We got out of it as fast as we could,' wrote Marianne. Travelling by train to Cairo, they found Dr and Mrs Charles Beke in the same carriage. Charles Beke was the author of many pamphlets and books on biblical geography and on his travels in Abyssinia to explore the sources of the Nile. Marianne was quite taken with his 'pretty young wife with her hair cut short and manners rather independent.'

They took rooms in the Hotel du Nil at £15 a day, and were very comfortable there. Most of their fellow-lodgers were 'German commercial gentlemen' but one was an Englishman, William Palgrave, an ex-Jesuit missionary in Syria and traveller in Arabia, and author of *Narrative of a Year's Journey in Central and Eastern Arabia*, published earlier in 1865. Both the Norths took to him at once. 'Palgrave has taken to sitting next to us at dinner, and most wonderfully agreeable he makes himself ... & a lively conversationalist,' wrote Frederick North. One night they were entertained by Edward (later Sir Edward) and Margaret Stanton — he had recently been appointed Agent and Consul in Cairo — and met a rich English couple at their house of whom Marianne wrote that they had difficulty finding a *dahabiyyah* large enough for themselves, their servants, their 'huge packages from Fortnum and Mason's, besides all the other encumbrances they had brought out from England.'

Frederick North had been somewhat apprehensive of the cost of a journey up the Nile. 'I see no good,' he wrote, 'in having a dragoman to ourselves from Syria. There are plenty of people about who speak English or French... The Nile expedition should only have been undertaken by Rich People, & not by poor XMPs.' There is little doubt that he made the journey to Egypt chiefly for Marianne's sake. 'Pop revels in having date palms to sketch from her window & minarets & wild architecture in every corner — which she can make "Pictures" of, as she calls them, for the worship of admiring friends.' He had been ill with a cold and sore throat but by the middle of the month it was improving, with the help of quinine. 'Going out however at sunset sets me all wrong again,' he wrote, 'I am ageing more rapidly than is pleasant. If Pop keeps up, however, through these journeyings, I will make no grievance of it.'

They spent two weeks in Cairo, Marianne usually riding a donkey, side-saddle, her father always walking. 'About after Pop sketching,' he wrote on 5 December, 'till I am nearly knocked up. She has her donkey & is busy, but I tire awfully.' They paid £5 a day for donkey hire, including a 'most efficient attendant'.

Frederick North decided to hire a *dahabiyyah* which could be shared with two others: 'it would be desirable to have more society, both for Pop and myself. Two people get querulous & tire of each other's sole company,' he wrote. By the end of November they had found a dragoman, Achmet Oman, who would take them and two companions up the Nile at a reasonable rate, and they had found two others to share their boat: a Frenchman, M. d'Annel, and an Englishman, Mr Spiers. Of the former, Frederick wrote: 'a very good fellow, but rather a flimsy weak Parisian egoist ... a somewhat trifling ... man of the genuine Narcissus order,' but Mr Spiers, turned out to be 'a capital comrade & he ... teaches Pop perspective.' Richard Phene Spiers was a young architect in Egypt on a Royal Academy travelling fellowship. Frederick implies some uncertainty as to whether he would go, as 'the English student still has difficulty about his cash,' but on 27 January the four set sail at 10 o'clock. At Aswan Mr Spiers made a sketch of Marianne painting, surrounded by children. She preserved it in her album, and it was later reproduced in *Some Further Recollections of a Happy Life*.[4]

Marianne speaks well of the crew of nine, including the cook who claimed to have cooked for the English for forty years, the ugly steersman who munched grass like a cow, the captain 'occasionally waking up and giving mild orders', and the sole member of the crew who 'said his prayers

---

[4] Marianne North, *Some Further Recollections*, 133.

regularly on a bit of old carpet.' She admits that 'the people and country I enjoyed far more than the old stones.'

They soon recognised that their dragoman was 'a regular brute'. When he offered to buy Marianne a little girl to wait on her, 'my father was furious.' At Minya on 11 March she bought calico to make a Union Jack.

> When we started, my father refused to have one, thinking it would hurt the Frenchman's feelings, but now to his horror he found he had hoisted the tricolor on board, and as both he and Achmet talked of buying slaves, my father thought it was time we had the English flag over our heads.

At Luxor they visited Mustapha Agha, whose house 'nestled in the middle of the finest group of columns.' He entertained her father and Mr Spiers to pipes and coffee, while Marianne was taken to see Lady Duff Gordon, a childhood friend. Lucie Duff Gordon refers to the meeting in a letter of 11 February to her mother: 'Fancy my surprise the other day ... In walked Miss North (Pop) whom I have not seen since she was a child ... She has done some sketches which, though unskilful, are absolutely true in colour and effect and are the very first that I have seen that are so.'[5]

At the end of January they reached Philae, 'even more enchanting than I expected', and pressed on to Wadi Halfa and Abu Simbel, where they spent three days painting and studying the ruins. Mr North bathed in the Nile, in spite of Achmet's warning about crocodiles (they had seen seven on the way up). Then they drifted slowly down stream. Once while sketching on shore, Marianne records, 'a nice black woman found her way up with her baby and sat by me as I worked. She examined the contents of all my pockets, but put everything carefully back.' They stopped for three days at Philae, 'but it was not so quiet as before: a party of Americans (three dahabiehs full) having come overland from Assouan to picnic there.'

They spent longer at Thebes on the way down, but Marianne found the tombs 'far too archaeological for modern humanity ... I hate walking where I cannot see my feet, or being hauled about even by the gentlest of

---

[5] Lucie Duff Gordon, *Letters from Egypt, with a memoir by her daughter, Janet Ross* (London: R. Brimley Johnson, 1902), 265.

Arab guides ... but argument and remonstrance were of no use, and I was hauled in by one hand, holding a candle in the other.' Her father 'felt the heat so much (the thermometer was eighty-two in his cabin after dark) that he decided to leave Thebes after a week, much to the disappointment of Mr Spiers.' Marianne felt she had 'had a mere taste of the wonders of Thebes', but she was worried about her father's health. They continued to Qena, rode from there to Denderah on 11 March, and stopped again at Abydos, 'to please Spiers', as Frederick North says. Between Beni Hasan and Memphis their *dahabiyyah* was visited by the notorious 'holy man' who came on board in 'a petticoat' and 'kissed all the natives, while we shrank closer into our cabin shell.' At last they reached Giza, where Marianne climbed the Great Pyramid. 'People make much unnecessary fuss about getting up ...' she writes, 'I did it in twenty minutes.' They were not sorry to reach the Hotel du Nil again, and have Mr Palgrave 'talk cleverly to us at dinner time instead of perpetual boat-grievances or archaeological arguments.'

A package from England which they had been expecting had not arrived, so they went to Suez for a rest at the seaside. The change did Frederick North 'a world of good, and we wandered on the sands for hours together.' They stayed in an American hotel there, where the other guests, all Anglo-Indians, were few but the traffic great. 'Over 400 people landed in one day to take tiffin, and then packed themselves into a train and went overland to Alexandria.' After a week at Suez they too travelled to Cairo by train, a three-hour journey, but the package had still not arrived, and they went on to Alexandria and embarked for Jaffa, which they reached on 9 April.

They were delighted to find that Ḥajji ʿAli, brother of Lady Duff Gordon's dragoman, had just returned from an engagement as guide to their friends Mr and Mrs Ewing, with a party of seven. Mr North engaged him on the spot, '& we slipped into their tents, horses, etc.,' he wrote, 'starting that very day at 3 p.m. So no time lost ... and he paid for everything, for £3 10s. a day.' Ḥajji Ali had excellent credentials, and they could not have been better served.

Fig. 14. Jerusalem, photograph reproduced by permission of Mr Tom North.

They reached Ramleh that night, and the next day, after a ten-hour ride, came to Jerusalem. They dismounted before entering the city by the Jaffa gate, and walked into the church of the Holy Sepulchre. They camped that night on the Mount of Olives. 'Our tents were on a ledge of the mountain, all among the grand old olives, a hundred yards above the garden of Gethsemane, into which we might almost have dropped a stone. ... The whole line of the city walls was opposite us, with the famous Dome of the Rock in front.'

The next day they went on to Jericho. At lunch time Marianne wanted to walk, but the Ḥajji advised against it, because there had been fighting there the previous day. Their tents were pitched that night on one of the old mounds of the ancient city with 'thirty square miles of croaking frogs all round us.' When they reached the Jordan they were again advised not to linger because of a hostile tribe nearby, so they rode to the Dead Sea, where Marianne bathed, since the Hajji told her that 'his ladies always liked to bathe' there; then over the hills to Mar Saba, spending the night in tents above the old monastery.

Fig. 15. Near Hebron, photograph reproduced by permission of Mr Tom North.

On 15 April they visited Bethlehem. 'Not a vestige of the simple manger,' wrote Marianne, 'but the situation remains unchanged and is very fine.' They took their lunch near Mamre (under the so-called oaks of Abraham), and camped just outside Hebron. 'The people of Hebron are proverbially uncivil to strangers,' wrote Marianne, 'the Hadji became nervous, and insisted on seeing us in front of him always, and my father was aggravating and *would* dart down side-streets.' Then they travelled north and pitched their tents by the lake at Tiberias on 28 April. Marianne took a bath there, walking straight out from the tent into the lake in her mackintosh cape, while her father bathed in the Roman hot

Tiberias on 30 April to the heights of Safed. 'And now,' Marianne writes, 'I must record the only unpleasant adventure that ever met my wanderings in any land, but the ludicrous share of the affair was so much greater than the disagreeable that I would hardly wish to have missed it.' She tells how she thought she would go up to the castle on her own, without disturbing her father or the Ḥajji, to make a sketch from the castle before sunset. Suddenly 'three rough creatures' bore down on her, dancing and yelling. Then

> one caught hold of my arm... but that was too much for a freeborn Briton to put up with; so I picked up a great stone, nearly as big as my head, ... and told them in good English to 'be off'. I did not swear, that would have been unladylike, but the words were effective ... and I walked with terrible dignity up the mound & pretended to sketch ... but somehow the pencil would not go straight.'

The rough creatures had run away, but alas! only to return on horseback. Marianne ran 'most ignominiously' down the hill, still clutching her stone. She escaped, but a shower of stones followed her. When the Ḥajji heard about it, he quickly took action, a prisoner was brought down, and proceedings put in hand, the stone being packaged as evidence; but all was resolved amicably in the morning with the help of 'backsheesh'.

The following day when they returned from the market at Safed they found all the Ḥajji's men being shaved. They were to witness the three-day Jewish Festival at Meiron. On 1 May they watched the 'endless procession of strange figures arrive up the hill... they continued to pour in all night and the next day, Jews from all countries, men, women and children ... not forgetting the poor woman from Liverpool married to the chief rabbi of Safed ... About sunset the ark was danced up the hill.' The next day the 'dancing, singing, praying, gossiping, fighting & drinking were incessant. Pistols & guns were continually being let off, but we heard of only one man actually killed.' That night they went on to a roof overlooking the courtyard, and stood between two of the domes there, and watched 'strange figures flinging their shawls off their heads & shoulders, their sashes & dresses, all heavy with gold & silver embroidery,' and throwing them into an altar like a font — 'others were throwing in bracelets, necklaces, & the gold coins off their heads, & oil

Fig. 16. Barber Saphed, photograph reproduced by permission of Mr Tom North.

was poured in, & the whole mass was set on fire...' Afterwards the Rabbi took possession of the mass of precious metal remaining on the altar, for distribution to the poor.

The next day they 'said farewell to our friends [at Safed], for I had made many among the Jewesses, their beauty captivated me ...' They kept to the high ground, lingering at the ruins of Kades, ancient Kadesh Naphtali, but eventually descending to the stifling plain, and pitching their tents at Banias.

The next day they were back in Damascus, which, Marianne wrote, 'needs no description from me ... When we wanted money, we were taken to a Dervish who kept an ironmonger's shop. He cashed a cheque without being able to understand it, or having any previous knowledge of our characters, & then ... treated us to ices.'

They camped that night near the ruins of a Christian village which the Turks had recently burned, and the next day they climbed in sleet and wind, and reached the Cedars of Lebanon by noon. 'Could we have found a more magnificent or holy church for our Whitsuntide devotions? I doubt it — & I refused to give a penny towards rebuilding the paltry Greek chapel under these sacred trees.'

The following day, 25 May, they descended to the plain, and camped on the brow of a cliff above Tripoli. They were the first party of the year to cross over the mountains, and were suspected by the local people of harbouring a Turkish outlaw, so that the Governor insisted on giving them an armed escort that night. In the morning they took the road to Beirut by the Dog River (Nahr al-Kalb). 'Our last camp!' wrote Frederick North in his diary. The entries had become fewer and briefer as they progressed. He was, after all, not a young man, and no doubt the exertion, fond though he was of exercise, and the unaccustomed nature of tent life, had taken their toll.

Fig. 17. Tripoli, photograph reproduced by permission of Mr Tom North.

But for Marianne, travels were just beginning. She had tasted a world beyond Europe, and had found an appetite for other cultures. She would not return to the Levant again, except to sail through the Suez Canal on her way to India, and she would not paint in watercolours again, but in her writing she would vividly record the experiences of mid-Victorian tourists in the Levant, with all their worries and prejudices, but above all, their enthusiasms.

Fig. 18. Jewish Festival at Meiron, 2 May 1865, photograph reproduced by permission of Mr Tom North.

From Pilgrimage to Budding Tourism: the role of Thomas Cook in the rediscovery of the Holy Land in the nineteenth century

Ruth Kark

Introduction

One of the dominant characteristics of modern times is the phenomenon of mass travel and tourism. Tourism is so widespread and accepted today, particularly in the Western world, that we tend to take it for granted. Travelling for pleasure in a foreign country by large numbers of people is a relatively modern occurrence, however, dating only from the early nineteenth century. Although travel for business, exploration, religious, cultural, educational, sport and medical purposes, and even for entertainment, can be found throughout human history, it was practised by a select few, and was limited in scope.

The beginnings of pre-modern cultural and pleasure tourism in the Western world date back to the sixteenth-century. The technological and social transitions associated with the Industrial Revolution brought about the development of new modes of travel and, eventually, the emergence of the holiday industry. According to Burkard and Medlik, the word *tourism* did not appear in the English language until the early nineteenth century. Mass tourism and inclusive package tours replaced the Grand Tour and the traditional pilgrimage. The train and steamer passage opened opportunities of travel not only to new socio-economic groups, such as the expanding middle class, but also changed attitudes towards gender and race. One of the main innovators in this sphere was Thomas Cook, who from 1841 onwards developed the modern business of tourism in England and abroad. By 1864 he claimed one million clients. Cook's 'Eastern Tours' were inaugurated shortly after this and helped to transform Palestine from being a *Terra Sancta* for pilgrims, as it had been for

Map 4. Cook's Tours to Egypt. The Nile, Turkey, Greece &c, 1873, Map 971(12), reproduced by permission of The British Library.

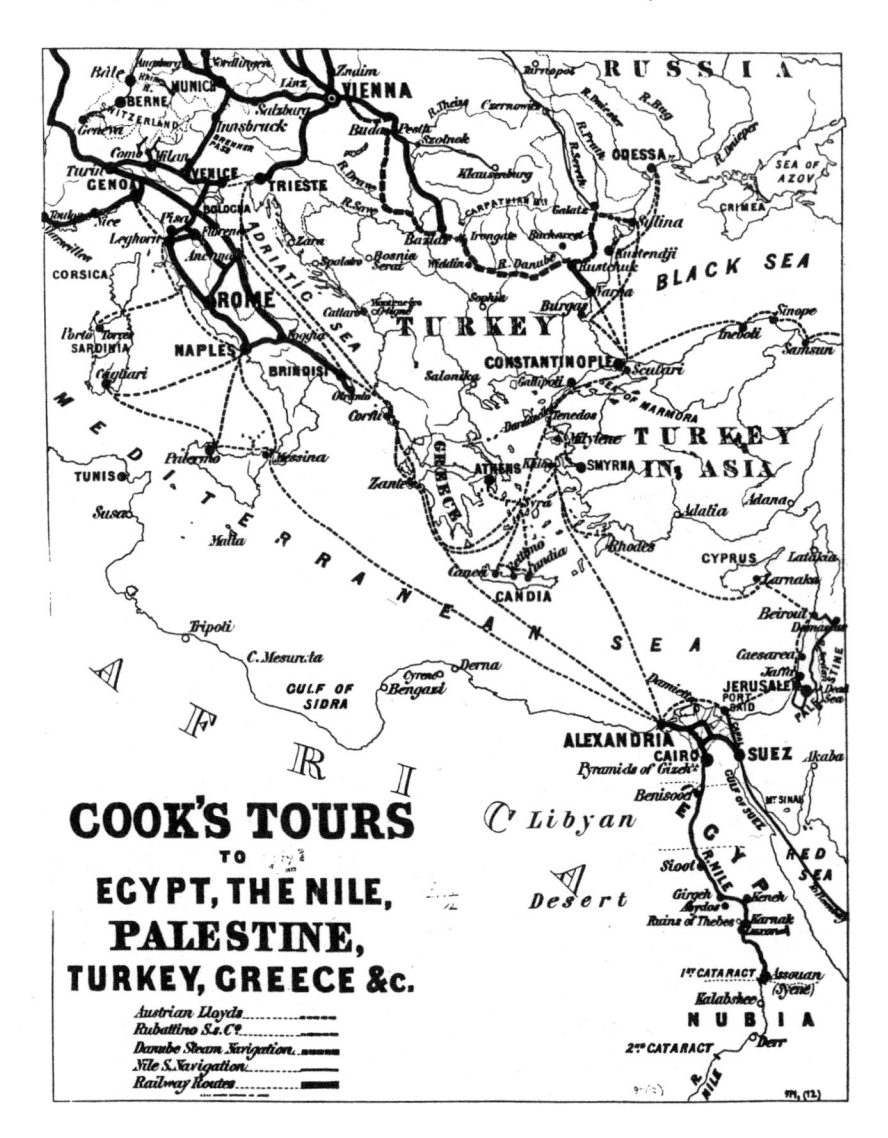

generations, into a destination for mass tourism.[1] This paper considers the role of Thomas Cook and Son in the modernisation and re-discovery through tourism of the Holy Land, and Cook's own ambition to combine piety with commerce in Palestine. The creation of new travel components by Cook, the land and sea routes and means of transportation chosen, the change in type, motivation and role of tourists, their biblical images, activity and experiences in the Holy Land, and their numbers will be discussed. His importance is attested to by the fact that four fifths of all British and American tourists who visited the country between 1881 and 1883 were brought by the Cook Agency. The impact of Cook's operation in Palestine on modernising the local economy and society, and on European and American culture and society will also be examined.

Thomas Cook: piety and innovative entrepreneurship in England

One of the main innovators in the sphere of tourism was Thomas Cook (1808-1892), English founder of the worldwide travel agency which bears his name. Cook, a printer, a Baptist missionary (1828) and an active pacifist, began by inventing package holidays that were known as Temperance Tours, designed to distract people from the evils of drink and nicotine. In 1841 he persuaded the Midland Counties Railway Company to run a special train between Leicester and Loughborough for a temperance meeting. It was believed to be the first publicly advertised excursion train in England. From 1841 Cook went on to develop modern tourism in England and abroad.[2]

---

[1] A.J. Burkard and S. Medlick, *Tourism* (Oxford and London: Heineman, 1995); Bill Cormack, *A History of Holiday, 1812-1990* (London: Routledge 1998), 1-49; John Towner, *An Historical Geography of Recreation and Tourism in the Western World, 1540-1940* (Chichester and New York: John Wiley, 1996), 96-138; Lynne Whithey, *Grand Tours and Cook's Tours: A History of Leisure Travel, 1750-1915* (New York: William Morrow, 1997), 1-134.

[2] C. Lamb, 'They didn't just book it — they Thomas Cooked it', *Financial Times* (13 January 1990), 18; *Encyclopaedia Britannica*, 3 (1885), 597; Edmund Swinglehurst, *Cook's Tours* (Poole, Dorset: Blandford, 1982).

By 1850 he was arranging tours for the English middle class to Paris, Italy and the Alps. In 1851 he scored his first big success when he was asked to organize visits to the Great Exhibition in Hyde Park, London. He transported 165,000 people, accommodating them in 'dormitories with clean towels and soap'. His method was to use the new railways and steamships, advance-purchasing tickets for resale, and to conduct the tours in person. He also published guidebooks, realizing that travellers needed hotel and restaurant recommendations. A coupon service was devised to provide hotel facilities and in 1873 Cook introduced circular notes, the forerunners of travellers' cheques, to save tourists carrying gold, which was both dangerous and inconvenient. His newspaper, the *Excursionist* (1851-1902) contained long articles directed at working men on the virtues of self-improvement through travel. Women tourists were also encouraged. Cook wrote about them:

> As to their energy, bravery and endurance of toil. ... they are fully equal to those of the opposite sex, while many of them frequently put to shame the 'masculine' effeminates. ... they push their way through all difficulty and acquire the perfection of tourist character.[3]

Such an attitude, put into practice, flattered middle-class women, who became an integral part of Cook's groups, increasing their general appeal to the middle classes.[4]

In 1867, Cook led the first excursion to the USA. At that time he estimated that in the twenty-seven years of the company's existence it had served nearly two million travellers, for whom 'God granted his protection'.[5] He took 75,000 visitors to the Paris exhibition of 1878. During the 1880s the firm took on military and postal services between Britain and Egypt.[6]

[3] Thomas Cook, 'Personal', *Cook's Excursionist*, Supplementary Number (25 November 1867).
[4] Maxine Feifer, *Tourism in History* (New York: Stein and Day, 1986), 170.
[5] Thomas Cook, 'Personal', *Cook's Excursionist*, Supplementary Number (25 November 1867), 2.
[6] L.J. Licorish and A.G. Kershaw, 'Tourism between 1840–1940', in Burkard and Medlick, *op. cit.*, 11–26.

Reminiscing in 1867 about his tourist initiative almost three decades earlier Thomas Cook related his success to enthusiasm and 'a passionate love for the great work' combined with 'the realisation of the thought that suddenly flashed across the mind, that the powers and appliances of steam and locomotion might be turned to useful account in the advancement of social and educational movements'.[7] These words reflect mid-nineteenth century missionary concepts and connotations. We may also gain some insight into Cook's self-perception from a short article in the 1873 *Excursionist*. He viewed himself as an original thinker and doer in the sphere of tourism:

> I never borrowed ideas of Tours from any one, though my original 'ideas' have been moulded into a good many Tourist systems of public companies; and as for individual speculators, they have made it their chief business to get hold of my arrangements, copy my Tickets, and then call them their own names.

When offered partnership in tours to the east by a Vienna contractor, he replied: 'that I always preferred to do my own work, in my own way, and to bear my own responsibility'.[8]

Many years later British statesman, William E. Gladstone (1809–1898), said:

> Among the humanising contrivances of the age I think notice is due to the system founded by Mr. Cook, and now largely in use, under which numbers of persons, and indeed whole classes have for the first time found easy access to foreign countries, and have acquired some of that familiarity with them which breeds not contempt but kindness.

This is consistent with Cohen's (1972) assertion:

> It seems mass tourism as a cultural phenomenon evolves as a result of a very basic change in man's attitude to the world beyond the boundaries of his native

---

[7] 'Personal', *op. cit.*
[8] 'Brief history of our Eastern Tours', *Cook's Excursionist* (24 November 1873).

habitat. So long as man remains largely ignorant of the existence of other societies, other cultures, he regards his own small world as the cosmos.[9]

Cook's 'Eastern and Holy Land Tours'

A trip to Jerusalem had been an ambition of Thomas Cook's since 1850, when travelling through the Highlands of Scotland, on one of his Highland Tours 'he fell in with a Clergyman just returned from the East, who gave much valuable information on Eastern travel and strongly urged the practicality of the project'. He sought advice about organizing a round trip to Egypt and Syria from James Silk Buckingham (1786-1855), a writer, traveller in the Middle East, and Member of Parliament who visited Palestine in 1816 and published a two-volume account in 1823. Around 1853 Thomas saw proposals advertised in Scottish periodicals, of a planned tour to Palestine, at a cost of about £200. Later his friend from Nottingham, Alderman Cullen, in a social gathering of Excursionists at Land's End, suggested that Cook should conduct his patrons to the Holy Land. The implementation of the idea was postponed until Cook had built up a solid American as well as British clientele, and the railway and steamship routes were sufficiently well established to cope with large groups. He kept the project in mind, and 'however silently the idea slept under the heavy load of other engagements, I had always anticipated that it must be done at some convenient season.' Between 1865 and 1867 a connection with a Mediterranean steamers company, strongly focused Cook's attention on the subject. Several letters were received from a writer in Constantinople, strongly urging the practicability of an eastern tour, and offering personal and other friendly assistance. As one of Thomas's principles was to make 'for his own guidance and satisfaction an exploratory visit' before announcing a new tour, he preferred 'in the great matter of an Eastern Tour ... to arrange and work out his own plans, availing himself of all practicable counsel and assistance.' He mentioned that one of the main reasons for not being able to apply this

---

[9] E. Cohen, 'Toward a sociology of international tourism' *Social Research*, 59 (1972), 164–81; Feifer, *op. cit.*

principle was 'isolation in my work, and the impossibility of leaving home for so long a period as 70 or 80 days'. He was thus able to advance the project two years after his son, John Mason Cook, joined the firm in 1864, and became competent to look after the home business. Thomas stressed proudly his role as 'originator' of the Eastern Tours: 'although in the arranging and carrying out of Tours to the East, I have had the instant and energetic co-operation of my Son, I adhere, for special reasons, to the personal pronoun in my brief notes of their origin, progress and results'[10]

In 1867 Thomas Cook made arrangements to spend the Christmas of 1868 in Jerusalem. He declared that before making an official announcement of a tour to Palestine he would go there himself to examine the conditions.

> The information to be obtained will include – the best time of the year for being in Palestine – the best travelling facilities, the best Hotel accommodation – the best Guides that can be engaged – the best places of interest to be visited – the routes to and from England – and the cost of the whole tour for two months. The entire cost is roughly estimated at £100 or 100 guineas.

Cook promised to pay attention to the gender aspect as well: 'How far it is practicable for ladies to undertake this tour, will constitute one of the interesting subjects of enquiry. The aim will be to provide for their company'.[11]

In September 1868, Thomas travelled via Italy and Constantinople to Smyrna, Beirut, Jaffa, and on to Alexandria and Cairo in order to negotiate future activity in the area with local agents. Although he planned to go to Jerusalem, and had letters of introduction to several of the most influential residents, he did not have enough time to go there. However, he made hotel and dragoman arrangements at Beirut and Jaffa, and in Beirut met several missionaries including Mrs Thompson, the founder of Beirut and Lebanon schools, and Mr and Mrs Mott. In Cairo he was approached by Alexander Howard (a Maronite from Beirut and Jaffa who Anglicised his name from Awad to Howard) and his partner

---

[10] 'Tour to Palestine', *Cook's Excursionist*, Supplementary Number (25 November 18670, 1–2; 'Brief history', *op. cit.* (24 November 1873).

[11] *Ibid.*

Abdullah Joseph, who asked Cook to give them a share of his future work, and be employed exclusively by him. Cook decided to hire Howard as a dragoman, and was very satisfied with his loyalty and performance.[12]

In 1869, the year in which the Suez Canal opened, Cook led the first party of ten travellers through the Holy Land and Egypt, whose adventures were recorded in her diary by one of the party, a Miss Riggs of Hampstead.[13] In later years the company organized the transport of groups of German Templars from Jaffa to Jerusalem (1874), transported over a thousand French Catholic pilgrims to the Holy Land and back (28 April-30 May, 1882), planned the tour of the second Shayara ('Convoy') of British Jews belonging to the Order of Ancient Maccabians (1897) and conducted Royalty around the Holy Land, the British princes Albert Victor and George (later George V) in 1882 and Kaiser Wilhelm II in 1898.[14] Although pilgrims had made their way to the Holy Land for centuries, the first organised tours began in the early 1850s: Roman Catholic groups from Italy travelling by the Lloyd Triestino steamship line, and parties organised by the order of St Vincent de Paul which set out twice yearly from Marseilles, at Easter and in August. The journey from France was prohibitively expensive and women were not admitted to these tours until after 1868. The first organised 'pleasure trip' to Palestine came, predictably, from the United States, part of a huge package deal; early in 1867, 150 Americans, organised by Henry Ward Beecher's Plymouth Church, planned to tour the continent of Europe and from

---

[12] R. Smyirk, 'Beginning of tourism to the Holy Land', in *The Second Million. Israeli Tourist Industry*, edited by Chaim H. Klein (Tel Aviv: Amir, 1973), 21; 'Brief history of our Eastern Tours', *Cook's Excursionist* (24 November 1873).

[13] N. Shepherd, *The Zealous Intruders: the western rediscovery of Palestine* (London: Collins, 1987), 173-5.

[14] *Cook's Excursionist* (1 November 1881) reports that a third generation of Cooks went on an excursion in the spring of 1880; R. Kark, 'The Kaiser in Jerusalem', *Etmol*, 23 (1998), 3-6; *Cook's Excursionist* (13 May 1882), 5; 'Maccabaean Pilgrimage to Palestine: Itinerary and Programme' (London: Thomas Cook and Son, 1897); Shepherd, *op. cit.*; N. Bentwich, 'The Anglo-Jewish travellers to Palestine in the nineteenth century', in *Essays Presented to E.N. Adler* (London: The Jewish Historical Society of England, 1942), 9-19.

there continue to the Holy Land and Egypt. This was the famous cruise of the 'Quaker City', described by Mark Twain.[15]

In the course of the nineteenth century, Palestine became a 'must' in the itineraries of many British and Americans travelling abroad. As Handy and Vogel have noted, although Protestant Christians placed less emphasis on pilgrimage, many sought out the scenes of Jesus' ministry and other sites with biblical associations as an act of faith. Others, who came mainly as observers of exotic lifestyles, were affected by the cultural and spiritual connotations of the Holy Land — as was even Mark Twain, who was undoubtedly one of the most cynical.[16]

The tourist trade to Palestine grew steadily, largely due to the efforts of Thomas Cook, whose advertisement, published in a guidebook from the Mandate period reminds potential tourists that: 'Cook's were established in Jerusalem long before there were railways and roads and when the only means of exploring the country was on horseback with camp'.[17]

A British missionary in Palestine, Reverend James Neil, gave in his book a very good description of the change in the 1870s:

> Nor must we omit to mention amongst the causes of the present improved condition of the country, the annual influx of a very great and increasing number of visitors. The entirely healthful mode of travelling it necessitates, with all the excitement and pleasure of camp life, the deep interest of its hallowed spots, the wide field it affords for exploration, and the wild beauty that still lingers everywhere on its natural features, combined to make Palestine a place of resort as soon as the modern facilities for travelling brought its shores to within an easy fortnight's distant from our own [...] Royal personages have been conspicuous among the number. Formerly only a few very wealthy travellers could accomplish the journey. Now it may be said to

---

[15] Shepherd, *op. cit.*

[16] R.T. Handy (ed.) *The Holy Land in American Protestant Life, 1800–1948* (New York: Arno Press, 1981), xvi–xviii; L. Vogel, *To See a Promised Land: Americans and the Holy Land in the 19th Century* (University Park, PA: Pennsylvania State University Press, 1997), 9–18.

[17] Harry Luke and Edward Keith-Roach, *The Handbook of Palestine and Trans-Jordan* (London: Macmillan, 1934), advertisements, 4. On tourism during the British Mandate period see K. Cohen-Hatab and Y. Katz, From Terra Sancta to tourism: the geographical-historical study of tourism and its contribution to the historiography of Eretz-Israel', *Cathedra*, 91 (1999), 113–36.

be within the reach of ordinary tourists. There are two well known conductors of travelling parties in England, Mr. Cook and Mr. Gaze, and one in Germany. The first of these repeats his visits four times during a single season, and in that of 1874 made arrangements for no less than 270 visitors to the Holy Land. Such is the number of Germans who flock to the country... American visitors, though they have to come three thousand miles further than others, are, to their credit be it said, the most numerous, and after them our countrymen furnish by far the largest contingent. This is, of course, excepting the Russian pilgrims, members of the Greek Church, who now, together with crowds from the neighboring countries, representatives of the Greek, Armenian, Syrian, Coptic, and almost all Oriental Churches, come up every year by thousands.[18]

Facilities for pilgrims were available in Palestine from early times and much improved when the rule of Muḥammad ʿAli (1831–1841) brought greater security. However, they were scarcely adequate to the mounting pressure generated by the sheer numbers of tourists, let alone their demands for physical comfort. Cook had to create proper hotels, find good guides, and solve hygienic problems of food, water and residence. The company's organisation of its Palestinian tours was based around the demands of its middle-class Protestant clientele, English and American, and they were often accompanied by Thomas or his son John. Almost everything was paid for in advance, reducing the risk of robbery. The dragomans were handpicked. In 1875, Cooks acquired a house and grounds near the Jaffa Gate of Jerusalem and threatened to concentrate their business there if local contractors and hoteliers 'do not treat our travellers and ourselves as they and we ought to be treated'. Among Cook's innovations were 'Biblical Educational and General Tours', 'designed specially for ministers and Sunday School teachers, and others engaged in promoting scriptural education', and 'educational tours for young gentlemen', later opened to others.[19]

A Cook's tour was not cheap; in the 1860s it averaged thirty-one shillings a day, including accommodation, dragoman, military escort and provisions imported from Britain. In 1873 for the journey out to Palestine Cooks used the railways to Genoa and Trieste or the Danube Steam Navigation to Varna on the Black Sea. From the Mediterranean ports

---

[18] James Neil, *Palestine Re-Peopled* (London: James Nisbet, 1883), 23–27.
[19] Shepherd, *op. cit.*, 180.

Austrian Lloyds or Rabattino S.S. Co. took travellers to Alexandria, Port Said and Jaffa, then back again from Beirut. Once arrived in Palestine, two tour routes were available. The short route took the tourists from Jaffa to Gaza, Beersheba, Jerusalem, on a round trip to the Dead Sea near Jericho, to Samaria, Nazareth, Cana, the Sea of Galilee, Damascus, Baalbek and Beirut. Another possibility was to start at Beirut, go down the coast to Sidon, Tyre, Haifa, Jaffa, and then on the short excursion. At the end of 1873, new routes to Moab and the Houran were added, going around the Dead Sea and north through Transjordan to Damascus via the Sea of Galilee or the Houran.[20] In 1891, the first edition of *Cook's Tourist's Handbook for Palestine and Syria* included 12 itineraries.

Thomas Cook & Son, and similar companies, like the one established in New York by Frank C. Clark (one of the children of the Adams American colonists at Jaffa), greatly increased the numbers of tourists visiting the Holy Land. The annual total rose from between 2,000 to 3,000 in the first half of the century to around 7,000 in the 1870s and around 30,000 on the eve of World War I.[21] Melman, who examined women travellers to the Middle East between the years 1719–1918, suggested that 13 per cent were tourists, typically Cook's tourists, or 'Cookites'.[22] In the 1830s it was said that between 10,000 and 12,000 pilgrims came to Jerusalem annually. The accuracy of this figure is difficult to ascertain, although it is similar to figures cited by the US consul in Jerusalem for 1868 (12,500 including 150 Englishmen and 250 Americans).

Between 1869 and 1883, Cooks brought about 4,500 travellers to Palestine; he claimed that this accounted for about two-thirds of the total number of tourists arriving from the West. By comparison, French Roman Catholics organised thirty-five caravans between 1853 and 1873 — which carried only 618 pilgrims — still vastly outnumbered, of course, by Eastern pilgrims from Russia, the Balkans and the Near East. Prior to

---

[20] *Cook's Excursionist* (22 September 1873), 4; *Cook's Tourist map of Palestine, Egypt and the Nile* (New York: Thos. Cook and Son, 1898).

[21] R. Kark, *American Consuls in the Holy Land, 1832–1914* (Detroit and Jerusalem: Wayne State University Press and Magnes, 1994), 235–40.

[22] B. Melman, *Women's Orient: English women and the Middle East, 1718–1918* (London: Macmillan, 1995), 40.

World War I, Baedeker and other sources estimated the number of annual visitors at between 15,000 and 25,000, of which about one quarter were tourists and the rest pilgrims. In 1910–1911, a total of 5,759 tourists and 20,000 pilgrims were reported; twenty-eight per cent of the tourists (1,625) were Americans.[23]

The local economy benefited from the increasing influx of tourists by importing foreign capital to religious institutions, stimulating demand for food, services and other products. Both the local population and the Ottoman authorities benefited from the increase in income. For example, Cook claimed 300 people and 200 horses and mules were serving the 300 tourists who visited Palestine at the beginning of 1880. According to Ruppin, visitors to Greater Syria brought in an annual sum of ten million francs (£400,000).[24]

Several towns in Palestine, but mainly Jerusalem and Jaffa, developed tourist infrastructure: hostels and hotels, catering services, money exchange, souvenirs, tourist guides and so on as they became pilgrimage and tourist centres. In the first half of the nineteenth century, pilgrims were often accommodated at monasteries. The first modern-style hotel, which offered some of the comforts of Europe, was opened in Jaffa in the 1850s by Kopel Blatner & Sons. Tourist accommodation improved further in the 1870s, when Cooks opened the Twelve Tribes Hotel in Jaffa. Additional modern hotels were opened in Jaffa from the 1870s onwards. Jerusalem had no hotels and only a few hostels, such as the Franciscan Casanova, in the mid-nineteenth century. A few big complexes, such as the Russian Compound and the Austrian Hospice

---

[23] Lorenzo M. Johnson, U.S. Acting Consul (Jerusalem) to William. H. Seward, Secretary of State, Washington D.C. (30 September 1868), USNA, RG59 T471/2; Kark, *American Consuls*, 235–6; R. Kark, *The Development of the Cities of Jerusalem and Jaffa from 1840 up to the First World War* (Jerusalem: Hebrew University, 1977), 181–2, 215–16; *Cook's Excursionist* (1 April 1880), 3.

[24] R. Kark, *Jaffa — A City in Evolution, 1799–1917* (Jerusalem: Yad Izhak Ben-Zvi, 1990), 285–8; *Cook's Excursionist* (1 November 1883), 3–4; Shepherd, *op. cit.*, 180; *Palestine Exploration Fund Quarterly Statement*, 25 (July 1893); Kark, *American Consuls*, 285–8; Letter of Cook's agent at Haifa to U.S. Vice-Consulate, Haifa (3 March 1903), USNA, RG84, Haifa Consular Agency, Misc. and Official Corres. Rec 1875–1917.

were built between 1850 and 1860 to accommodate pilgrims. Cook allocated a camping area for his groups outside the Jaffa and Damascus Gates of the old city. In the second half of the century, however, many new hostels and hotels were built. Several hotels — the Jerusalem, Mediterranean, New Grand and Fast Hotels — had an annual contract, or some kind of arrangement with Cooks' and Clark's travel agencies: in 1903 Cook had three branch offices in Palestine (Jerusalem in David Street, Jaffa in the German Colony and Haifa near Hotel Carmel).[25] Twenty-eight hostels and hotels, of which some were luxurious and modern, were counted by Yellin in Jerusalem in 1898.[26]

By the end of the nineteenth century, the major travel agencies handling tourists were Cook, Tadras, Clark, Hamburg, Barakat, and Nasir and Farajalla. Commissioners could be hired to help passengers disembark, release luggage from customs, and secure lodgings, horses and carriages. Ferrying and wagon services were available, as well as hundreds of porters, guides and escorts, and over twenty-three caravansarays in Jaffa alone in 1905. Local firms proliferated. Restaurants and cafés multiplied: in Jaffa there were sixty-four restaurants and eighty-one coffeehouses in 1905.[27]

---

[25] Kark, *Jaffa*, Programme of Tours in Egypt and the Holy Land, arranged and personally managed by Messrs. Nissaire, Farajallah and Co. (n.d., c. 1910–1911); Maoz Haviv, 'Thomas Cook's Company and the Holy Land', a seminar paper (Jerusalem: n.d.), 25.

[26] Palmer Parsons (ed.), *Letters from Palestine: 1868–1912*, written by Rolla Floyd (USA: Privately Published, 1981), 106–107; J. Ahtola, 'Thomas Cook and Son and the Egyptian season', in *Travel Patterns: Past and Present. Three Studies*, edited by J. Ahtola and T. Toivonen (Savonlinna: Finnish University Network for Tourism Studies, 1999), 7–32; P. Brendon, *Thomas Cook; 150 years of popular tourism* (London: Secker and Warburg, 1991), 182–200.

[27] Kark, *Jaffa*; Programme of Tours in Egypt and the Holy land, arranged and personally managed by Messrs. Nissaire, Farjallah and Co. (n.d., c. 1910–1911); Maoz Haviv, 'Thomas Cook's Company and the Holy Land' a seminar paper (Jerusalem: n.d.), 25.

Map 5. Cook's Tours in Palestine, 1873, British Library Map 48840(40), reproduced by permission of The British Library.

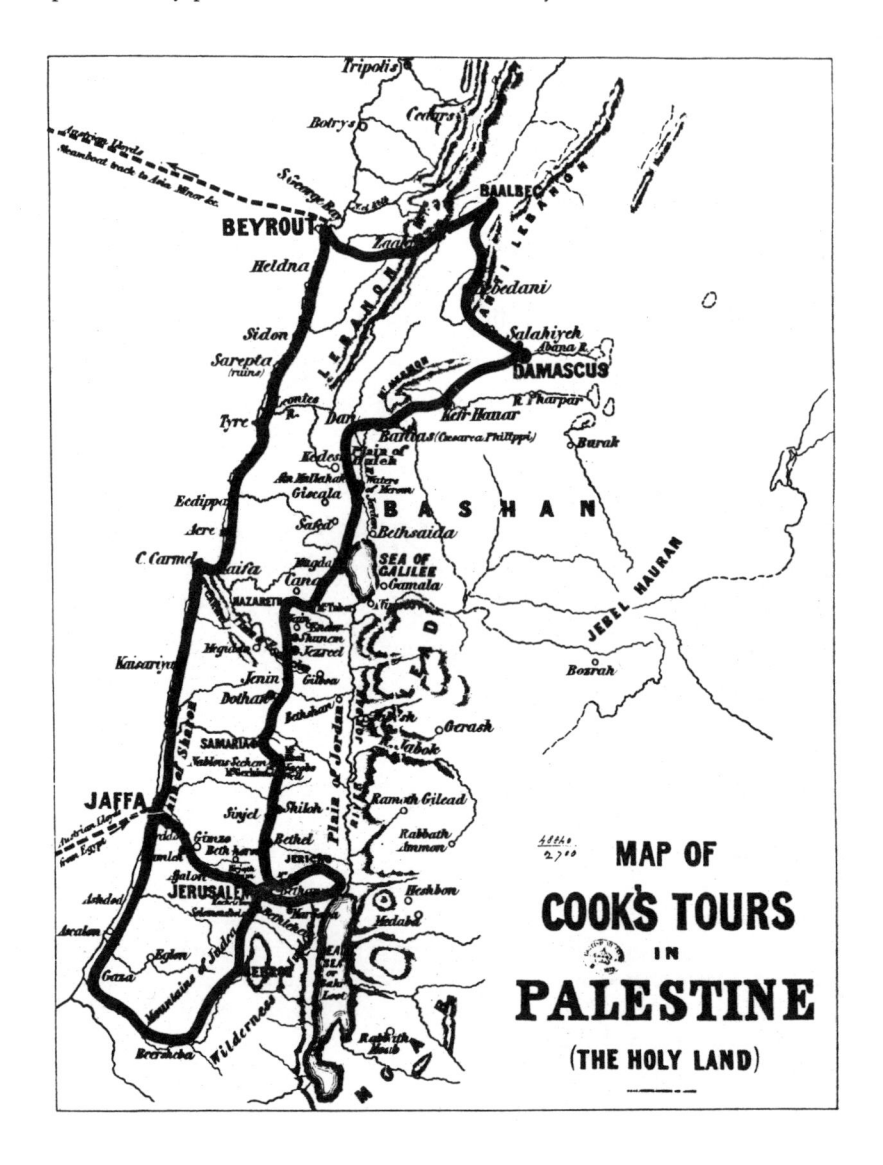

Combining piety and philanthropy with commerce in the Holy Land: Cook and Holy Land Protestant and British activities

In his operation in the Holy Land, Thomas Cook always had in mind his missionary background. On the eve of his reconnaissance trip to Palestine, Cook expressed his pious feelings towards Jerusalem and the Holy Land:

> the vision is certainly an enchanting one to be near the spot with which are associated the Star of Bethlehem, the song of the Angels, the adoration of the Magi, the wonder of the shepherds, and all those other New Testament incidents and associations comprehended in the fulfillment [sic] of all the prophecies which centred upon the Nativity.[28]

In a personal confession he wrote: 'It will be a joyous event to see the "mountains round about Jerusalem" but its culminating glory would be to look beyond those mountain ranges to the "Jerusalem above" and if a tour to famed attractions of Palestine should inspire all who accompany us to seek the "better land", a rich reward crowns our labours'.[29]

Cook's tours combined visits to the Holy Places, the missions and their schools, and 'biblical excavations'; the parties carried not only maps and guide books but bibles and hymn books, and sang as they went. Mention has already been made to the 'Biblical Educational and General Tours', but it is worth noting that in the first edition of Cook's *Tourist's Handbook* (1891), the editor 'endeavoured [sic] to incorporate ... not merely the references to the passages of Scripture descriptive of places of interest, but the words of the sacred text also.[30]

Cook also used his tours to support philanthropic work in Palestine. For example there was one stop on the advertised schedule for 1877, at Miss Arnott's Mission School in Jaffa, a property which Cook had

---

[28] 'Tour to Palestine, *Cook's Excursionist*, Supplement Number (25 November 1867).

[29] Thomas Cook, 'Personal', *Cook's Excursionist*, Supplementary Number (25 November, 1867), 2.

[30] *Cook's Tourist's* [*Traveller's* in later editions] *Handbook for Palestine and Syria* (London: Thomas Cook and Son, 1891), v-vi.

purchased for the mission, and another in Nablus, at the house of Selim el Karey, who had converted from the Greek Orthodox faith to Protestantism.[31] The Jaffa Tabeetha Mission School, founded by Miss Walker Arnott, a Scottish Presbyterian, in 1863, was one of the first Arab girls' schools in Palestine; Miss Arnott remained involved until her death in 1911 [1912?]. In 1877 the Tabeetha Mission Committee was formed in Edinburgh to help run the school. Miss Arnott also received an annual grant from the Society for Promoting Women's Education in the East, a ladies' voluntary group near Glasgow and, more substantially, a grant from Thomas Cook and Son. In the 1870s, Thomas Cook purchased a sizeable tract of land on a hill outside Jaffa town wall, not far from the new gate. Here he erected a two-storey building as the headquarters of the mission and school. According to Nile, the massive sandstones used for the building were from the Jaffa old town wall pulled down by order of the Governor and sold as building material for the new school house[32] The building was rectangular in shape with an open inner courtyard and a tiled roof. For eighteen years Cook also maintained a number of Arab scholars, at his own expense. The building, located in today's Yefet Street in Jaffa, is still an Anglican girl's school.[33] Cook's *Excursionist* also published appeals for help for the school.[34]

The Excursionist published in 1869 a report of the annual meeting of the Palestine Exploration Fund (PEF, established in 1865), and announced the collection of contributions for the Fund, by the Cook office in London and Miss Cook in Leicester. The newspaper reported on the progress of the Survey of Western Palestine and later the Survey of Eastern Palestine being undertaken by the PEF.[35]

Cook's support was also instrumental in setting up the PEF's geological expedition of 1883 to 1884 to Arabia Petraea, the Arabah and Western

---

[31] Shepherd, *co. cit.*
[32] Neil, *op. cit.*
[33] Kark, *Jaffa*, op. cit., *97, 169079;* Melman, op. cit., 54.
[34] *Cook's Excursionist* (29 October 1874), 3; *Cook's Excursionist* (26 January 1876), 2–3.
[35] 'Palestine Exploration Fund', *Cook's Excursionist* (10 July, 1869), 3; *Cook's Excursionist* (6 June, 1877), 5; (16 December 1880); (2 February 1881), 5; (1 November 1882), 4, 11–18; (22 July 1882), 4.

Palestine, headed by the Irish Professor, Edward Hull. Cook's philanthropy is evident from Hull's report, the company taking upon itself all the travelling arrangements by land or sea, to provide tents, food and attendants, and to advance money when needed 'without the slightest profit, directly or indirectly to the firm.' When the expedition members left London by train on their way to Dover and Egypt, John Mason Cook was on the platform at Ludgate Hill Station, to wish them a good journey.[36]

A decision to open a British Hospice and Ophthalmic Dispensary was reached in London on July 1882. It was opened in 1883 by the English League of the Order of St John of Jerusalem, to give free care to all nations and races. Cooks took upon itself to collect contributions for the hospital.[37] From the 'First Annual Report of the British Hospice and Ophthalmic Dispensary in Jerusalem, under the Management of St. John of Jerusalem (English Langue)', whose patron was the Prince of Wales, we learn that John Mason Cook was one of three members of the institution's local committee in Jerusalem, together with the British Consul, Noel Temple Moore, and Thomas Chaplin, M.D. The local committee, including Cook, and Sir Edmund Lechmore, the vice-chairman of the British Order, and Lady Lechmere, who came to Jerusalem, selected a site with a building, at a cost of £1,050.[38] In his report to the General Assembly, written in 1883, Lechmere wrote: 'and our thanks are specially due to Mr. J.M. Cook, who has, from the first, rendered us essential service by the generous manner in which he has placed the resources of his establishment at Jerusalem, and the services of his agents at our disposal'.[39] From this report we learn that Thomas Cook and Son 'very handsomely undertook to send out our Surgeon at the net cost, and to see that on arrival in Jerusalem suitable quarters were provided for him.' We also see that John Mason Cook's donation of £100

---

[36] E.G. Hull, 'Narrative of an expedition through Arabia Petraea, the Valley of the Arabah, and Western Palestine', *Palestine Exploration Fund Quarterly Statement* 16 (1884), 114–17.
[37] *Cook's Excursionist* (1 May 1883), 3.
[38] *First Annual Report* (1883), The Order of St John's Archive, London, 3–5.
[39] Lechmere, *op. cit.*, 10–11.

for that year was the highest received. From additional correspondence between John Cook and Lechmere in 1889, found in the archives of the Order in London, we see that Cook persisted in his support of the Jerusalem Hospital.[40]

Cooks continued to take an interest in the development of Palestine even after the founders had departed the scene. Following the famous declaration in 1917 by the Foreign Secretary, Arthur Balfour, that the British government would 'view with favour the establishment of a national home for the Jews ...', the company's *Traveller's Gazette, Excursionist and Tourist Advertiser* welcomed the move as practical, of 'world-wide importance', and allowing 'the Jews to have a place where they can have conditions in accordance with their religious precepts, and where the surroundings are hallowed by their Bible story'.[41]

Conclusion

The nineteenth century marked a decisive turning point in the modern history of Palestine, and the beginning of change and modernisation in many spheres. This paper deals with the role of Thomas Cook and his impact on Palestine during the period of transformation from traditional journey and pilgrimage to the Holy Land to semi-modern tourism. The distinction of the Holy Land with its unique history and religion inspired attempts to create a special content to the tourist experience, differing substantially from travel plans for other foreign destinations. Leisure and recreation were not the only aim. Thomas Cook was a businessman and a talented organiser, who perceived brilliantly the potential of tourism in Europe and America. But he was also a man of faith and vision regarding

---

[40] J.M. Cook to Sir E. Lechmere (8 March, 1889), Volume — Hospice, The Order of St John's Archive, London. Cook advised the Order on the attitudes of the Pasha and the Ottomans: 'I am convinced the Turkish Government at the present time is not desirous of allowing Christians or Europeans to do anything that they can possibly prevent.'

[41] 'Palestine for the Jews', *The Traveller's Gazette*, 67 (January 1917), 6.

tourism in the Holy Land. He insisted on preserving and subsidising these tours, although they were not economically viable.

His activities in Palestine reflected his personality and his intention to combine his tourist business with Christian activities. He was personally involved in funding missionary health and educational institutions, as well as other British organisations such as the Palestine Exploration Fund, often not to the liking of his more hard-headed son and partner, John Mason Cook, though he too played a part. The creation of new institutional frameworks and travel components by the company went hand in hand with the changing perceptions, images and motivations of the travellers, and change in the type of tourists brought to the Holy Land (including women, Protestants, Catholics, British Zionist Jews, princes and kaisers) and in the tour routes and means of transportation. Cooks' operation in Palestine affected the modernisation of the local economy and local society, on the one hand, and European and American culture and society, on the other.

Bibliography

Ahtola, J. and T. Toivonen (eds), *Travel Patterns: Past and Present. Three Studies* (Savonlinna: Finnish University Network for Tourism Studies, 1999).

Bentwich, N., 'The Anglo-Jewish travellers to Palestine in the nineteenth century', in *Essays Presented to E.N. Adler* (London: The Jewish Historical Society of England, 1942), 9–19.

Brendon, P, *Thomas Cook; 150 years of popular tourism* (Secker and Warburg, 1991).

Burkard, A.J. and S. Medlick, *Tourism* (Oxford and London: Heineman, 1995).

Cohen, E., 'Toward a sociology of international tourism' *Social Research*, 59 (1972), 164–81.

Cohen-Hatab, K. and Y. Katz, 'From Terra Sancta to tourism: the geographical-historical study of tourism and its contribution to the historiography of Eretz-Israel', *Cathedra*, 91 (1999), 113–36.

Cook, Thomas, 'Personal', *Cook's Excursionist*, Supplementary Number (25 November, 1867), 2.

Cook's Tourist's [Traveller's in later editions] *Handbook for Palestine and Syria* (London: Thomas Cook and Son, 1891).

Cormack, Bill, *A History of Holiday, 1812-1990* (London: Routledge 1998).

Feifer, Maxine, *Tourism in History* (New York: Stein and Day, 1986).

Handy, R.T. (ed.) *The Holy Land in American Protestant Life, 1800-1948* (New York: Arno Press, 1981).

Hull, E.G., 'Narrative of an expedition through Arabia Petraea, the Valley of the Arabah, and Western Palestine', *Palestine Exploration Fund Quarterly Statement*, 16 (1884), 114-17.

Kark, R., *The Development of the Cities of Jerusalem and Jaffa from 1840 up to the First World War* (Jerusalem: Hebrew University, 1977).

Kark, R., *Jaffa – A City in Evolution, 1799-1917* (Jerusalem: Yad Izhak Ben-Zvi, 1990).

Kark, R., *American Consuls in the Holy Land, 1832-1914* (Detroit and Jerusalem: Wayne State University Press and Magnes, 1994).

Kark, R., 'The Kaiser in Jerusalem', *Etmol*, 23 (1998), 3-6.

Klein, Chaim H. (ed.), *The Second Million. Israeli Tourist Industry* (Tel Aviv: Amir, 1973).

Lamb, C., 'They didn't just book it – they Thomas Cooked it', *Financial Times* (13 January 1990), 18.

Luke, Harry and Edward Keith-Roach, *The Handbook of Palestine and Trans-Jordan* (London: Macmillan, 1934).

Melman, B., *Women's Orient: English women and the Middle East, 1718-1918* (London: Macmillan, 1995).

Neil, James, *Palestine Re-Peopled* (London: James Nisbet, 1883).

'Palestine for the Jews', *The Traveller's Gazette* 67 (January 1917), 6.

'Palestine Exploration Fund', *Cook's Excursionist* (10 July, 1869), 3, and other articles in this periodical.

Parsons, H. Palmer (ed.), *Letters from Palestine: 1868-1912, written by Rolla Floyd* (USA: Privately Published, 1981).

Shepherd, N., *The Zealous Intruders: the western rediscovery of Palestine* (London: Collins, 1987).

Swinglehurst, Edmund, *Cook's Tours* (Poole, Dorset: Blandford, 1982).

Towner, John, *An Historical Geography of Recreation and Tourism in the Western World, 1540-1940*, (Chichester and New York: John Wiley, 1996).

Vogel, L., *To See a Promised Land: Americans and the Holy Land in the 19th Century* (University Park, PA: Pennsylvania State University Press, 1997).

Whithey, Lynne, *Grand Tours and Cook's Tours: A History of Leisure Travel, 1750-1915*, (New York: William Morrow, 1997).

Fact and Fantasy

In this third section we see the how development of travel — pilgrimage, professional, cultural — to the Near East encouraged that secondary development of Orientalism, a phenomenon relevant to the next three papers on the artists J.F. Lewis and Edward Lear and the novelist Gérard de Nerval. J.F. Lewis was the first of the three to visit the region, settling in an Ottoman house in Cairo between 1841 and 1851. The region had begun to attract a number of professional artists; Lewis was perhaps inspired by earlier visits to Morocco, Spain and the eastern Mediterranean. During his Cairo decade Lewis produced some 600 sketches and watercolours that later, on his return to London, he worked up into elaborate paintings of oriental life, catering to the tastes of a Victorian public already under the influence of a unique description of Lewis by Thackeray who had visited him in Cairo in 1844 and famously described him as living the life of 'a languid lotus eater'. This was an image well suited to the tastes of Lewis' late Victorian public, a taste which was also fed by his paintings. Weeks argues that the paintings deliberately reinforced Thackeray's account to the detriment of the more rounded view of Lewis that his skilful manipulation of the London art market deserved.

In contrast Edward Lear's paintings of the region, the result of three visits between 1849 and 1867, are more strictly topographical. Many of his Palestinian and Sinai watercolours were of biblical sites, catering to the would-be pilgrim or tourist; these often included friends of Lear's who commissioned oil paintings on the basis of sketches made on the spot. Khatib points out that it is clear from Lear's letters that he purchased photographs to ensure accuracy, a medium becoming increasingly accessible from mid-century.

Gérard de Nerval was a novelist with first-hand experience of the Levant; he visited the area extensively in 1843, publishing an account of the contemporary scene, *Le Voyage en Orient*, on his return to France. He also published two novellas around characters from the history of the region, one inspired by the eccentric Caliph al-Hakim who ruled Egypt and Palestine in the early eleventh century, and the other even more tenuously based on the story of King Solomon and the Queen of Sheba. The contrast between the fact of Nerval's travel account and the fiction of his novellas is a striking demonstration of the Orientalist manipulation of the Near Eastern scene, both past and present, to cater for a public taste already primed by the many translations — into English as well as French — of 'A Thousand and One Nights'. Taymonova argues that Nerval used myth and legend to develop his own philosophical symbolism based on the interaction of European and oriental cultures, popular with his public but outlasting its cultural or indeed political relevance.

John Frederick Lewis (1805–1876): mythology as biography, or dis-orienting the 'languid Lotus-eater'

Emily M. Weeks

Relatively little is known about John Frederick Lewis's ten-year stay in Egypt, from 1841 to 1851. Unlike many other nineteenth-century artist travellers, such as Sir David Wilkie (1785–1841) and David Roberts (1796–1864), Lewis left no diary or journal detailing his activities and had no contemporary biographers. He wrote few letters to his friends and relatives while abroad, and maintained an unusual degree of distance from his compatriots in Cairo. The informational void that results from Lewis's uncommunicative and antisocial nature is, however, not absolute. There is one lengthy description of Lewis in Cairo, written by an old friend of his in the 1840s, which has maintained its popularity with art historians and biographers for over a century. Though undeniably fascinating and at first glance illuminating, I would like to suggest that this account has actually done more harm than good in scholars' attempts to gain a knowledge of the elusive British painter John Frederick Lewis.

In 1846, William Makepeace Thackeray (1811–1863) published a humorous travel essay. *Notes of a Journey from Cornhill to Grand Cairo*, which had begun inauspiciously as five short contributions to *Punch*, became one of Thackeray's most popular literary works.[1] In its final pages, Thackeray provided an account of a visit with his friend J—, believed to be John Frederick Lewis, which took place in Cairo in October 1844. To his great surprise, the author found the artist living 'like

---

[1] William Makepeace Thackeray, *Notes of a Journey from Cornhill to Grand Cairo* (London: Chapman and Hall, 1846; Heathfield: Cockbird Press, 1991). All page numbers cited here are taken from the 1991 edition of Thackeray's text.

a languid Lotus-eater, a dreamy, hazy, tobaccofied life'.² He stood in awe before J—'s enormous Islamic house, located 'far away from the haunts of European civilization',³ and raved about the wonderful meal of 'delicate cucumbers stuffed with forced meats' and 'yellow smoking pilaffs [*sic*]' prepared by J–'s Egyptian female cook, that he enjoyed there.⁴ Most memorable, however, was Thackeray's rather bewildered description of J— himself:

> A man — in a long yellow gown, with a long beard somewhat tinged with gray, with his head shaved, and wearing on it first a white wadded cotton nightcap, second, a red tarboosh — made his appearance and welcomed me cordially. It was some time, as the Americans say, before I could 'realise' the semillant J. of old times. He shuffled off his outer slippers before he curled up on the divan beside me. He clapped his hands, and languidly called 'Mustapha'. Mustapha came with more lights, pipes, and coffee; and then we fell to talking about London, and I gave him the last news of the comrades in that dear city. As we talked, his Oriental coolness and languor gave way to British cordiality; he was the most amusing companion of the — club once more. He has adopted himself outwardly, however, to the Oriental life. When he goes abroad he rides a gray horse with red housings, and has two servants to walk beside him. He wears a very handsome, grave costume of dark blue, consisting of an embroidered jacket and gaiters, and a pair of trousers, which would make a set of dresses for an English family. His beard curls nobly over his chest, his Damascus scimitar on his thigh. His red cap gives him a venerable and Bey-like appearance. ... We ... sat smoking in solemn divan.⁵

Thackeray's colourful account has been repeated in nearly all of the literature on Lewis, from the nineteenth century until today. No qualifications are made of its terms; no context is given for its creation; no cautionary words are written. Rather, readers are encouraged to rely on it as a factual, evidential archive. While it is difficult to challenge the veracity of Thackeray's description in the absence of alternative biographical resources, it is not difficult to question scholars' continued dependence upon it, or the authoritative status that they have granted it.

2   Thackeray, 146.
3   *Ibid.*, 142.
4   *Ibid.*, 145.
5   *Ibid.*, 144–5.

This paper questions the implications and consequences of these tendencies, arguing that they have allowed a mythical, atemporal, and rather two-dimensional, John Frederick Lewis to take the place of a multi-faceted historical figure. Moreover, Thackeray's words have not only influenced an understanding of Lewis himself, but they have also conditioned the reception of his pictures from the nineteenth century until today.

The art historian Marcia Pointon best expresses the underlying methodological concern of this paper. In her essay, 'The Artist as Ethnographer: Holman Hunt and the Holy Land', Pointon addresses the question of intertextuality — how texts (be they paintings, verbal accounts, institutional proceedings or historic events) relate to each other, and how these relations change through time, as the ideologies which create and surround them change.[6] Comparisons become a means of registering difference and identifying the process of meaning making over time, not simply a way of distinguishing 'right' versions from 'wrong'. Consequently, then, although one may doubt the reliability of Thackeray's account, this does not negate its evidential value. Whether true or false or, most probably, somewhere in between, it is inherently valuable as an object of study and comparison in a broader network of representation and in the more general context of historiographical analysis. Its circulation and (mis)-use over the course of two centuries can be juxtaposed with the circumstances surrounding other pieces of biographical information, however vague or fragmentary, in order to understand better how a particular image of Lewis came to be created.

Lewis was born in London, the son of a German engraver, in 1805. By the age of twenty-one, after some favourable recognition as an animal painter, he decided to concentrate upon painting in watercolour, the medium with which he achieved his fame. Though popular in England, Lewis did not remain there. He travelled for almost two years in Spain and Morocco from 1832 to 1834, earning the nickname 'Spanish Lewis'.

---

[6] Marcia Pointon, 'The Artist as Ethnographer: Holman Hunt and the Holy Land', in *Pre-Raphaelites Re-Viewed*, edited by Marcia Pointon (Manchester & New York: Manchester University Press, 1989), 22-43.

In 1837 he again left England, this time to travel through Italy, Greece and Turkey, before settling in Cairo in 1841. From this date on, for nearly a decade, Lewis communicated little with friends and family. Determined to become a sort of 'participant observer' in Egyptian society, Lewis apparently retreated from his own, English one, and devoted his energies to recording and embracing the country and culture around him.

In addition to the account given by William Makepeace Thackeray, related above, other fragmentary references to Lewis exist from the 1840s. The most often repeated of these come from contemporary artists' patrons. In 1842, Thomas Philips, the patron of the artist Richard Dadd (1817–1886), visited Cairo and mentioned that Lewis had 'not been very usefully employed hitherto'.[7] This fits well with Thackeray's comments regarding Lewis's life of indulgence and leisure in that city. Lord Elphinstone (1807–1860), Governor of Madras and Bombay and the patron of one of Lewis's younger brothers (the painter Frederick Christian, or 'Indian', Lewis, Jnr.), wrote to the latter in 1844:

> I had again the pleasure of seeing your brother on my way out last winter. He was living in the most Ottoman quarter of Cairo — in a house which might supply materials for half the Oriental annuals and manuals of Eastern architecture that appear in London and Paris. He showed me a very spirited sketch of Mehemet Ali [then Pasha of Egypt] — the best and in fact the only good likeness I have seen.'[8]

The description of Lewis's house and neighbourhood, if not his artistic activity, again conforms to Thackeray's text.

In 1851 Lewis returned to England and set up house outside London with his young wife Marian Harper, whom he had married in Alexandria in 1847.[9] In the remaining years of his life, Lewis produced his most famous pictures, all of which were inspired by his years in Egypt. These included domestic subjects, desert encampments and street scenes, based loosely on the six hundred or so sketches he had brought back to England

[7] Quoted in Major General Michael Lewis, *John Frederick Lewis, 1805–1876* (Leigh-on-Sea: F. Lewis, 1978), 33.
[8] *Ibid.*, 34.
[9] *Ibid.*, 21. Unfortunately, very little is known about Lewis's wife and no correspondence of her own survives.

with him. Lewis continued to earn great critical acclaim for his extraordinary watercolours, notably from the most significant critic of the era, John Ruskin (1819–1900), but he was disheartened by the lack of financial reward and turned to oil paintings in the late 1850s. He resigned as president of the Old Watercolour Society in 1858 and became a regular contributor to the Royal Academy, to which he was elected an associate in 1859 and a full member in 1865. The renewed presence and popularity of his work in London after 1851, however, did little to change Lewis's social habits: he continued to avoid the city, attending public events only infrequently and missing several Royal Academy functions. Lewis died in his home in Walton-on-Thames, Surrey, in 1876.

As this brief biography suggests, Lewis was a complex figure in nineteenth-century Victorian society, one who both distanced himself from its norms and expectations and successfully negotiated with its demands. He was at once an eccentric, peripheral figure in metropolitan London and a prominent, prolific painter, operating at its heart; he was at once a curiosity and a widely recognised name.

Two photographs of Lewis in his later years help to illustrate these distinctive sides of Lewis's personality and the tension that exists between them. In the photograph of Lewis taken by Elliott and Fry (National Portrait Gallery, London) (Fig. 19), the artist is shown as a reserved gentleman, starched and buttoned-up in the latest respectable attire. The second photograph, however, of just a few years earlier, reveals a very different Lewis (private collection) (Fig. 20). Here, he is dressed in 'Turkish' clothing and strikes a dramatic pose, his scimitar at his side. His embroidered jacket and wide trousers are remarkably similar to those described by Thackeray. These disparate images of J.F. Lewis, which clearly warrant critical attention, are rarely acknowledged together in standard accounts of his biography or in discussions of his work. Though both photographs were meant to project a certain image to a contemporary Victorian audience, and therefore played a significant role in the construction of Lewis's artistic identity and public persona, no attempt has been made to reconcile them. Instead, the image of Lewis in exotic dress is focused upon, to the exclusion of all else.

Fig. 19. Photograph of J.F. Lewis, undated — photographed by Elliott and Fry (National Portrait Gallery, London).

Fig. 20. Photograph (albumin print) of J.F. Lewis in Eastern dress, undated, photographer anonymous (Private Collection).

Fig. 21. John Frederick Lewis — 'The Hosh [Courtyard] of the House of the Coptic Patriarch, Cairo', 1864, oil on canvas (Private Collection).

Fig. 22. John Frederick Lewis — 'The Mid-Day Meal', 1875, oil on canvas (Private Collection).

The consequences of this biographical lopsidedness, in which the lotus-eating 'Turk' described by Thackeray is privileged unfairly, are especially vivid for art history. Briony Llewellyn, for example, who believes Thackeray's description of the artist to be 'acutely perceptive', has claimed a similarity between Lewis's painting of 1864, *The Hosh (Courtyard) of the House of the Coptic Patriarch, Cairo* (private collection) (Fig. 21) and Thackeray's description of Lewis's own house in that city.[10] Indeed, she notes that the 'ogling black eyes' of Lewis's Egyptian servant girl, whom Thackeray speculates teasingly about, are just visible in the painting, through the second-story *mashribiyya* (turned wood) window.[11] A similar correspondence is observed between Thackeray's textual account of his sumptuous dinner with J— and Lewis's visual rendering of *The Mid-day Meal* (private collection) (Fig. 22), painted about three decades later.[12] Rather than interrogating this curious and anachronistic parallel between literature and art, or exploring the nature of the relationship between writer and painter, the author uses Lewis's pictures to elaborate on — and, consequently, to 'verify' — Thackeray's textual account. The limitations this methodological approach imposes on the reading of the images are obvious: Lewis's pictures are read inductively, rather than deductively, a prescriptive process that discourages other, more provocative questions from being asked of them.

The temptation to reduce Lewis or his pictures to the words of William Makepeace Thackeray, and thereby restrict them to a particular historical and literary moment, cannot be traced to one author alone. As early as 1969, art historians seemed reluctant to admit that Lewis, like many other artists, travelled energetically about Egypt, sketching *en plein air* in Luxor

---

[10] Briony Llewellyn, 'Two Interpretations of Islamic Domestic Interiors in Cairo: John Frederick Lewis and Frank Dillon,' *Travellers in Egypt*, edited by Paul and Janet Starkey (London & New York: I.B. Tauris, 1998), 150.

[11] See also, Thackeray, 143 and *passim*.

[12] The 'similarities' between text and painting are noted in Llewellyn's captions to the illustrations in the 1991 edition of Thackeray's *From Cornhill to Grand Cairo* (pages 143 and 145, respectively). Llewellyn also makes passing references to the connections between text and pictures in her article, 'Two Interpretations' (*op. cit.*, 150–1).

and Aswan.¹³ The image of the 'languid Lotus-eater' that they had firmly in mind was a much more romantic one to promote. In another example, Lewis's famous watercolour of 1856, *A Frank Encampment in the Desert of Mount Sinai, 1842* (Yale Center for British Art) (Fig. 23), is again co-opted to serve as an illustration to Thackeray's text. Kenneth Paul Bendiner reads it as a projection of the artist's ideal life, as it was 'confided' to Thackeray in 1844.¹⁴ The complexity and significance of the painting is diminished, in favour of reinforcing the status and credibility of Thackeray's account. The possibility that other influences were operating on Lewis, and that they had more to do with England than with his alleged lifestyle in Egypt, is dismissed.

Fig. 23. John Frederick Lewis — 'A Frank Encampment in the Desert of Mount Sinai, 1842 ... ', 1856, watercolour and bodycolour (Yale Center for British Art, Hew Havant, CT).

[13] See, for example, Jeremy Maas, *Victorian Painters* (London: Cresset Press, 1969), 92.
[14] Kenneth Paul Bendiner, 'The Portrayal of the Middle East in British Painting, 1835–1860', Ph.D. dissertation, Columbia University (Ann Arbor: UMI, 1979), 223.

The formative influence of Thackeray on nineteenth-century discourse about Lewis is also worth considering in the light of these concerns. In 1892, a writer in *The Portfolio* articulated clearly the significance of Thackeray's description of Lewis for contemporary readers, and the influence it had had upon them: 'Lewis stands before us as a living figure in his strange metamorphosis from the Western dandy into the bearded, grave and reverend Oriental, taking his part *au grand serieux*, and both dressing and playing it to perfection without the slightest tinge of the amateur ill at ease in his unwonted trappings.'[15] Though Thackeray's own suggestion of the 'complete transformation' of Lewis from Englishman to Egyptian had been somewhat more subtle: 'As you will be glad to know how an Oriental nobleman (such as J. undoubtedly is) is lodged and garnished, let me describe the contents of [his] hall of audience',[16] the widespread belief that Lewis had successfully 'gone native' in Egypt cannot be overestimated. He was now believed to have insights into Egyptian life and culture that passing tourists simply did not. The artist and poet Edward Lear (1812–1888), for example, could write without hesitation in 1875 that: 'there have never been, and there never will be any works depicting Oriental life — more truly beautiful and excellent... for besides the exquisite and conscientious workmanship, the subjects painted by J.F. Lewis *were perfect as representations of real scenes and people.*'[17]

Thackeray's repeated and persuasive insistence on the success of Lewis's 'Oriental' masquerade, then — his clothes, his house, even the food he ate — was apparently enough to convince many contemporaries to accept the realism of his pictures and dismiss the possibility of his deliberate manipulation, or fictionalisation, of Egyptian scenery and culture. This conviction influenced the reception of Lewis's paintings during and shortly after his life, as Lear's remark makes clear and therefore, in important and unexpected ways, served to guarantee their success in the Victorian art world. As reputable documents put forth by an 'insider', Lewis's Orientalist works were to be respected, believed in, and, most

---

[15] *The Portfolio*, 1892, 94.
[16] Thackeray, *op. cit.*, 144.
[17] Quoted in Lewis, *op. cit.*, 61 [italics mine].

importantly, purchased, above all others. Though current scholars are no longer willing to accept these pictures as 'realistic', their understanding of them has been no less shaped and determined by the words of William Makepeace Thackeray.

As these examples demonstrate, Thackeray's text has positioned itself as a canonical framework, and has thereby discouraged alternative critical appraisals and investigations of the artist and his work. The publication of *From Cornhill to Grand Cairo*, it must be remembered, was compromised by commercial interests and other, ulterior motivations on Thackeray's part.[18] The structure and content of its description of Lewis, moreover, follows a long tradition of (often-fictionalised) biographical accounts of artists.[19] Clearly, it cannot be regarded as an objective document in the Lewis archive.

How then might Thackeray's text be used more cautiously and productively by scholars, in order to explore Lewis and his work, rather than impose preconceived frameworks upon them? Upon his return to England in 1851, Lewis must have been aware of Thackeray's already famous account of his life and activity in Egypt. The impact this had on the artist and/or on his works, and on his subsequent self-fashioning, have yet to be examined. Lewis's decision to remain silent about his years abroad and allow Thackeray's account of it to circulate unchallenged, must be considered for the economic, personal and professional advantages and disadvantages this had on the artist. The photograph of Lewis in 'Turkish' dress, for example, may have been meant to perpetuate an obviously popular, seductive and therefore marketable image that Thackeray had already established. The similarity between Thackeray's description of Lewis's clothes and those chosen for the picture is now easily explained. Thackeray's text, moreover, may have served as a source for Lewis's later work — whether its contents were based on reality or not, its established commercial success virtually guaranteed the popularity

[18] See Edgar F. Harden (ed.), *The Selected Letters of William Makepeace Thackeray* (New York: New York University Press, 1996).
[19] See, for example, Ernst Kris and Otto Kurz, *Legend, Myth, and Magic in the Image of the Artist: an historical experiment* (New Haven: Yale University Press, 1979).

of Lewis's subject matter. Rather than attempting to verify Thackeray's text through Lewis's paintings, or reconstruct his life in Egypt based on its engaging anecdotes, then, scholars can reverse the direction of their gaze and their chronological preoccupations, and consider the influence of the author on the artist after 1851.

Focusing on the problematic nature of Thackeray's text (its biases, its economic motivations and so on) can also prove enlightening, rather than merely destructive. Scholars, seduced by the compelling image of the 'languid Lotus-eater', have failed to remember that 'John Frederick Lewis' is itself a construction, a text as intricately crafted as Thackeray's own. The awareness of this fact offers a second, potential solution to the problem of incorporating Thackeray's text into the Lewis literature.

As a counterpoint to this discussion of Lewis and Thackeray, it is useful to consider a parallel case of biographical myth making, in which recent scholarship has been more effective in demystifying its subject and interrogating the texts that helped to construct him or her. Though any number of examples could have been chosen, from a variety of different periods (Leonardo da Vinci, Michelangelo, David Livingstone, General Charles George Gordon, Lawrence of Arabia, even Jackson Pollock come to mind), the English poet, Lord Byron (1788–1824), is of special interest. Lewis's appreciation of the poet is well documented: in 1869, he added verses of Byron's 'Maid of Athens' to the catalogue entry for his painting *An Intercepted Correspondence* (private collection)[20] and, years earlier, had fulfilled a commission to draw several illustrations for *Byron's Beauties*, published in London in 1835.[21] To allege that Lewis was well aware of the posthumous reputation of the poet and the process of his idolisation is not unwarranted.

The phenomenon of 'Byronism' has been recognised as a paradigm of how a carefully constructed identity can take on a life of its own, quite separate from that of the person him or herself. Indeed, Frances Wilson notes that Byron complained frequently that he had become unrecognisable, 'fed upon out of all recognition by an entire industry of

---

[20] Bendiner, *op. cit.*, 200.
[21] *Ibid.*, 86.

writers, reader, reviewers and revengers.'²² Byron's recognition of the power of his mythic image, much of it self-made, is obvious. To Lady Blessington, he remarked, 'People take for gospel all I say, and go away continually with false impressions.'²³ One such 'false impression' is the series of pictures of Lord Byron in Albanian dress painted by Sir Thomas Phillips. Byron sat for Phillips several times in 1813 and 1814. Phillips producing many portraits in the process. The portrait illustrated here, based on a picture exhibited at the Royal Academy in 1814, was painted long after Byron's death (Fig. 24). Though Byron wore Albanian dress very little and never in England, except to pose for Phillips's pictures, this image is undoubtedly familiar to many.²⁴

Phillips' calculated repetition of particularly resonant themes and costumes helped to perpetuate a romantic image of the poet long after his death, one that did not necessarily reflect reality. The drawing of 1823, by the Count d'Orsay (Fig. 25), on the other hand, is perhaps less so. Though more accurate in terms of Byron's dress and ever-fluctuating weight, viewers today would understandably be hard pressed to identify the slender, conservatively dressed figure portrayed here.

Doris Langley Moore explains the reason for the mis-recognition most eloquently: 'There is the style we know as Byronic, the draped cloak, the open collar, the hair swept back from the temples. There is the kind of dress Byron actually wore, and there is the influence these real and supposed appearances had...'²⁵ These three separate strands, she maintains — the historical figure, the personality and the public perception — must be recognised, distinguished one from another, and incorporated into a responsible biographical account, if the complexity of the figure and the

---

[22] Frances Wilson (ed.), *Byromania: portraits of the artist in nineteenth- and twentieth-century culture* (London: Macmillan; New York: St. Martin's Press, 1999), 3.
[23] Wilson, *op. cit.*, xii.
[24] Doris Langley Moore, 'Byronic Dress', *Costume: The Journal of the Costume Society*, 5 (London: Society of the Victoria & Albert Museum, 1971), 8.
[25] *Ibid.*, 1.

Fig. 24. Sir Thomas Phillips — 'Lord Byron in Albanian dress', after 1835, oil on canvas (National Portrait Gallery, London).

Fig. 25. Count d'Orsay — pencil drawing of Lord Byron, 1823 — location unknown, reproduced in Doris Langley Moore , 'Byronic Dress', *Costume: The Journal of the Costume Society*, 5 (London: Society of the Victoria & Albert Museum, 1971), 1-13.

reasons for popular confusion about him or her are to be understood. Scholars can exercise their deconstructive energies, in short, to achieve evidentially productive ends: Here, the visual disparity between the painting of Byron and the drawing, and the confusion that it causes, can be explained by 'unpacking' various formative texts. The figure in the historical record can usefully be opposed to public perceptions, both contemporary and posthumous.

Thackeray's account, as one of the 'strands' in Lewis's biography, can then, and should, occupy an important place in the critical scholarship. The repeated intertwining of Lewis and Thackeray and the omission of the other strands, however, is problematic. As the above examples have demonstrated, Lewis's biography is regularly condensed into a paragraph-long excerpt. His status as a brilliant technician and a sophisticated manipulator of the Victorian art market, indeed his interaction with English society in general, is ignored. His paintings have been interpreted only in relation to a single text of 1846, and not for their involvement with the pressing cultural, political and/or socio-economic issues that were circulating during their creation, long after his return from Egypt. Life before and after Thackeray's visit seems not to matter.

With the simple addition of other recorded incidents and commentaries, however, or the inclusion of other 'strands', the figure of John Frederick Lewis is transformed. His turn from watercolours to the more lucrative medium of oils in the late 1850s, his intimate (and opinionated) interactions with dealers, artists, art critics and patrons, and the calculated repetition of his most popular subject matter allow the 'languid' artist to take on an economically motivated, actively self-promotional and professionally canny, dimension. His work becomes less concerned with the historical realities of Egypt and more with the demands of the Victorian art world. Compositional mistakes, glossed over in light of Lewis's alleged ethnographic knowledge and precision, as posited by Thackeray, now invite important political and social readings.

A revisionist account of John Frederick Lewis's work, such as this paper proposes, that moves beyond Thackeray's powerful but limiting literary trope and engages with the man photographed by Elliott and Fry, re-introduces the sophisticated and celebrated member of the London art world of the 1850s, 1860s and 1870s to the discussion. Lewis's work, rich and layered with meaning as it is, can be read in a variety of contexts — in terms of debates about style, British imperialism, issues of race and gender in the period — rather than being reduced to mere illustrations of a nicely-turned journalistic phrase. This 'dis-orientation' of the 'languid Lotus-eater' and the firm placement of him back in London, and beyond the years 1841 to 1851, results in a deeper, more nuanced understanding of this complex and fascinating nineteenth-century British painter and his work. Moreover, it encourages a critical re-examination of other travellers' accounts and an awareness of the vicissitudes of historiography, whether the discussion involves a renowned literary figure, a highly accomplished artist or a 'languid Lotus-eater'.

Bibliography

Bendiner, Kenneth Paul, 'The Portrayal of the Middle East in British Painting, 1835–60', Ph.D. dissertation, Columbia University (Ann Arbor: UMI, 1979).

Harden, Edgar F. (ed.), *The Selected Letters of William Makepeace Thackeray* (New York: New York University Press, 1996).

Kris, Ernst and Otto Kurz, *Legend, Myth, and Magic in the Image of the Artist: an historical experiment* (New Haven: Yale University Press, 1979).

Lewis, Major General Michael, *John Frederick Lewis, 1805–1876* (Leigh-on-Sea: F. Lewis, 1978).

Llewellyn, Briony, 'Two Interpretations of Islamic Domestic Interiors in Cairo: John Frederick Lewis and Frank Dillon,' in *Travellers in Egypt*, edited by Paul and Janet Starkey (London and New York: I.B. Tauris, 1998), 148–56.

Maas, Jeremy, *Victorian Painters* (London: Cresset Press, 1969).

Moore, Doris Langley, 'Byronic Dress', *Costume: The Journal of the Costume Society*, 5 (London: Victoria & Albert Museum, 1971), 1–13.

Pointon, Marcia, 'The Artist as Ethnographer: Holman Hunt and the Holy Land,' in *The Pre-Raphaelites Re-Viewed*, edited by Marcia Pointon (Manchester and New York: Manchester University Press, 1989), 22–43.

Ray, Gordon N. (ed.), *The Letters and Private Papers of William Makepeace Thackeray*, 4 vols (Cambridge, Mass.: Harvard University Press, 1945–1946).

Thackeray, William Makepeace, *Notes of a Journey from Cornhill to Grand Cairo* (London: Chapman and Hall, 1846; Heathfield: Cockbird Press, 1991).

Wilson, Francis (ed.), *Byromania: portraits of the artist in nineteenth- and twentieth-century culture* (London: Macmillan; New York: St Martin's Press, 1999).

Edward Lear's Travels to the Holy Land: visits to Mount Sinai, Petra and Jerusalem

Hisham Khatib

This is not intended to be an introduction to Edward Lear (1812-1888). Lear is well known to most art lovers in Europe. However, he is little recognised in Egypt and the Levant, in spite of his many contributions in depicting the landscape of Egypt, the Holy Land, Syria and Lebanon. While one will find reprints of the lithographs of David Roberts (1796-1864) all over the Levant, one rarely finds anyone who has heard of Lear, let alone own or even seen, any of his works. Lear, no doubt, has been a more accomplished traveller and painter than Roberts. He travelled widely, all over the world, often in the Near East, yet he made no lithographic records of his Near East travels.

Lear published six European travel books with lithographic plates. These depicted scenes from Italy, Albania, Calabria/Naples, Corsica and the seven Ionian Islands. Had Lear published any lithographic works of his Near Eastern drawings, these would have been a great success, and would have introduced Lear to many households and art lovers in the Near East. Unfortunately, this did not happen so that Lear is seldom recognised in the Near East, in spite of his tremendous artistic contributions. It is enough to recall that when the Royal Academy of Arts held the Edward Lear Exhibition[1] from 20 April to 14 July 1985 it showed Lear's oil painting of 'Jerusalem from the Mount of Olives — 1859' as the Exhibition's poster (Fig. 26). Another poster depicted 'The Pyramid's Road, Gizeh 1873'. This testifies that the Near East paintings which Lear left to the nation were some of his very best.

---

[1] Vivien Noakes, *Edward Lear (1812-1888)* (London: Royal Academy of Arts, 1985).

Fig. 26. Edward Lear — 'Jerusalem from Mount of Olives, Sunrise', 1859, oil on canvas.

Edward Lear

Edward Lear's contributions are well documented in the literature and reflected in the bibliography. It is enough to mention that he was described by one of his contemporaries, his friend, Chichester Fortescue, as a 'man of versatile and original genius'. He was an ornithological draughtsman compared in his own time with Audubon, a superb landscape draughtsman, a traveller and musician. He was also the creator of a genre of children's writing in which as Nonsense Poet, he stands supreme. It is not only his versatility that is extraordinary, but also his productivity. When Lear died he left at least 7,000 watercolours, made on his travels; about 2,000 studio watercolours including the sets of illustrations to Tennysons's poems; more than 300 oil paintings; two books of natural history illustrations and more than a hundred additional published ornithological lithographs; five travel books and five or six travel manuscripts prepared for publication; four books of Nonsense; extensive diaries and thousands of delightful and useful letters. Hundreds of his paintings as well as some of his letters relate to his experiences in Egypt and the Near East.

Of interest in this chapter are Lear's paintings and his letters.[2] Lear's letters about the places he visited and his impression and description of these places are as delightful to review as his paintings. Many a time they go beyond mere chit-chat to become a historical record of events and people he encountered at that time. Some of these letters contained drawings of the places he was describing and intended to paint, although some were only thumb-nail sketches.

Lear was described by his friend William Holman Hunt (1827–1910) as 'the most indomitable being in encountering danger and hardship'.[3] Many of these dangers and hardships were encountered in his visits to the Holy Land. Lear first met Hunt in 1852; Hunt being the more accomplished oil painter gave Lear advice about oil painting. Lear considered himself to be a second generation Pre-Raphaelite Brother. Hunt was also a traveller

---

[2] Vivien Noakes, *Edward Lear: selected letters* (Oxford: Clarendon Press, 1988).
[3] William Holman Hunt, *Pre-Raphaelitism and the Pre-Raphaelite Brotherhood*, 2 vols (London: Macmillan, 1905).

having visited the Holy Land four times. They planned to visit Jerusalem and the Holy Land together. Unfortunately, this did not materialise.

Lear's Visits to Egypt and the Holy Land

Although Lear was an epileptic, he undertook three journeys to the Near East. The first trip was from January to February 1849 when he travelled to Cairo, Suez and Sinai. His second journey was from March to June 1858 when he travelled to Bethlehem, Hebron, Petra, the Dead Sea, Jerusalem, Syria and Lebanon. From December 1866 to March 1866 Lear travelled to Egypt and up the Nile as far as Wadi Halfa. In the following month, April 1867, he visited Gaza and Jerusalem before returning to England in June 1867. Therefore Lear visited Sinai once, Petra once and Jerusalem twice. These travels demanded high levels of endurance that would have exhausted most healthy men, particularly at a time when journeys in Sinai and Petra were quite dangerous. Yet Lear's biographer, Vivien Noakes, explains that being on the move helped to reduce the frequency of his epileptic attacks.[4]

Visit to Sinai

Lear visited Sinai once, on his first journey to the Near East. He travelled from Suez on 17 January 1849, accompanied on that trip by his travel companion, John Cross. They intended to travel via Sinai to Beirut. He reached, on the 25th of the month, the great plain of El-Raha below the immense mountain of Sinai, Mt Horeb. Lear was very impressed by the location which universal tradition has affixed as the site of Moses' Camp. He wrote a letter, on 1 February, to his sister Ann saying 'the excessive and wonderful grandeur of the spot is not to be described, though I hope to shew you drawings of it ... A convent — a Greek establishment was built in the sixth century.' Lear was here referring to the Convent of St Catherine's at Mount Sinai, where he stayed for three nights.

[4] Vivien Noakes, *Edward Lear: the life of a wanderer* (London: BBC, 1968; 3rd ed. London: Ariel Books, 1985).

Fig. 27. Edward Lear — 'Mount Sinai', watercolour.

Apparently Lear was enchanted by the plain of El-Raha and Mount Sinai. Most of his drawings in Sinai depict this plain overshadowed by the mountain. In my collection there is a large Lear oil painting of this scene as well as two small watercolours (Fig. 27). This oil painting was commissioned by Lt General Sir William Thomas Denison (1804–1871), who was married to the second daughter of Admiral Sir Phillips Hornby, an old friend of Lear and a kinsman of the Earls of Derby.[5] Lear also depicted the same location in many of his oils and quick pencil and ink-wash drawings — and returned to it many times during his career. Two of these oils were small and another a large circular painting, yet such circular paintings were not a common feature of Lear's work.

Although other painters such as David Roberts,[6] William Henry Bartlett[7] (1805–1854) and others made many drawings of different sites in Sinai apart from the plain of El-Raha and Mount Horeb as well as drawings of St Catherine's Convent, Lear concentrated most of his artistic efforts in drawing the plain of El-Raha with Mount Horeb filling the background. Beside the three oil paintings, there are at least ten ink wash drawings depicting the same scene and from the same spot, with only very minor modifications. To my knowledge, no other single landscape was exactly repeated so often in his drawings. These drawings along with his letters to Ann show what a profound impression the location must have had on him.

Lear's first journey to the Holy Land and Sinai was apparently pleasant and with few problems other than the weather which forced him to go back to Suez on 4 February and recommence his visit to Palestine via Gaza. However, prevented by severe weather and his own illness, these plans were not fulfilled at the time. He had to wait another nine years before he could visit Jerusalem. He never went back to Sinai.

---

[5] Vivien Noakes, private letter to the author, 1 August 1988.
[6] David Roberts, *The Holy Land* (1842–1844), III.
[7] William Henry Bartlett, *Forty Days in the Desert* (1848).

Visit to Petra

In 1858 Lady Waldegrave commissioned Lear to produce two paintings of the Holy Land. One had to be of Jerusalem, the other subject matter was left open. He commenced his journey in March 1858 and visited Jerusalem, Bethlehem, Hebron, the Dead Sea and Petra. On the same trip he also visited Lebanon and Damascus. He wrote a very interesting and revealing letter to Lady Waldegrave on 27 May, after which she chose Masada for the subject of the second painting.

It was in this context that Lear made his only and most dangerous trip to Petra, the unique Nabataean rock-cut city. At the time, law and order was very lax in the Holy Land. Travelling beyond the cities and main roads was hazardous,[8] with local tribes controlling practically the whole countryside, particularly the Jordan valley and the area east of the River Jordan, and demanding protection money from every traveller.

He left Jerusalem on 2 April and travelled to Petra through Bethlehem and Hebron. He crossed the north of Wadi Araba and reached Petra after six days' travel, on 8 April 1858. Lear, like all other travellers to Petra, was greatly surprised and impressed by what he saw and wrote to his sister Ann: 'I found a new world, but my art is helpless to recall it to others or to represent it to those who have never seen it — But I will try'. He also wrote in his diary:

> I sat down at noon to draw and did so uninterruptedly until it grew too dark to see the marks of my pencil or the colours I was using ... I worked on the whole view of the valley looking to eastward to the great cliff, then the bed stream among its flowering shrubs, then on one of the higher terraces where a mass of fallen columns lie in profuse confusion and gathered scraps and coloured effects of the whole scene from various points.[9]

But Lear did not have much time to paint. He stayed in Petra for less than a day and a half. Next day, after his arrival, he had a lot of trouble from the local tribesmen who were competing with each other for his

---

[8] Y. Ben Arieh, *The Rediscovery of the Holy Land in the Nineteenth Century* (2nd ed., Jerusalem: Magnes Press, 1983).
[9] 'The Journey to Petra — a Leaf from the Journals of a Landscape Painter', *Macmillans Magazine* (April 1897).

protection money. He was robbed of all his money and most of his other belongings and was lucky to leave the site of Petra without injury. Therefore, he had very little time to record the splendour of the many sites at Petra, which David Roberts, for instance, who stayed longer, was able to depict in many of his watercolours and lithographs (most houses and offices in Jordan today display reproductions and postcards of them). For example, Lear did not visit the splendid site of al-Deir [the Monastery]. This would have demanded a full day's journey and tough ascent of about 930 stairs to the top of the mountains which surround Petra. Nor did he visit the summit of Mount Haroun.

Nevertheless, Lear did manage to make a few oil paintings and many watercolours and sketches of the attractions of Petra. Probably the most important is a large oil painting of the amphitheatre (Fig. 28) which is in a private collection in Jordan[10] and another coloured sketch of al-Khazna [the Treasury] (Fig. 29).[11] The colouring of the oil painting, although slightly exaggerated, nevertheless depicts the unique colours of the red-rose city. There are other watercolours, pencil sketches and sepia ink drawings of the Petra ravine, with some its monuments and caves.

It was unfortunate for posterity that Lear's visit to Petra was so curtailed and dangerous. His records of the trip in his letters and his drawings were severely restricted by the shortness of his stay and the hazardous circumstances. He never went back.

[10] Jordan National Gallery, *On the Banks of the Jordan*, catalogue of an exhibition (Amman, 1986).
[11] Gerald Ackerman, *Les Orientalistes de l'école britannique* (Paris: ACR Edition, 1991).

Fig. 28. Edward Lear — 'Petra — the amphitheatre', oil on canvas.

Fig. 29. Edward Lear — 'Petra — The Treasury', 13 April 1858, pencil and watercolour.

Visit to Jerusalem

Lear visited Jerusalem twice, in 1858 and on a second visit in 1867. Both visits were in April, probably the best month to visit the city for the weather is fine and most of the countryside is green. Lady Waldegrave had commissioned him to paint an oil colour of Jerusalem at sunset. This was not easy. Jerusalem's panorama is best viewed from the east and in the morning from the Mount of Olives, from which a commanding view of the city can be seen. In order to compromise, and after a thorough search, Lear chose a spot in the north eastern corner of the city in order to undertake his painting. Correspondingly, Lear could only paint the central and southern parts of the city, that is, most of the area south of St Stephen's Gate. The painting contained the important sites: the Muslim Dome of the Rock, the Church of the Holy Sepulchre and Jerusalem's two synagogues.

In 1859 he made another painting for Sir James Reid called 'Jerusalem from the Mount of Olives—Sunrise'. This painting is one of the best recorded paintings of Jerusalem for it is detailed and fairly accurate.[12]

From his letters, it is clear that Lear used photographs he had purchased to assist him to attain an accurate painting of details of the city. By the middle of the nineteenth century the use of photographs by landscape painters was slowly becoming accepted practice. Thomas Seddon (1821-1856), for example, utilised photographs extensively, when he painted his 'Valley of Jehoshophat' masterpiece.[13] Lear's painting of the Jerusalem panorama (Fig. 30) definitely surpassed, in quality and use of colours, those of other, well known painters of Jerusalem. Earlier painters, David Roberts, for instance, did not have the advantage of having access to photographic prints.

Lear made many other rapid pencil and ink wash sketches of which he was such a master, as well as watercolour drawings of Jerusalem and its

---

[12] Mary Anne Stevens, *The Orientalists: Delacroix to Matisse* (London: Royal Academy of Arts, 1984).
[13] Christopher Wood, *The Pre-Raphaelites* (London: Book Club Associates, 1981).

Fig. 30. Edward Lear — 'Jerusalem from the Mount of Olives', watercolour heightened with white.

surroundings. Some of these paintings were commercially mass-produced watercolours specifically made for sale, part of what Lear called his Tyrants (Fig. 30).

Lear never attained the same success and importance as other painters such as David Roberts, who recorded different sites and location in Jerusalem in forty detailed lithographs which are undoubtedly the best known historical record of the city. Even a modest painter like W.H. Bartlett attained a higher reputation for his drawings of different scenes in Jerusalem in the nineteenth century.

Lear's impressions of the conditions of the city in 1857 were not very complimentary. Jerusalem, at that time, was no more than a backwater of the decaying Ottoman Empire, neglected and in a sad state. The invasion of Palestine by Napoleon Bonaparte in 1799 had drawn the attention of the world to the Holy Land but after the defeat of Bonaparte in Acre, Jerusalem and the Holy Land reverted back to its old status as a forgotten part of the Ottoman Empire. The country, because of outside interest, slowly began to change and modernise from the middle of the nineteenth century and increasingly towards the end of the century. Edward Lear's letter to Lady Waldegrave, written in Damascus on 27 May 1858, after his trip to Jerusalem, is most revealing of the unfortunate state of the city of Jerusalem at that time.

> Oh my nose! O my eyes! O my feet! How you all suffered in that vile place! For let me tell you, physically Jerusalem is the foulest and odious place on earth. A bitter doleful soul-ague comes over you in its streets. And your memories of its interior are but horrid dreams of squalor & filth, clamour & uneasiness, hatred & malice & all uncharitableness. But the outside is full of melancholy glory, exquisite beauty & a world of past history of all ages:-every point forcing you to think on a vastly dim receding past, or a time of Roman war & splendour, (for Aelia Capitolium was a fine city) or a smash of Moslem & Crusader years, with long long dull winter of deep decay through centuries of misrule. The Arab & his sheep are alone the wanderers on the pleasant vallies and breezy hills round Zion:- the file of slow camels all that brings to mind the commerce of Tyre & other bygone merchandize ... My stay at Bethlehem delighted me greatly. And I then hoped to have got similar

drawings of all the Holy land. All the country near it is lovely and you see Ruth in the fields all day below those dark olives.[14]

In spite of this uncomplimentary description of the city, he said in this letter that 'with all this and in spite of all this there is enough in Jerusalem to set a man thinking for life, and I am deeply glad that I have been there'.[15]

Lear's second trip to Jerusalem was in April 1867. He travelled to Jerusalem from Egypt via Gaza, arriving there on 13 April. He stayed only two days. His paintings and records of this second visit are both limited in comparison to those of his previous visit. Nevertheless, during that stay he painted a magnificent view of the garden of Gethsemene, with its marvellous old olive trees.

Lear's travels to the Holy Land were some of the most enduring and dangerous journeys he undertook in his career. Due to his persistence and courage we are rewarded not only with some of his best oils and colourful watercolours, but also insight into the Holy Land: Palestine, Petra and Sinai, during the mid-nineteenth century. Lear's works are probably more realistic and descriptive of existing conditions in the Holy Land than exotic depictions of the 'orientalist'. It is unfortunate that his great artistic and literary contributions are still little recognised in that part of the world compared to those of his less talented, but more popular contemporaries, such as David Roberts and William Henry Bartlett.

Bibliography

Baring, M. 'Edward Lear', *Punch and Judy and Other Essays* (London: Heinemann, 1924), 255-60.

Davidson, A. *Edward Lear: landscape painter and nonsense poet (1812-1888)* (London: John Murray, 1938; second edn 1968).

Hewett, O.W. (ed.), *And Mr Fortescue* (London: John Murray, 1958). Excerpts from the diaries of Chichester Fortescue, Lord Carlingford, 1851-1862.

---

[14] Lear to Lady Waldegrave, Damascus. 27 May 1858, in *Letters of Edward Lear* (London: 1907).

[15] *Ibid.*

Hoper, P., *Edward Lear* (Oxford and New York: Oxford University Press, 1962).

Hunt, W. Holman, *Pre-Raphaelitism and the Pre-Raphaelite Brotherhood*, 2 vols (London: Macmillan, 1905).

Kelen, E., *Mr. Nonsense: a life of Edward Lear* (Nashville; Thomas Nelson, 1973).

Lehmann, J., *Edward Lear and his World* (London: Thames and Husdon, 1977).

Noakes, V., *Edward Lear: the life of a wanderer* (London: Collins, 1968; revised edn Fontanta, 1979; revised edn, London: BBC Publications, 1985).

Richardson, J. *Edward Lear*, Writers and their Work, no. 184 (London: Longmans, Green, 1965).

——, 'Edward Lear: man of letters', *Ariel*, 1 (1970), 18–28.

Slade, B.C. (ed.), *Edward Lear on My shelves* (New York: privately printed for W.B. Osgood Field, 1933).

Oriental Novellas in the *Le Voyage en Orient* by Gérard de Nerval

Mariana Taymanova

In 1843 Gérard de Nerval undertook a long journey across the Levant. Unlike his predecessors, Châteaubriand and A. de Lamartine, neither the Biblical nor the ancient Orient attracted him; he was interested in the modern Levant, its cities, its peoples, their rites and traditions, so different from European ones. Nerval was the first of the French Romantics to consider the Orient without prejudice and preconception. He was able to find there mystery and freshness, as well as the occult traditions which offered him new insights in his perception of the world.

Back in France, Nerval published his travel notes, which later formed the book *Le Voyage en Orient*. In 1847 and 1850 he added to this predominantly documentary account of his travel two fictional novellas: *Histoire du Calife Hakem* and *Histoire de la reine du Matin et de Soliman, prince des Génies*. These two legends, rich in philosophical meaning, brought additional local flavour to his account. In these novellas Nerval explored the biblical and Islamic past of the Orient but it is interesting to note that the Queen of Sheba, King Solomon, and Caliph al-Hakim did not interest him as historical figures; they were rather symbols or mythological characters. The writer used myth and legend as a plot to develop a philosophical concept.

In *Le Voyage en Orient* the story is told in the first person — by a traveller who is the narrator, and who in the reader's perception personified the writer himself. Yet to make the story sound more plausible, the two novellas were related by strangers: in the first case by the Shaykh of the Druzes who explains to a foreigner the fundamentals of his religion and, in the second case, by a Turkish story-teller who, like Sheherezade, day after day entertains his listeners in a Turkish coffee-house. In doing so, Nerval achieved a double effect: a genuine nineteenth-century Orient served as a frame for the picture of biblical Palestine and eleventh-century Egypt.

The main character of the *Histoire du Calife Hakem* (1847) was unknown to European readers. It was established that in writing this novella Nerval used various sources which included Sylvestre de Sacy's *Exposé de la religion des Druzes* (1837), Herbelot's *Bibliothèque Orientale* (1776), as well as the works of Arab historians al-Makin, al-Maqrizi, al-Nuwayri.[1] Al-Hakim bi-amr Allah [Ruler by God's Command] (AD 985–1021) was the sixth ruler of the Egyptian Fatimid dynasty, noted for his eccentricity and cruelty, and considered by some of his subjects as a divine incarnation. After his mysterious disappearance his adherents in Lebanon and Syria, who believed in his divinity, developed the Druze religion. Despite the fact that Hakem was an historical figure, Nerval did not try to be chronologically precise and interpreted rather freely the facts of his life. Following the principles of Romanticism, Nerval displaced the character in time and space. The hero of the story disguised as a peasant (*fellah*) walks unrecognised among his subjects, trying to persuade them that he is a god. But no one except a blind beggar believes him. As a result of a conspiracy of his chief minister Argévan, Hakem was confined to the Maristan, a madhouse, where the lunatics not only identify him as a Caliph but also recognise his divinity. They stage a rebellion to gain their freedom. In the course of this rebellion, a fire breaks out in Cairo. Hakem, reinstalled as Caliph, intends to marry his own sister Sitt al-Mulk: (considering himself a god Hakem puts himself above human social norms). Yet arriving at the wedding he finds a double in his place. The wedding is cancelled and subsequently three assassins sent by Sitt al-Mulk kill Hakem. That is, in essence, the plot of the story.

Nerval once jokingly remarked to Victor Hugo that he professed at least seventeen religions: he was a Muslim in Egypt, a pantheist among the Druzes and worshipped the Chaldean star-gods when on the high seas.

---

[1] Al-Makin, *Histoire mahométane, ou les Quarante-neuf khaliphes du Macine* (Paris: R. Soubret, 1657); Al-Maqrizi, *Histoire de khaliphate de Hakem* (Paris, 1806); al-Nuwayri, *Nihayat al-arab fi funun al-adab*, 21 vols (al-Qahirah : Dar al-Kutub al-Misriyah , 1923–1976).

Richer[2] argued that the syncretism and mysticism in which the Druzes enveloped their religion made it particularly attractive to Nerval.

Viewing Hakem as a symbol rather than an historical character, Nerval on several occasions deviates from historical authenticity, e.g. Argévan was executed nine years prior to the events described, the mosque where, according to Nerval, Hakem gave his speech was built only in 1285, the fire in Cairo colourfully depicted in the book, occurred at a different time, the hashish that Hakem enjoyed smoking was imported to Egypt two years later, not a single Caliph has ever built a palace on the island of Rawdha and so on. Nerval also avoided the facts regarding the cruelty and tyrannical behaviour of the living god. The real events were of secondary importance for Nerval, for they were merely the background against which he analysed the human characters.

German Romanticism influenced Nerval more strongly than it did any other French writer. This was at least partly due to his knowledge of the German language; his translation of Goethe's *Faust* as well as his enthusiasm for Ernst T.A. Hoffmann[3] were widely known. Like Hoffman, Nerval was much attracted by the theory of doubles developed by Franz Mesmer.[4] This interest, akin to his fascination with Orientalism in general terms, was partly dictated by prevailing fashion and for many Romantics this was a suitable form of self-expression. The psychoanalyst Otto Rank[5] (1925) suggested that the theme of doubles was primarily developed by writers who themselves suffered from various psychic

---

2   J. Richer, *Gérard de Nerval et les doctrines ésotériques* (Paris: Griffon d'Or, 1947).
3   Ernst Theodor Amadeus Hoffman (1776–1822), German writer, composer and painter; known for his stories in which supernatural and sinister characters move in and out of men's lives, ironically revealing tragic or grotesque sides of human nature.
4   Franz Anton Mesmer (1734–1815), German physician whose system of therapeutics, known as mesmerism, was the forerunner of the modern practice of hypnotism. He has advanced a theory of a duel consciousness, of the magnetic union of souls.
5   Otto Rank (1884–1939), Austrian psychologist who extended psychoanalytic theory to the study of legend, myth, art and creativity and who suggested that the basis of anxiety neurosis is a psychological trauma occurring during the birth of the individual. Otto Rank, *The Double* (University of North Carolina Press, 1971).

suffice to mention Hoffmann and Edgar Allan Poe, Guy de Maupassant and Fiodor Dostoevsky). In the majority of cases, the dualism results from a psychological division, and an inability to adapt to a hostile social environment. In this respect the story of Hakem's folly and physical duplication may be viewed as a revolt against a hostile society. In contrast to that, the appearance of Yusuf, Hakem's double, may be seen as a traditional Romantic device. The theme of dual existence, half-reality, half-dream underlines the duality in the consciousness of the main hero; this too is an important principle of the romantic perception in the world.

In this novella both male characters share a strong physical resemblance, which they fail to notice when they first meet to smoke hashish. Only later, on the day of Hakem's wedding with his sister, the Caliph is astonished to find a double by the side of the bride. He takes him for a *ferouer* (the word is borrowed from the Persian religious belief), and in the Orient the double is a symbol of ill will. It is significant that this scene is Nerval's pure invention, not being recorded in any known source. On the other hand, the motif of a legal fiancé witnessing the wedding of his bride to another man is fairly common in European folklore. In this case Nerval skilfully rearranged the motif, setting it in an Oriental environment.

It is also curious to note that *Histoire du Calife Hakem* is the only work where Nerval made a concession to the conventional view of the Orient as it existed in European Romantic literature. The stylisation in the manner of the *Arabian Nights*, theatrical descriptions of splendid palaces, with their colourful interiors, beautiful gardens, and luxurious dresses, all that has little in common with the real Orient as described by Nerval in his *Voyage en Orient*. The intentionally artificial Orient emphasises the unreal character of the setting.

At the same time Hakem, rebellious by nature, is a typical Romantic character. As Clouard, the French literary critic put it, there is something Baudelairian in Hakem's personality. Oriental folklore formed for Nerval the basis on which he developed generalisations. The Romantics often referred to history and legends; the very genre of the historical novel was a Romantic creation. Yet, unlike Prosper Merimée, Sir Walter Scott or Alexandre Dumas, Nerval took no interest in purely historical facts; he was attracted rather by an outstanding personality unwilling to abide by the conventions of his time, the character to whom he ascribes the best Romantic features.

We may suggest that Hakem had yet another double, Nerval himself. As Richer wrote: 'Les légendes orientales arrangées par lui participent à son enterprise de transformation du réel.'[6] Marie-Jeanne Durry argues that while Oriental travels were a venture into an external world, the legends could be considered as voyages into the writer's inner self, the expression of Nerval's most intimate feelings.[7]

It is well known Nerval suffered from mental instability and three times during his lifetime underwent treatment in the psychiatric hospital of Dr Blanche in Passy. The account of the Caliph's stay in the lunatic asylum is viewed as highly confessional, reflecting Nerval's own bitter experience (in *Aurélia* Nerval gave yet more precise details of his mental state). Hakem, unable to bear his own subjects treating him as insane, tries to persuade them that he is in good health and is a god. This painful topic is fairly common in Nerval's works, and again, in the character of the oriental Caliph of the eleventh century his personal emotions come to the fore. The physical perception of the *alter ego* realised in the form of a double was not only a literary device; it was rather an expression of the duality in the writer's consciousness, his rejection of reality, his escape from it.

In spite of the great difference in time and space, the life and experience of Hakem and Nerval are strangely similar. As we have already mentioned, both were confined to lunatic asylums, both were unable to win the heart of the woman they loved and witnessed her wedding with a double. Like Hakem, Nerval wandered in Cairo dressed as a *fellah* to avoid being recognised. Even the scene of hashish smoking was probably based on the personal experience of the writer. Of course, one cannot directly interpret the story-line of the novella in terms of Nerval's biography. But these events have a paramount significance for the writer's works. In proclaiming himself god, Hakem, like many Romantic heroes,

---

[6] *Op. cit.* (1947), 370.
[7] J.M. Durry, *Gérard de Nerval et le mythe* (Paris: Flammarion, 1957), 5.

was seeking true values not in the outside world but within his own self. Nerval was mainly interested in the inner conflict of his hero, the disarray in his relation to the social environment.

The second novella *Histoire de la reine du Matin et de Soliman prince des Génies* (1850) may also be called a journey into the inner world of Nerval. The image of the mysterious Queen Bilkis has teased the imagination of writers and artists of the past and present: Charles Gounod and Georg Handel in music, Paolo Veronese, Raphael, Jacobi Tintoretto, Marc Chagall in painting, architects of the cathedrals in Amiens, Strasbourg, Chartres and Parma; Charles Nodier, Gustave Flaubert, Heinrich Heine, Aleksandr Kuprin, Vyacheslav Ivanov in literature gave their own perception of the biblical queen.[8] The image of the Arabian queen had attracted Nerval since his youth. The short story by Nodier, *La Fée aux miettes*,[9] may be considered as a starting point for this interest.

Tormented by an unrequited passion for the actress Jenny Colon and trying to obtain her sympathy, in the late 1830s Nerval wrote a libretto for an opera on the Queen of Sheba tailor-made for the actress. Nerval took his task seriously. As Théophile Gautier recalls: '... it is difficult to

---

[8] Charles Gounod (1818–1893), French composer noted particularly for his operas, of which the most famous is *Faust*; Georg Frederic Handel (1685–1759), German-born English composer of the late baroque era noted for his operas, oratorios and instrumental compositions; Paolo Veronese (1528–1588), one of the major painters of the sixteenth-century Venetian school; Raffaelo Sanzio [Raphael] (1483–1520), Italian master painter and architect of the high Renaissance; Jacopo Robusti Tintoretto (1518–1594), Venetian painter; Marc Chagall (1887–1985), Belorussian-born French painter, printmaker and designer; Charles Nodier (1780–1844), French writer who was influenced by the *roman noir*; Gustave Flaubert (1821–1880), novelist regarded as the prime member of the Realist school of French literature; Heinrich Heine (1797–1856), German poet whose international literary reputation and influence were established by the *Buch der Lieder* [Book of Songs] (1827), frequently set to music, though the more sombre poems of his last years are also highly regarded; Aleksandr Ivanovich (1870–1938), Russian novelist and short-story writer, one of the last exponents of the great tradition of Russian critical realism; Vyacheslav Ivanovich Ivanov (1866–1949), philosopher, classical scholar, and leading poet of the Russian Symbolist movement.

[9] Charles Nodier, *Fée aux miettes*, in *Contes fantasiques* (Paris: Classiques Garnier, 1961).

imagine how many books he had read ... what amount of information he had collected to write this play. The Bible, the Talmud, Sankoniaton, Hermès ... the entire *Bibliothèque orientale* by Herbelot, all were studied by him'.[10] Nerval offered the libretto to the composer of the day, Meyerbeer, but he rejected it and the writer presented the tale as a separate novella. Three years later, the image of a southern queen reappeared in his short story *Aurélia* and the same year, 1850, yet again in his poem *El Desdichado*.[11]

The beautiful and wise Queen of Sheba arrives in the land of the Israelites to visit King Solomon. Her aim is to find for herself a royal spouse to produce heirs worthy of her own high status. But she meets there Adoniram, a talented architect of the temple of Solomon and falls in love with him. Jealous Solomon sends three killers who murder the architect.

Using the legend of the Queen of Sheba as a plot for his novella, Nerval based himself on both the Bible and the Qur'an, according to which Bilkis, a pagan queen and a worshipper of the Sun, came to the kingdom of Solomon and, overwhelmed by his wisdom, was converted to the true faith. According to Arab tradition, the Queen of Sheba is a daughter of a *jinn* and her demonic ancestry was reflected in her goat's legs as revealed by the astute Solomon. Traditionally Solomon symbolised the wise, creative element while the queen embodied the rebellious, wild side of the human nature. In their conflict, wisdom triumphs.

Nerval took his material from various sources: the Bible (Genesis; I Kings chapters 1–11; I Chronicles chapters 28, 29: II Chronicles 1–9; Job 6:19; the Song of Songs 7:8); the Qur'an (Suras XXVIII, XXVII, XXXIV); the non-canonical Arabic source 'The Book of Prophets' (eleventh century AD),[12] Ethiopian folklore, the German scholar Weil.[13] As a result, he created his own version of the legend giving paramount importance to the

---

[10] Théophile Gautier, *Portraits et souvenirs littéraires* (Paris: Michel Lévy, 1875), 19.
[11] Gérard de Nerval, *Œuvres*, 2 vols (Paris: Classiques Garnier, 1958), I, 693.
[12] Al-Kisai, as-Salebi (or at-Talebim).
[13] Gustav Weil (1808–1889), German orientalist, translated the 'Arabian Nights' into German. Gustav Weil, *Biblische Legenden der Muselmänner* (Berlin, 1845).

conflict between creativity and mediocrity, the creator and the created work. Contrary to tradition, the protagonist in Nerval's story is not Solomon, an arrogant and selfish old man, but Adoniram. Being a rebel, he struggled against both the cruel God Jehovah and King Solomon and defeated them, as they both were vulnerable to time. Adoniram was the creator and true creativity is immortal as it implies an endless reproduction of itself. That is the reason why creators rather than rulers are immortal. The main idea of the legend was used by Nerval to assert the inner freedom of the artist.

The image of Adoniram reflects the syncretic philosophy of Nerval which combined elements of both the classical European and the Oriental traditions. Adoniram was a descendent of Cain who was banished by God for fratricide from the settled land and doomed to wander eternally. He and all his stock became outcasts. Inspired by noble motives they tried in vain to assist mankind by teaching them crafts, arts and basic knowledge. Yet the men were unable to comprehend 'the children of fire', tormented by their own greatness. They were doomed to a short life, to incomprehension and contempt; only after their death would humans venerate their tombs. A similar destiny was reserved for the proud outcast Adoniram in whom Nerval has merged the features of Hiram, the builder of the temple of Solomon (I Kings chapter 3-8) and those of Jeroboam, the rebel (I Kings 11:26). Apart from them the Bible mentions another Adoniram, a tax inspector (I Kings 4:6), who supervised the workmen felling the cedars of Lebanon for the Temple (I Kings 5:15).

According to ancient Persian tradition, Cain, the distant ancestor of Adoniram, was not of human origin, but a descendent of Iblis, the angel of light and the son of fire. Cain's grandson was Tubalcain, who made all kind of tools out of bronze and iron (Genesis 4:22). He was also the progenitor of the tribe of 'children of fire'. One should add in this respect that the motive of fire, one of the four elements in classical philosophy, is omnipresent in Nerval's works. For Nerval fire was a superior element, a symbol of universal love. Bilkis also belonged to the tribe of children of fire, being also a descendant of Cain. One may suggest that Nerval was familiar with one of the numerous Muslim versions of the legend published in 1850 by Nicholas Perron, the French orientalist whom

Nerval had met in Egypt and who introduced him to various aspects of Islam. According to this version the newly born Bilkis was thrown by her mother into the fire which performed the function of a wet-nurse. Nerval too considered himself a descendent of Cain and one of the children of fire directly related to Adoniram and Tubalcain. [In his letter to Dr Blanche in 1851 he wrote that he knew the secret places in Paris where the metal was hidden....][14] According to Nerval's version the Queen of Sheba falls in love with the genial architect and not with Solomon. They were the spiritual brother and sister who were destined by God to meet each other. In this case, as in the legend of Hakem, Nerval returned to his favourite theme: the predestined union of two superior beings. But this union failed to last long. The Queen of Sheba, in the words of Nerval, like Sylvie, Aurélia and Salema in the novel *Voyage en Orient*, personifies an ideal female archetype, a symbol of a poetically superior love to which Nerval aspired all his life and which he was unable to attain. The concept of Adoniram, like that of Hakem, is deeply biographical; Berance has referred to both *Aurélia* and the legend of Bilkis as the key for understanding the personal tragedy of Nerval.[15] Adoniram, a rebel rejected by human kind, is similar to Lord Byron's Cain and Hugo's Hernani.[16]

As in his first novella Nerval was very attentive to detail. The list of the sources he studied prior to the writing of the novella of Bilkis is very impressive. It included not only works by European Orientalists, but also Arabic sources (Nerval studied both the Arabic and Persian languages). The Egyptian scholar, Taha Ḥusayn, indicated that in the transcription of proper names, Nerval always followed Qur'anic tradition: Soliman Ben-Daoud; Moussa Ben-Amran, Bilkis, Héva [Eve] and so on.[17] Yet although he was rigorously correct in subtleties, Nerval was at the same time guilty

---

[14] When Nerval had mental disturbances and hallucinations he was permanently obsessed by the image of the Queen of Sheba and all the entourage related to this topic.
[15] François Berance, 'Fils de Cain', *Nouvelles littéraires* (29 May 1958).
[16] *Hernani*, a play by Victor Hugo (1802-1885) presented in 1830 in Théâtre Français, Paris, where the main character is a Spanish rebel. This drama was regarded as a manifesto of Romanticism and its victory over Classicism.
[17] Taha Hussein, 'Moënis', *Le romantisme français et l'Islam* (Beirut; Dar al-Ma'aref, 1960).

of chronological inaccuracies: it is well known that the Queen of Sheba visited Solomon when the Temple was already completed and the 'copper sea' was cast. Had Nerval followed this order of events, he would have been unable to convey the main concept of the legend.

This novella about Bilkis has another profound meaning in connection with freemasonry. Despite the fact that in discussing this work Nerval called himself a freemason, the critics could not find any proof of this statement. In the legend one may find complex associations with the symbolism, rites and general concepts of freemasonry. Several scholars find this in the life of Hiram, who was assassinated by three workmen to whom he had refused to show the holy books. The Bible ascribes to Hiram the casting of the 'copper sea', which in Nerval's novella was created by Adoniram. According to other traditions, Adoniram and Hiram were the same person, the originator of freemasonry (as Nerval put it in his comments for the novella 'Adoni' means 'master', so the name sounds like 'master Hiram'). As is well known, freemasons call themselves 'the sons of the widow': Hiram was the son of the widow. Other scholars insist that the Queen of Sheba was the widow of Adoniram. Nerval agreed: 'Mais tu sais que je suis moi-même l'un des enfants de la veuve, un louveteau qui était nourri dans l'horreur du meurtre d'Adoniram et dans l'admiration du saint Temple dont les colonnes ont été des cèdres du mont Liban.'[18]

Apart from these direct allusions to freemasonry, there are also numerous indirect references: to three major degrees of freemasons: the Apprentice, the Fellow of the Craft and the Master Mason which date back to the construction of the Temple of Solomon; a symbolic sign 'tau' accepted by the freemasons, which was referred to by Adoniram; the columns of carved cedar wood, called 'Solomon columns' for the decoration of masonic lodges. Nerval was referring to the teaching that combined morality and charity with the traditions of chivalry and brotherhood, spiritual aspirations which were of great significance to Adoniram. This hidden symbolism forms a mystic aura enveloping the novella.

[18] Nerval, Gérard de, *Œuvres*, 2 vols (Paris: Classiques Garnier, 1958), II, 479.

There are numerous elements common to both novellas. The plot in each case is dramatic and includes a beautiful woman, two rivals, three killers, each story ending in the tragic death of the main character and an unconsummated love between the spiritual brother and sister; in each novella one can find similarities with the life of Nerval himself. Both novellas develop as dramas (it was not by chance that the legend of Bilkis was originally designed as an opera). Like a painter, Nerval creates giant frescoes through his writing to convey the burning of Cairo, a wedding as a magic show, the casting of the copper sea, the descent into the underworld alternate with lyrical landscapes and more subdued scenes. Both novellas reflect Nerval's evolution as writer and thinker. It is significant that the story of Bilkis, written after the legend of Hakem, is more complex and contains philosophical revelations, which anticipate the spiritual quest of future generations. Adoniram and the writer-traveller are the only characters in the novel that have undergone inner development. For Nerval the Oriental legends served as a literary mould in which he was able to cast his aesthetic and philosophical credo, transgressing the frames of a conventional plot.

The interaction of European and Oriental cultures goes both ways. The oriental legends used in European literature enabled the French writer to express his aesthetic credo. But an opposite example is also known: when European motives were reworked in Oriental culture. In 1950 Tawfiq al-Hakim, the founder of contemporary Egyptian drama, published in Paris, in the collection *Le Théâtre Arabe*, his play *Solomon le Sage* which puzzled the critics. Describing the meeting of King Solomon and the Queen of Sheba, Hakem completely avoided the traditional version of the legend. In this play Bilkis, who is madly in love with her slave, rejects Solomon. One may suggest, that the Egyptian playwright was inspired by Nerval's interpretation of this legend and in his turn represented the old plot not as a conflict between two religions but as a drama of two strong passionate characters and as a great human tragedy. This peculiar chain of literary interaction (the Orient–West–Orient) shows once more that a true writer is able to elevate any artistic generalisation to the level of universal values.

Bibliography

Berance F., 'Fils de Cain', *Nouvelles littéraires* (29 May 1958), 5.

Durry, J.M., *Gérard de Nerval et le mythe* (Paris: Flammarion, 1957).

Gautier, T., *Portraits et souvenirs littéraires* (Paris: Michel Lévy, 1875).

al-Makin, *Histoire mahométane, ou les Quarante-neuf khaliphes du Macine* (Paris: R. Soubret, 1657).

Al-Maqrizi, *Histoire de khaliphate de Hakem* (Paris, 1806).

Nerval, Gérard de, *Œuvres*, 2 vols (Paris: Classiques Garnier, 1958).

Nodier, Charles, *Fée aux miettes*, in *Contes fantasiques* (Paris: Classiques Garnier, 1961).

al-Nuwayri, Ahmad ibn ʿAbd al-Wahhab (1279–1332?), *Nihayat al-arab fi funun al-adab*, 21 vols (Cairo: Dar al-Kutub al-Misriyah , 1923–1976).

Rank, Otto, *The Double* (1925: Chapel Hill: University of North Carolina Press, [1971]).

Richer, J., *Gérard de Nerval et les doctrines ésotériques* (Paris: Griffon d'Or, 1947).

Taha Hussein, 'Moënis', *Le romantisme français et l'Islam* (Beirut; Dar al-Ma'aref, 1960).

Weil, Gustav, *Biblische Legenden der Muselmänner* (Frankfurt a. M.: Literarische anstalt (J. Rutten), 1845).

List of Contributors

Barbara Codacci, Florence University, is an expert on Italian travellers to the Middle East and contributed to *Unfolding the Orient* (Reading: Ithaca, 2001) with Marta Petricioli.

Hugh C.S. Ferguson, architect. Lecturer in Architecture History at Strathclyde University and Glasgow School of Art, 1960–1990. Member of the British School at Athens. Publications on Greek architecture, topography and travel. Recent book: *Glasgow School of Art: The History* (1995).

Peter Frankopan was Schiff Foundation Scholar at Jesus College, Cambridge, and then Senior Scholar at Corpus Christi College, Oxford where he wrote his doctorate on the political history of the Mediterranean, Adriatic and the Aegean in the eleventh and twelfth centuries. He is currently Senior Research Fellow at Worcester College, Oxford.

Yehoshu'a Frenkel teaches Medieval Islamic History at the University of Haifa. His courses deal with social, juridical and political topics in the Fertile Crescent and the Maghrib, from the emergence of Islam to the dawn of the colonial period. He has contributed several articles on these subjects to journals and books.

Davina Huxley worked on excavations and as an archaeological draughtsman in Cyprus, Chios, Crete, Lerna, the Athenian Agora and Kythera. Her interest in Leake dates from three years spent in Greece with opportunities to follow in his footsteps, and with ready access to the rare book travel collection of the Gennadius Library

Ruth Kark, Professor of Geography at the Hebrew University of Jerusalem, has written and edited fifteen books and about 100 articles on the history and historical geography of Palestine and Israel. Her research interests include the study of concepts of land, land use, and patterns of land ownership in Palestine/Israel in the 19th and 20th centuries, urban and rural settlement processes, and Western interests in the Holy Land and interactions with its local populations.

Hisham Khatib. Jordanian art collector. The Khatib collection is on Jerusalem, the Holy Land, and Egypt during the Ottoman period. This collection includes paintings, travel books, plate books, engravings, photographs, maps and atlases. It is the largest in the Middle East and one of the most important still in private hands.

Norman N. Lewis. Wartime service in Middle East; M.A. Cantab. Principal Instructor Middle East Centre for Arab Studies, Shemlan, Lebanon, 1948-1955. Government Agreements Department, Gulf Eastern Co. 1955-81. Author of *Nomads and Settlers in Syria and Jordan, 1800–1980,* C.U.P. 1987 and numerous articles on Syrian history and related topics.

Brenda Moon. Formerly University Librarian, University of Edinburgh.

Charles Plouviez, M.A. (Edin.) graduated in Eng. Lit. in 1950. Spent 34 years in advertising, from copywriter to chair. Since retirement in 1984 has written and published on various literary and other subjects, including three biographies for New *Dictionary of National Biography.*

Sarah Searight. Prolific traveller throughout the Middle East and author of numerous books on the Middle East including *The British in the Middle East* (London, 1969; New York, Athenaeum, 1970; reprinted 1979) and *Steaming East* (1991).

Marianna Taymanova lectures in Russian Literature at the University of Durham. Previously lived in St Petersburg where she translated French novels into Russian, and lectured on French Literature at its University.

Malcolm Wagstaff is Professor Emeritus in the University of Southampton and Visiting Professor in its Department of Geography where he taught historical geography and the regional geography of the Middle East until his retirement. He has a particular interest in the historical geography of Greece and Turkey.

Emily M. Weeks is a doctoral student in the Department of the History of Art Department. Her research focusses on nineteenth-century British artists in Egypt and issues of Orientalism. She received her BA in Art History from the University of Washington in 1995 and her MA and M.Phil degrees from Yale University in 1997 and 1999, respectively. Her thesis, 'The "Egyptian Years" of John Frederick Lewis (1805–1876): An Orientalist Painter Reviewed', will be submitted in October 2001.

Berit Wells is an Associate Professor of Lund University in Classical Archaeology and Ancient History. Since 1994 she has been Director of the Swedish Institute at Athens. She is an active field archaeologist, at present focussing on the investigations of the Poseidon Sanctuary at Kalaureia (modern Poros) in the Saronic Gulf.

Ionian Expedition *see* Ionian Mission
Ionian Islands 9, 35, 38, 197
Ionian Mission xii, 1, 45–49, 55
Iran 110, 112
Iraq 110, 112
Istanbul *see* Constantinople
Italy 111, 158, 161, 180, 197

Jaffa 6, 124, 128–9, 148, 161, 162, 165–7, 170; Miss Arnott's Mission School 169–70; Tabeetha Mission School 170; Twelve Tribes Hotel 166
Jamal al-Din b. Nubata 111
Jericho 129, 149, 165
Jerusalem 6, 69, 85–86, 90–95, 110, 113–16, 118, 123, 124, 125, 129–32, 134, 149, 162–7, 169, 171, 197, 200, 202, 203, 207, 210; al-Aqsa Mosque 114, 116, 125; Church of the Holy Sepulchre 90, 91, 92, 116, 125, 131, 135, 149, 207; Dome of the Rock 114, 125, 131, 149, 207; Gethsemane 149, 210; Jaffa Gate 164, 167; Jerusalem Hospital 172; Mount of Olives 149, 197–8, 207; Order of St John of 171, 172; Saint Stephen's Gate 207; Temple Mount 131; Via Dolorosa 125; Wailing Wall 125, 134; 'Umar Mosque *see* Dome of the Rock
John, Bishop of Parma 92
John XXIII, Pope *see* Roncalli
Jordan, river 85, 129, 133, 150, 203
Judaea 124, 129
Judeich, Walter 32
Judith of Bavaria 92

Kadesh 152
Kapsali 38, 39
Khalid b. 'Isa al-Balawi 111, 112, 114
Kinglake, A.W. 67, 144
Kingston Lacy 62
Kléber, General Jean-Baptiste 6
Koehler, General George Frederick 6
Komnenos, Alexios I, Byzantine Emperor 94, 98
Kopel, Blatner & Sons, hoteliers 166

Kythera 1, 5, 7, 8, 35–41

Lake District 43
Lamartine, A. de 213
Larissa 79, 80
Latakia [Lattaqia] [Laodicea] 63, 93
Leake, Lieutenant-Colonel William Martin xii, xiii, xiv, 1–41, 49, 53, 76
Lear, Edward xiii, 1, 175, 188, 197–212
Lebanon 58, 62, 126, 127, 129, 153, 200, 214; cedars of 153, 220
Lechmere, Sir Edmund 171–2
Leipzig 80
Lethaby, W.R. 54
Levant Company 17
Lewis, John Frederick xii–xiv, 175, 177–96
Libanus *see* Lebanon
Lietbert, bishop of Cambrai 93
Linné, Carl von (Linneaus) 81
Liudprand of Cremona 97
Lloyd Triestino, steamship line 162
London: Athenaeum Club 25; Bank of England 22; British Museum 20, 24, 26, 31; Eaton Square 23; Euston Propylaeum 24; Great Exhibition (1851) 158; Hyde Park Ionic Screen 25; Kew Gardens 141; National Gallery 21; Pantechnicon 26; Reform Club 25; St Pancras 33; St Paul's Cathedral 22; University College 21
Lovisolo, Giuseppe 126, 128, 130
Lusieri, Giovanni 36
Luxor 147, 186

Madina 115
Mainz, archbishop of 96
al-Makin 214
Malta 5, 7, 36
Mamluk period 110, 114
Mamre 150
Manzikert 100
al-Maqrizi 214
Mar Saba 150
Masada 203
Massaia, Guglielmo 125, 130
Maupassant, Guy de 216

Index

186–9, 194, 197, 199, 200, 210, 214, 215, 221
Egyptian Exploration Society xii
El-Raha, plain 200, 202
Eldridge, Mr 143
Elgin, Lord 1, 7, 20, 31, 35, 36
Elgin Marbles 25, 26, 31, 35, 38, 51
Ellenborough, Lady *aka* Madame Digby 144
Elphinstone, Lord 180
Ephesus 127
Ewing, Mr and Mrs 148

Failoni, Giovanni 126
Fauvel, M^r 36
Fez 115
Finco, Gaetano 126
Fiott, John 69
Franciscan Order 124, 125, 166
freemasonry 222
futuḥat 112

Galilee 124, 129, 165
Gandy, J.M. 46
Gandy, John Peter 46, 50, 53, 54
Gautier, Théophile 218
Gaza 111, 112, 165, 200, 202, 210
Gaze, Mr 164
Gell, Sir William xii, xiv, 1, 42–56
Genoa 89, 100, 164
Genocchi, padre 127, 130, 133
George V, King of England 162
German Templars 162
Ghislanzoni, Narciso 127, 128, 130
Giorgi, Isidoro 126
Giza 148, 197; Great Pyramid 148
Gjörwell, Carl Christoffer 74, 75, 77, 79
Gladstone, Wm E. 159
Glasgow 170
Goethe, Johann Wolfgang von 215
Gordon, Lady Duff 147, 148
Gothic Revival 24
Gounod, Charles 218
Granada 117
Grand Tour 17, 71, 121, 155; Grand Tourists 17, 45
Greece xi, 1, 3, 7–12, 17–22, 24, 28, 32, 36, 39, 44, 46, 54, 63, 71, 76, 180

Greek Revival architecture xiv, 1, 17–34
Greek War of Independence 3, 18, 28, 32
Grenville, Sir Richard 66
Gubernatis, Angelo De 122, 123, 127, 131, 135–7
Gustav III, king of Sweden 71, 73, 75

ḥadith 112, 117
Haifa 127, 165, 167; Hotel Carmel 167
ḥajj 110–11, 113, 115
al-Hakim bi-amr Allah, Fatimid ruler 92, 176, 213, 214, 216–18
Hamburg, travel agency 167
Hamilton, William Richard 7, 11, 18, 31, 35, 36
Handel, Georg 218
Harper, Marian 180
Hawkins, John 11
Hebron 85, 110, 129, 150, 200, 203
Heliopolis, battle of 7
Herodotus 39
al-Hijaz 112
Hittorff, Jacques-Ignace 30
Hobhouse, John Cam *later* Lord Broughton de Gyfford 12
Hoffer, Joseph 28
Hoffmann, Ernst T.A. 215, 216
Holy Land xii, xiv, 90, 92, 95, 96, 103, 110–13, 122, 123, 155–74, 179, 197–212
Holy Places 90, 98, 115, 116, 128–32
Homs 109
Hornby, Admiral Sir Phillips 202
Houran 165
Howard, Alexander 161
Hugo, Victor 214, 221
Hull, Edward 171
Hungary 91
Hunt, William Holman 179, 199–200
Ḥusayn, Taha 221

Ibn al-ʿArabi 112, 115, 117
Ibn Baṭṭuṭa 110, 118
Ibn Khaldun 116
Iceland 102
India 110
Inwood, H.W. 33

Beni Hasan 148
Bernardi, Jacopo 126
Bethany 129
Bethlehem 6, 85, 129, 135, 150, 169, 200, 203, 209
Bilad al-Sham *see* Syria
Bilkis, Queen 218, 221-3, *see also* Sheba, Queen of
Björnståhl, Jacob Jonas xii, xiv, 2, 71-84
Black Sea 99, 164
Blessington, Lady 191
Blomberg, Carl Peter 74
Bonaparte, Napoleon 5, 13, 17, 209
Bonomelli, Geremia 127, 130, 135
Bracebridge, Charles Holte 30
Brindisi 91
British Hospice and Ophthalmic Dispensary 171
British Military Mission to Turkey 5
Bruce, Michael 57, 60, 68
Buckingham, James Silk 2, 66, 160
Burckhardt, John Lewis xii, 2, 57-61, 65, 66, 68, 69
Burton, Decimus 25
Buselli, Bonaventura 127
Byron, Lord 12, 44, 51, 190-1, 194, 221
Byronism 190
Byzantium 91, 92, 96-100

Cairo 7, 58, 59, 65, 111, 114, 116, 117, 145, 146, 148, 161, 175, 177, 180, 200, 214, 215, 217, 223; Hotel du Nil 145, 148
Calabria 197
Calucci, Emanuel 38
Cardona, Filippo 127
casanovas 124, 166, 171
Celsing, Ulric 74
Chandler, Richard 45, 46, 50-52, 76
Chaplin, Thomas 171
Châteaubriand, François-René 213
Cherville, Asselin de 59
Clark, Frank C., travel agent 165, 167
Clarke, Edward Daniel 43, 51, 76, 83

Clay, Edith 45
Cockerell, Charles Robert 19, 21-23, 26, 29, 31, 32
Colocci, Adriano 127, 131
Conrad of Constance 92
Constantine, Emperor 90
Constantinople 6, 8, 17, 22, 35, 63, 65, 71, 74-76, 79, 85, 87, 89, 90, 91, 95, 96-103, 160-1
Cook, John Mason 161, 164, 171-3
Cook, Thomas 155-74
Craven, Richard Keppel 46, 55
Crete xi, 35, 91
Crimean War 134
Cross, John 200
Crusaders 96; First Crusade 88, 98, 101
Curzon, Robert 81
Cyprus xi, 6, 66, 81, 93, 127

Dadd, Richard 180
Damascus 61, 64, 65, 69, 85, 109, 110, 112, 114, 117, 122, 127, 133, 143, 144, 152, 165, 167, 203, 209; house of Dimitri 144
Damonte, Perpetuo Dionigi 123, 127, 132, 134
Danube Steam Navigation 164
Dardanelles 75
Dead Sea 129, 150, 165, 200, 203
Deering, J.P. *see* Gandy, John Peter
Denderah 148
Denison, Sir William Thomas 202
Dilettanti, Society of xii, 1, 2, 11, 13, 20, 21, 45, 46, 48-55
Dodwell, Edward 30, 76
Donaldson, Thomas L. 26, 27-32
Dostoevsky, Fiodor 216
Druzes 213, 214
Dumas, Alexandre 216
Dyrrakhion [Durazzo/Durrës] 91

Edinburgh: Parthenon 22
Egypt xi, 5, 6, 17, 18, 36, 55, 58-61, 111, 115, 121, 123, 127-8, 145-8, 158, 160, 162, 163, 176, 177, 180,

Index

Abercromby, Lieutenant General Sir Ralph 7
Aberdeen, Lord 'Athenian' 11
Abu 'Abd Allah Muḥammad al-'Abdari 111, 112
Abu 'Abd Allah Muḥammad b. 'Umar b. Rashid al-Fihri al-Sabti 115
Abu al-Hasan 'Ali al-Qalṣadi 115, 117
Abu Salim al-'Ayyashi 116
Abu Simbel 147
Abydos 148
Abyssinia 145
Académie des Beaux Arts 30
Acre 209
Acre, St Jean d' 127
Adhemar of Chabannes 92
Aegean Sea xi, 111
African Association [Association for Promoting the Discovery of the Interior parts of Africa] 2, 12
Albania 8, 9, 13, 197
Albert Victor, prince 162
Aleppo 109, 114
Alexandria 17, 58, 90, 111, 145, 148, 161, 165, 180
'Ali Pasha of Yannina 9, 10, 22
Almeria 114
Almoravids 117
Amalfi 100
Ambelakia 79, 80
Amiens, Peace of 8, 38
Anatolia *see* Asia Minor
Andalucia 117
Annel, M. d' 146
Antioch 90
Araba, wadi 170, 203
Arabia 61, 111, 112, 115, 117, 145; Arabia Petraea 170
Arabian Nights *see* Orientalism

al-Arish, Convention of 6
Arnott, Miss Walker 169, 170
Asia Minor xi, 3, 6, 20, 21, 32, 39, 45, 46, 48, 49, 65, 91, 93, 95, 100, 110, 122, 127
Aswan [Assouan] 7, 146, 187
Athens 7, 18-20, 23-26, 28, 30, 32, 33, 36, 48, 50; Parthenon 20, 21, 25, 28, 29, 30, 73
Austrian Lloyds 165
Avlemon 35, 36, 40

Baalbek 61, 127, 144, 145, 165
Baedeker 166
Baghdad 93
Balfour, Arthur 172
Balkans 8, 165
Banias 152
Bankes, William John xii, 2, 57, 61-67
Banks, Sir Joseph 60, 66
Barakat, travel agency 167
Barker, John 66, 69
Barry, Sir Charles 25
Bartlett, William Henry 202, 209, 210
Barzini, Luigi 122, 123, 127, 132, 133, 137
Basil II, Byzantine Emperor 100
Bassi, Alessandro 126
Bedford, Francis 46, 50, 53, 54
beduin 65, 133
Beecher, Henry Ward 162
Beersheba 165
Beirut 122, 126, 127, 143, 145, 153, 161, 165, 200; Oriental Hotel 143
Beke, Charles 145
Belgioioso, Cristina di, Princess of *see* Trivulzio, Princess Cristina
Belmore, second Earl of 60
Beltrame, Giovanni 126

Mecca 113, 115, 118
Mediterranean xi, 87–89, 91, 111, 121, 150, 164, 175
Meiron 151–2
Melos 39
Memphis 148
Mentor, Lord Elgin's vessel 7, 35, 36
Merimée, Prosper 216
Meryon, Dr Charles 2, 57–60, 62–64, 68–69
Mesmer, Franz 215
Meteora 71, 76, 80–82; Grand Meteora 81, 82
Minghelli, Alfonso Maria 127–8, 134
Minya 147
Missett, Col. Edward 59
Moab 165
Montagu, Edward Wortley 76
Moore, Noel Temple, consul 171
Moore, Tom 44
Morea *see* Peloponnese
Morocco 175, 179
Morritt, John 11
Mott, Mr and Mrs 161
Mount Athos 71, 74, 76, 81
Mount Carmel 129
Mount Lebanon 86, *see also* Lebanon
Mount Olympos 80, 82
Mount Ossa 80, 83
Mount Tabor 120, 129
Muḥammad b. Jabr al-Wadi Ashi 111
Muḥammad b. Rushayd al-Fihri 111
Muḥammad ʿAli 164
Muḥammad Alfi Bey 7

Nablus 170
Nahr al-Kalb, river 153
Naples 197
Napoleonic Wars 17, 22
Nasir and Farajalla, travel agency 167
Nazareth 129, 165
Neil, Revd James 163
Nelson, Admiral Lord Horatio 17, 38
Neo Grec see Greek Revival
Nerval, Gérard de xii, xiii, 175, 176, 213–23
Nicaea 94
Nile 5, 7, 36, 111, 127, 145–8, 200

North Africa 110, 112, 115
North, Frederick xi, 141–53
North, Marianne xi, xiii, 86, 141–54
Nubia 7, 61
al-Nuwayri 214

Olivari, Leonida 126
Olmi, Gaspero 125
Orientalism 124, 175, 215, 216, 223
Orientalist 176
Orientalist art 186–8
Orientalists 221
Orsay, Count d' 191
Oxford: Ashmolean Museum, 22; Taylorian Institute 22

Palestine xi, 5, 57, 71, 85, 86, 90, 109–39, 155, 157, 160–7, 169, 170–3, 175, 176, 202, 209, 210, 214
Palestine Exploration Fund xii, 170–1, 173
Palgrave, William 145, 148
Palmyra 2, 45, 64, 65
Paris 158; Exhibition (1878) 158
Pars, William 45
Parthenon: casts 31; Parthenon sculptures *see* Elgin Marbles
Paton, J.M 33
Pausanias 39, 44
Peloponnese [Peloponnisos] [Morea] 8, 94
Pennethorne, John 28
Perigord 92
Perinaldo, Francesco Cassini da 126
Perron, Nicholas 220
Petra 200, 203–204, 210; al-Deir [The Monastery] 204; al-Khazna [The Treasury] 204, 206; Mount Haroun 204
Philae 147
Philippopolis 93
Phillips, Sir Thomas 180, 191
pilgrimage 85, 113, 134, 155–73
pilgrims xi–xii, 85–103, 113–14, 121, 124–5, 128, 130, 131, 132, 134, 135, 155, 164–7; *see also ḥajj*
Pisa 100

Pittakis, Kyriakos 28, 29
Placereani, Leonardo 125
Playfair, W.H. 22
Poe, Edgar Allan 216
Pompeii 44
Port Said 145, 165
Pouqueville, F.C.H.L. 76, 77
Pullan, R.P. 53

Qena 148

Rabattino S.S. Co. 165
Raggi, Giuseppe Salvago 122, 127, 131, 137
Ramleh 149
Ramsay, W.M. 32
Rawdha, island 215
Reid, Sir James 207
Renouard, George 58
Revett, Nicholas 45, see also Stuart and Revett
Rhine 5
Rhodes 127
riḥla xiii, 109–18
Robert of Normandy 96
Roberts, David 177, 197, 202, 204, 207, 209, 210
Rogers, Mr 143
Romani, Giuseppe 126, 134
Rome 18, 91
Roncalli, Angelo, later Pope John XXIII 122, 127, 137
Ross, Ludwig 28
Rossi, Luigi 126, 128, 133, 134
Royal Academy of Arts 21, 181, 191, 197
Royal College of Surgeons 25
Royal Geographical Society xiii, 12
Royal Institute of British Architects (RIBA) 21, 27, 30, 53
Royal Society of Literature 13, 41
Rudbeck, Carl Fredrik 75
Rudbeck, family 73
Ruskin, John 181
Rus' 99

Russia 165

Sacy, Sylvestre de 214
Safed 151-2
Saint Cybard, monastery 92
Saint Petersburg 75
Saint Vincent de Paul, order of 162
Saintonge 92
Salah al-Din al-Ayyubi 114
Salonica see Thessaloniki
Samaria 165
Samos 48, 52
Schaubert, Eduard 28
Scott, Sir Walter 44, 216
Seddon, Thomas 207
Seljuk period 93, 100
Serao, Matilde 122, 125, 126, 128, 135, 137
Seville 117
Shayara ('Convoy') 162
Sheba, Queen of 176, 213, 218, 219, 221, 222, 223, see also Bilkis
Sicily 5, 18, 20, 30
Sidon 58, 61, 63, 127, 165
Sinai 6, 61, 111, 175, 200–202, 210; Mount Horeb 200, 202; Mount Sinai 197, 202; St Catherine's Monastery 111, 200, 202
sira 112
Smirke, Robert 19–20
Smyrna 48, 127
Soane, Sir John 19
Society for Promoting Women's Education in the East 170
Solomon, King 176, 213, 219, 220, 222, 223
Spain 110, 112, 175, 179
Sparta 94
Spiers, Richard Phene 146, 148
Squire, Lt later Lt. Col. John 18, 36
Stanhope, Lady Hester xii, xiv, 2, 57–70
Stanton, later Sir, Edward 145
Stanton, Margaret 145
Stevens, G.P. 33
Stoppani, Pietro 124, 127, 129, 132, 136

Strambio, Alessandro 126, 130
Stuart and Revett 23, 24, 30, 33, 46, 50
Stuart, James 24, *see also* Stuart and Revett
Suchtelen, Jan Pieter van 75
Suez 148, 200, 202
Suez Canal 145, 154, 162
Survey of Eastern Palestine 170
Survey of Western Palestine 170
Sweden 73
Switzerland 5
Syria xi, 5, 7, 36, 61, 62, 63, 65, 68, 69, 85, 86, 93, 109–20, 122, 123, 127, 136, 143, 145, 160, 166, 197, 200, 214

Tadras, travel agency 167
Taillefer, William, of Angoulême 92
Tedeschi, Radini 122
Tempe, valley/vale of 2, 79, 82, 83
Temperance Tours 157
Thackeray, Sir William Makepeace xii, xiii, 175, 177–81, 186–90, 194
Thebes 147
Thessaloniki 9, 73, 74, 79, 91
Thessaly 2, 71, 74–83
Thomas Cook [& Son] xii, 85, 86, 155–73
Thompson, Mrs 161
Thucydides 39
Tiberias, lake of 129, 135, 150, 165
Tornielli, Giorgio 126, 128
tourism 85, 86, 155–73
tourists 86, 86, 141, 157, 164, 166, 172–3
Transjordan 165
travellers, in general 112–14, 118, 121–37, 213
Trieste 164
Trikkala 79, 81
Tripoli (Lebanon) 62, 153
Trivulzio, Princess Cristina 122, 127, 129, 131, 134, 136, 137
Twain, Mark xiii, 163
Tyre 126, 127, 165, 209

Umayyad dynasty 110, 114
Urban II, Pope 98
Ussing, J.L. 77

Valiani, Luigi 126, 137
Varna 164
Venice 89, 91, 100
Vienna 80; Congress of 121
Vigoni, Giuseppe 127, 129, 133, 137

Wadi Halfa 147, 200
Waldegrave, Lady 203, 207, 209
Walpole, Horace 45
Weil, Gustav 219
Wheler, Sir George 25
Wilhelm II, Kaiser 86, 162
Wilkie, Sir David 177
Wilkins, William 19, 20–21, 30, 32, 49, 50, 53
Wilkinson, Sir John Gardner 44
Wood, Robert 45
Woods, Joseph 30
Wordsworth, Christopher 30
Wordsworth, William 43–44

Xanthian Marbles Committee 31–32
xenodochia 94
Xenophon 39

Zante 38, 48
Zionism 134
Zionist 136
Zunini, Enrico 127, 129, 131, 135, 136, 137